GERALD MONSMAN

COLONIAL VOICES

THE ANGLO-AFRICAN

HIGH ROMANCE

OF EMPIRE

UNIVERSITY PRESS
OF THE SOUTH

2021

Copyright Gerald Monsman 2021.

All rights reserved. No part of this publication may be reproduced, stored in a retrieval system, or transmitted, in any form or by any means, electronic, mechanical, photocopying, recording or otherwise, without the prior written permission of the Publisher.
Published in the United States by The University Press of the South. Printed in France by Monbeaulivre.fr
E-mails: unprsouth@aol.com; universitypresssouth@gmail.com

Gerald Monsman.
Colonial Voices. The Anglo-African High Romance of Empire.
Second Edition. In English. African Studies, 20.
Cover Art: 'African Mask, Cote d'Ivoire Senoufo.' Maker unknown. Reproduced with the author's permission.
viii + 292 pages. Bibliography; Index.

1. South Africa. 2. Literature. 3. Anglo-African Writer's Club. 4. Bertram Mitford. 5. Literary Society. 6. British Imperial Society. 7. Boer Imperial Society. 8. H.Rider Haggard. 9. W.C. Scully. 10. H.A. Bryden.

ISBN: 978-1-889431-55-9 (First US Edition, 2010)
ISBN: 978-1-952799-24-2 (Second European Edition, 2021)

This one is

for

Nancy

A ma vie de coeur entier

CONTENTS

Preface	vii
Authors of Empire	1
1. Anglo-African Writers' Club	3
2. A Profile of Bertram Mitford	39
Pre-Colonial *Imperia*	73
3. Shield and Assegai: Warriors	75
4. Love and Magic: Wives	109
Colonial Settlement	143
5. The Farm and the Colony	145
6. The Land and its Riches	175
Colonial Bloodshed	209
7. Renegades and Rebels	211
8. Cannibals and Slaves	241
Author's Afterword	273
Bibliography	279
Index	287

PREFACE

Ever since the nineteenth-century the imperial romance has been understood, on some level, not merely as a self-evident genre of adventure capable of producing an aesthetic experience but as a political construction of ideological identifications and exclusions. There is a serious dearth of critical work on late-imperial writers of popular romances written about the Anglo-African colonies and the regions beyond their imperial frontiers. A growing interest in Africa now means that even the Anglo-imperialist using the voices of the original inhabitants to write about Africa is no longer a forgettable novelist from an insignificant corner of the globe. The strategic move in *Colonial Voices* is to re-evaluate "voice" in terms of "landscape," in which natural space and cultural space are interdefining, though radically different for indigenous and capitalistic societies. Thus when economic globalization invaded diverse indigenous habitats, it redefined the land as a capitalistic resource. Tribes were progressively displaced from their traditional physical homelands which served as the framework for their cultural voices–for myths, songs, ceremonies, visions. By the end of the nineteenth century this land was a vanishing presence in their lives.

Critics have suggested that discourse about indigenous populations in the language of the colonizer cannot establish an authentic relatedness between the tribal lives these authors describe and Western experience. This view considers colonial English an instrumentality bound by doctrinaire political and religious principles, a collection of whitened words like bones in a sepulcher. But *Colonial Voices* argues that contemporary disapproval over the appropriation of indigenous subject matter by white writers fails to take into consideration such co-relations and connections within historical experience as those that allow simultaneous, multiple social perspectives. The empire author's ideological stance is tempered both by scrutinizing divergent African and Western cultural concepts and by utilizing abundant historical and multi-textual tethers with which to ground his fiction. To revalue these writers, it is necessary to read their fiction both with and against the grain of imperial ideology; that is, to read their literal content also in the light of counter-imperial contexts as reflected in the land and its different voices. It is this relation of landscape to voice and of voice to written text that will give the work of these empire writers their audacity of vision and a heuristic value of achievement.

This monograph particularly brings an important and neglected figure back into the canon–Bertram Mitford (1855-1914). Mitford explores the cultural differences between Western and African perspectives with respect to spirituality, social organization, justice, women's roles, and civic duty. His work is measured against somewhat better known Anglo-African writers, including H. Rider Haggard, Olive Schreiner, John Buchan and W. C. Scully, as well Sol Plaatje, an indigenous novelist writing in English. After the second chapter, each subsequent section compares Mitford's fiction to other narratives by one or more near contemporaries. These Anglo-African narratives are treated in terms of their divergent "voices"–the inflections and social identities of authorial, narrational, characterological, and historical speakers–as they comment on the events, cultural rituals, and beliefs of the original inhabitants or settlers in conflict or (sadly less frequently) in harmony. The varied styles of discourse by which the narrators tell their stories include elements of camp-fire tales, ancient myths, heroic narratives of warfare, colonial turns of phrase, and "dark talking" between tribal chiefs or banter by black servants. Both their multiplicity and their conflicting goals challenged the empire's socially constructed assumptions about power. And they suggest alternative modes and values to define settler and subaltern identities.

In analyzing these voices of the Zulu, Ndebele, and British *imperia*, this study utilizes new primary materials from Africa, the United Kingdom, and the United States to work through their deeds and legacies. Although I resist turning what is essentially a literary history into a theory-driven discussion, an informed awareness of contemporary global scholarship and debate will be apparent in this discussion. Anyone in the twenty-first century reading the primary texts of the nineteenth will find the spellings and accepted terms for ethnic groups in South Africa deeply enmeshed in the politics of usage. Within the context of British imperialism, nouns such as *native* or *Hottentot* (a Dutch derivative, "to stammer," from the clicking sound of the Khoisan speech) evoke a disparaging or patronizing stereotype of backwardness. But although I will endeavor to establish clearly the valencies and currency of my terminology and to be accurate in referring to the historical polities and geography of Southern Africa, consistent maintenance of contemporary usage (often taken from Nguni or other African language groups) must on occasion yield to imperial usages (their English forms). In certain places the contrast of recent socio-political terminology would jar with the nineteenth-century historical atmosphere, and the reader is invited to suspend contemporary perspectives in order to experience Africa as the authors lived it.

Originally undertaken as the "2007 Lectures" for the History of Ideas Institute, this series is now brought to publication with the assistance of a timely Award from the Office of the Dean of the College of Humanities, University of Arizona. I am happy also to thank Professor Robert Langenfeld, editor and publisher of *English Literature in Transition, 1880-1920* and ELT Press, for permission to utilize for this current study biographical material in the Appendix of my *H. Rider Haggard on the Imperial Frontier* (ELT Press, 2006). Also, I wish to thank Professor Paul Niemeyer and "Mitfordians" Brian Stringer, Jay Jenkins, Kent Rasmussen, and Jim Armstrong. To them I owe much in the way of encouragement, sage advice and a few pub drinks. Diana deKrijger-Monsman, who through songs when I was a child taught me enough Dutch so that fortuitously I could muddle through Afrikaans in later years, was the beginning of it all. Much more recently I set about acquiring a basic knowledge of isiZulu, of phonology and grammar, but unlike old Africa hands, I can't sing any hymns in isiZulu–yet.

PART I

AUTHORS OF EMPIRE

CHAPTER 1
THE ANGLO-AFRICAN WRITERS' CLUB

Among current questions of canonicity and the rehabilitation of less "mainstream" kinds of texts, Part I, Authors of Empire, proposes that the fiction of Bertram Mitford, H. Rider Haggard, and other Anglo-African writers such as W.C. Scully, H. A. Bryden, and John Buchan, may be prime candidates for consideration, inasmuch as their work has depth as well as an accessible, popular appeal. This "adventure" category includes heroic struggles in settler life, sagas such as those of the Ndebele-Zulu peoples, the tension of suspense or the passion of adventure and romance, and the paranormal. Until recently, and in some quarters currently, "popular" nineteenth-century empire writers and their readers have been marginalized as practitioners and enthusiasts of a formulaic and trivial genre. Yet because so many people read and were influenced by these works, they provide us with insights into the cultural trends and ideologies of that era. Still, traditional markers between serious and popular literature are becoming more blurred or complicated by a growing awareness in critical discourse that popular works also may be artistic. A process of critical re-evaluation, focusing on the range of adventure romance's contributions–on its narrative voices, its sophisticated, complex characterizations, and its use of irony, particularly in presenting British and Boer imperial societies–would bring a new appreciation of these authors "more often named than read, and more often read than profitably studied" (Eliot, "Metaphysical" 669).

John Buchan's definition of "the romance" as an adventure tale "where the incidents defy the probabilities, and march just inside the borders of the possible" (*Steps* 5) is apposite. Later in this same narrative, Buchan's protagonist recounts a horrible murder:

> "You're looking for adventure," I cried; "well, you've found it here. The devils are after me, and the police are after them. It's a race that I mean to win."

> "By God!" he whispered, drawing his breath in sharply, "it is all pure Rider Haggard and Conan Doyle."
> "You believe me," I said gratefully.
> "Of course I do," and he held out his hand. "I believe everything out of the common. The only thing to distrust is the normal."(*Steps* 70)

One tends to think of Shakespeare's plays, even the romances, as embodying the beliefs of his Tudor era, but one is less likely to assume the adventures and occult happenings in Haggard or Doyle express any sort of practical political philosophy or effective cultural commentary. Popular and serious works of literature alike can be vehicles of political comment and social vision, and any separation of higher and lower is often exaggerated.

This present critical examination begins at the metropolitan center of empire with the speakers and topics at the "Anglo-African Writers' Club," a filter through which the mysterious "other" on the frontiers of empire was represented. Mary Louise Pratt has suggested an unequal dialectic in which the urban center "habitually blinds itself to the ways in which the periphery determines the metropolis–beginning, perhaps, with the latter's obsessive need to present and re-present its peripheries and its others continually to itself" (Pratt 6). Statements on the white man's burden in Victorian schools, editorials in newspapers, and sermons by vicars, created even in the club a popular belief in "the Divine right of a great civilizing race such as ours " (*Times* 17 May 1898:11). Nevertheless, fiction by several of the club writers on the British presence in Africa challenges at least some of the assumptions of jingoistic imperialism. The best empire romances are neither wholly conservative, like G. A. Henty's fiction, nor confrontationally polemical, like Olive Schreiner's *Trooper Halket of Mashonaland* (1897).[1] Rather, the best of this fiction questions the ideology of empire, even while maintaining an

---

1. This value judgment debatably assumes that when character, action, and image are intended to persuade readers to adopt a particular position or action on a topical issue, the æsthetic element is diminished–in Schreiner's story, an attack on Rhodes's policies.

ostensible consensus on its generic structure and readership as defined by class, gender, age and geography. That such works have formulaic moments–hair's-breadth escapes, sickness, hunger, death, and the reconciliation of lovers–is undeniable. Such motifs, however, are equally present in mainstream fiction and, even, in non-fictional works of travel, hunting and exploration, and missionary accounts. The complaint that popular works fail to explore the social norms from which they originate is simply untrue. The fact is that the use of history and ideology in popular fiction has been inadequately recognized and articulated. Canonical literature of quality certainly has an agenda beyond entertainment, but so does popular fiction. Moreover, highbrow novels cannot match empire romance for responsiveness to the cultural anxieties and urgencies within a broad, popular base of readers. These romances of empire reflect how readers expected to see that world: "In spite of all its apparent peace and restfulness, its smiling beauty and magic charm of scenery, there is never absent in Africa the note of passion, the undertone of the fierce warfare between nature and life, between man and animal, between man and man. And it is perhaps this note of tragedy, this element of passion which gives to Africa its thrilling interest" (Smuts vii-viii). Far-off in time as Britain's crown colonies may be, it is easy to visualize the impact of nineteenth-century imperialism on Ndebele and Zulu political power. It is a drama that opens our eyes to our own human ambitions and flaws. Not only does this fiction portray with authentic local color the sudden changes wrought by British imperialism upon traditional, indigenous ways of life, these narratives also convey the weight and interest of pivotal human moments–of life lived in the presence of death or of passion or of duty, of guilt and innocence, and of the ironies of unfeeling circumstance.

Although such fiction graphically depicted the clash of cultures, current uneasiness with its dramatization may well obscure the original force and tenor of the scenes. Because neither Mitford nor his fellow Anglo-African writers explicitly condemned the British presence in Africa, they were (and still are) considered "patriotic" writers who praised the manly virtues of the Empire against tribal Africans and Boers. Mitford kept an ironic distance from the jingos of the proletariat, and his authorial voice currently is relevant for its shrewd attitudes and interpretations of those historical events. Significantly, his plots are more often presented from the perspective of colonist or indigenous African struggling for survival in the colonized land than from G.A. Henty's transoceanic perspective of *With Buller in Natal* (1900) or *With Roberts to Pretoria* (1902). When Henty writes in the preface to this latter novel that "the Boers had not the heart to venture even once to face the British in the open" (vi), Mitford unhesitatingly burlesques this "consuming love of fair play" in *The Curse of Clement Waynflete* (1894): "Sergeant Clark's idea, you see, was thoroughly characteristic of his nationality, viz., that naked savages armed only with spears . . . ought by every law of fairness to stand out and do themselves the honour of being shot down by the latest improvement in breech-loading weapons of precision in the hands of Englishmen. Failing this they were 'crawling, cowardly, greasy rascals'" (7). Actually, Mitford realized that Clark's type of crafty warrior was the Zulus' ancient standard (*Zulu Country* 145) and so far from disparaging them, he is allowing Clark actually to credit the Zulus with adapting tactics to pragmatic necessities. The imperial scorn of the Zulu language (Nguni form: isiZulu) as "native jabber" or "monkey chatter" by those who hadn't learned it strikes the same ironic note as the popular glorification of military action as "nigger-shooting," mere "fun," or what Royston, an imperial dim-wit in *Waynflete*, rationalizes to King Cetywayo (no less!) as merely his desire for "adventure."

 Colonial Voices: The Anglo-AfricanHigh Romance of Empire is a companion study to my *H. Rider Haggard on the Imperial Frontier* (2006) and will introduce pivotal novels by Bertram Mitford, reading his texts both "with the grain," to explore how the patriotic nineteenth-century public understood his political meanings, and simultaneously reading "against the grain" to identify those covert ambiguities, unspoken preferences, and subtle inconsistencies that subvert the dominant imperial ideology. Both Mitford's language, stylistics, and the interrelated images as well as his social, political, and literary contexts will be explored. Ever since Odysseus met Polyphemus, the confrontation between "god-fearing" European culture and "wild savages" (Homer 9: 177-78)–between reason and passion–has presented itself in literature and life according to an imperial agenda or "script" foreshadowed here by Homer. This scenario of deceit and technological force unfolds according to a sequence of actions, neither willingly admitted nor openly orchestrated, but which yet appear as scripted as if it were a play. The wonderful Gikuyu parable in Jomo Kenyatta's *Facing Mount Kenya: The Tribal Life of the Gikuyu* (1938) illustrates exactly this sort of aggressive imperial appropriation of Africa's ostensibly unoccupied land. Recounting this oral tale of his people–a beast fable, later titled by Chiuna Achebe "The Gentlemen of the Jungle"–Kenyatta illustrates the British attitude towards tribal Africans as calculatedly dishonest (47-52). The British "gentlemen" are the "animals" of the jungle, the "man" is the African; and although the jungle "gentlemen" know that untenanted land is used at least part of the year by shifting cultivators, they enable one of their own, the elephant, to force the "man" out–a script that now will end with a political backlash.

The first great imperialist in Western literature may be Odysseus. Although as Homer describes him, he pridefully taunts the aboriginal Polyphemus, yet as Tennyson in "Ulysses" pictures him, he has much else in common with the British imperialist, "roaming with a hungry heart." Neither Ithaca nor England as insular habitations could contain that lusting spirit of exploration, travel, and progress: "'Tis not too late to seek a newer world." This voice of Tennyson's Ulysses became also the voice of Britain's nineteenth-century empire–but not the only one. Mitford and his contemporaries introduce a wide spectrum of characters, with immensely different racial or gender histories, who talk about the world and themselves diversely. Many Anglo-African writers knew the novelist cannot have just the one story of colonial society, even if it be the seemingly benign story of the missionary. He or she must listen to the many voices of children, women, and of the land and its indigenous inhabitants. Indirectly, these voices also bespeak a distinguishable authorial presence, who stages how these figures are depicted, who speaks with intentionality for them, and who creates for his readers a sympathetic closeness to them or an ironic distance from them. The elephant sticking his trunk into the colonial room or lying on the verandah–to summarize Kenyatta's hilariously satiric Gikuyu parable–seems always to be for the imperial author, given that the ideal of cultural superiority may be flawed and that colonial rule may not be benign or just, whether and to what extent black resistance or violence towards white society is justified.

The present study examines the agreement or conflicts between African and imperial speakers and, through them, the refracted intentions of the authors of the narratives here considered. The characters' differing values and social viewpoints–religious, political, economic, racial or historical–either reinforce or controvert each other. Each voice must be construed against the backdrop of all the other voices, not to mention the roaring of beasts and the thunder that is the voice of God. And each must be read with or against the grain not only of such multifarious voices within each particular text, but, equally, read with or against the larger contexts of Anglo-African political analysis and social discourse. If "high romance" implies a tale of larger-than-life love and adventure–one rather less realistic than the usual vein in which things occur–in this fiction of empire situational contrasts, ambiguities, and ironies often subvert the conventional romance elements. Descriptions of social values that expose fundamental tensions are integral to the authors' intent and create for the reader a complex response. For this reason, in both generically dissimilar adventure tales and in works of realism, common concerns with local cross-cultural interactions, framed by the broader imperium, show how gendered and subaltern voices, no less than more-canonical ones, attested to the alteration, renegotiation or maintenance of complex identities. Narratives by Sol Plaatje, Olive Schreiner, and Joseph Conrad (who all have attained canonical or quasi-canonical status) are compared to the romance adventure to provide, in terms of a thematic and formal convergence between genres, a more dynamically expressive definition of empire fiction. That these writers have been part of the canon for various lengths of time, demonstrates the continuity of Mitford's thematic and imagistic values within the canonical range of Anglo-African literature in the High Victorian and Edwardian eras. This will be the *procedure* of the present study. The contemplated *outcome* of this study, which breaks new ground critically and biographically, aims to "mainstream" Mitford and his fellow African and Anglo-African writers, so that in future they can be read alongside Dickens or any other Victorian or Edwardian novelist, not merely considered special-topic local colorists. I suggest that Mitford and his fellow writers hold a unique place in relation to Homer's epic, inasmuch as their fiction reflects a time when the *last* habitable places on earth were being discovered, explored, and colonized. Yet these stories of seeking "newer worlds," from the time of Homer to that of these Anglo-African writers, have an astonishing contemporary resonance in our twenty-first century world of nation- and empire-building.

§

From the agoras of ancient Greece to the parks and pubs of Victorian England, centralized spaces of concentration and mixture promoted locally diverse contacts, mobility and opportunity. The same is true of imperial capitols; indeed, the emperors in Rome placed symbolic importance on their city as a center to counterpoise the inescapable loss of power in their far-flung empire. In the late nineteenth century, the buildings of major European cities that assumed the function of imperial capitols competed with and copied each other. British architects lamented London's falling behind rival national models for the imperial metropolis. Paris had Baron Haussmann's publicly supported reconstruction proclaiming the power of Napoleon III's state; Brussels boasted the grandiose and ambitious plans of King Leopold II for the city's rebuilding. Of London it was observed that the various locales within the city served differing functions of empire. In such cities, money for far-flung trading networks was centralized and no full understanding of an empire without its functioning social-economic-political center and its ostensibly dependent periphery can be reached. The significance of even a regional governmental center is testified to in a novella that will be discussed later, W.C. Scully's *A Vendetta of the Desert* (1898). Writing of the Cape Colony, Scully observes: "For centuries the government tried to prevent the expansion of the Colony to a distance from the central authority at Cape Town, but the efforts were as useless as though one were to try to control quicksilver on a slanting board with the hand. The enactment of the most stringent laws was of no avail to prevent the more adventurous spirits from seeking their fortune in the vast, mysterious hinterland. Such men looked upon the heathen as their inheritance and on the wilderness as their portion" (49). This dynamic of central control and peripheral independence, finally even tribal rebellion, is the essence of the three-way British, Boer, and African struggle.

In connection with the high romance of Empire, it may therefore not seem too strange to describe a gathering of writers at monthly dinners in the Grand Hotel, Northumberland Avenue, London. If there was a home for England's novels of Africa–an ideological center of journalistic opinion and literary production–it may well have been here at the Anglo-African Writers' Club in Westminster. For most of the club's existence, H. Rider Haggard seems to have been its Chairman, active at its monthly dinners from its inception in 1895 to the early years of the following century.[2] In his autobiography, *The Days of My Life* (1926), Haggard refers, perhaps a bit dispassionately, to this group of which he was elected chairman as "a pleasant and useful dining society" (2: 110). Literary members included Bertram Mitford, author of many African novels, including *Sign of the Spider* (1896), W.C. Scully, author of *Kafir Stories* (1895) and *Between Sun and Sand* (1898), H. A. Bryden, author of *Tales of South Africa* (1896), and numerous other writers. A slighting reference in *The New York Times* opens the possibility that F. C. Selous, narrator of hunting adventures, and Olive Schreiner, writer of *The Story of an African Farm* (1883), attended the club meetings.[3]

---

2. *The San Francisco Call* noted that the Anglo-African Writers' Club was "recently formed in London" with Rider Haggard as its President (1 July 1895: 6). Apparently, William Eglinton, who gave up mediumship and spiritualism for journalism, was the club's vice-chairman in 1895 and chairman in 1896, having in 1890 hunted extensively in South Africa ("Eglinton").

3. "Mr. Kipling was the guest at a recent dinner of the Anglo-African Writers'

Haggard, along with the Secretary of the Anglo-African club, on one occasion called on Schreiner at her apartment, much to the landlady's displeasure at a single woman entertaining gentlemen callers. Haggard initially had made Schreiner's acquaintance when he sent her a copy of his first novel in testimonial to the impression that her novel of farm life on the karoo, the arid, semi-desert tableland of southern Africa, had made upon him, which subsequently in "About Fiction" he priased as a notable narrative of "spiritual intensity." In a letter to his brother, Haggard somewhat contradictorily observed "that he was attracted by Schreiner's intellect, but admitted that he was repelled by her 'complete and overpowering atheism'" (Stiebel 380; Haggard, "About Fiction" 180).

Pleasant and useful the club undoubtedly was, but the largest share of excitement was generated by politics. When three African chiefs came to London to entreat Queen Victoria to halt appropriation of their territory by Cecil Rhodes's British South African Company,

> pro-native and prosettler traditions clashed, literally, in a barroom brawl inside Rider Haggard's Anglo-African Club in London, just before the Bechuana chiefs left England. Prosettlers, led by the French traveler Lionel Décle, clashed with pro-natives led by H. A. Bryden, who in the pages of the *Saturday Review* had accused "Mr. Rhodes and the monopolists" of trying to seize and suck the three chiefs dry. (Parsons 258)

This event reflected a vigorous exchange of these gentlemen's opinions as reported in "The Smoking Room" column of *The African Review* for 16 November 1895:

> It was hoped that Khama with his companions would be the guests of the Anglo-African Writers' Club at the monthly dinner this week, but although they were very anxious to accept the

---

Club. The Anglo-African writers are, so far as is known, Mr. Rider Haggard, Mr. Selous, and Miss Olive Schreiner. These appear to have taken to themselves a sufficient number of Anglo-Africans, who hope some of these days to write, and they have formed a club that from time to time gives capital dinners" (Alden BR388).

invitation–which, by their special request, was kept open for a week–they were unable to do so, as they are now practically in the hands of the Government. Mr. A. Wilmot was also asked, but he has gone over to Rome–actually, not religiously. Khama would have enjoyed himself, I think, but though it is a well-known fact that all members of the Anglo-African Writers' Club are teetotalers, it does not follow that their friends are, and I fear the chief would have been shocked at the "dead men" on the table on Wednesday evening.

    The evening was a pleasant one. Mr. Bertram Mitford presided, and near him sat Mr. Cust, the Editor of the *Pall Mall*, M. Lionel Dècle, and Mr. Stevens, also from that paper. . . . M. Dècle followed [Mr. Cust's speech] with some very trenchant remarks upon "l'affaire Stokes,"[4] branching off into a somewhat strong denunciation of Khama, whom the celebrated explorer evidently does not like. M. Dècle explained that he once bought some oxen from Khama, and had to pay £8 for each beast. Some months later, wishing to dispose of them, he asked Khama to buy them back, and could only get £3 for each beast. I am bound to say that nearly everybody who heard this story seemed to think that the Chief was an extremely good business man, and I fancy that he went up considerably in their estimation. Mr. H. A. Bryden defended Khama warmly, but there was no fight, and then we had some music and some more speeches. . . .

    One of the events of the evening was the arrival of Lobengula, the *Pall Mall Gazette* bulldog, who was sent for by Mr. Cust, and who came in charge of a gorgeously-dressed black boy. Lobengula was an appropriate and a welcome guest, and his beauty was much admired. (867)

One must not take everything at face value; Lobengúla was probably the only teetotaler there–and, of course, "boy" in colonial usage could be an adult servant.

    The article by Bryden in the *Saturday Review*, entitled "Schreiner *v.* Rhodes," dealt with Olive Schreiner's "impeachment of Mr. Rhodes and his policy" in "The Political Situation," *Cape Times*, 28 August 1895, for allowing "a small band of monopolists" to

---

4. In 1895 Charles Henry Stokes, a British-born ivory trader, was summarily tried and hanged in King Leopold's Congo Free State not for an alleged sale of firearms but as retaliation for lost ivory commissions.

appropriate the mineral resources of Southern Africa for personal profit: "She shows but too plainly that under the Rhodes *régime* South Africa has been in effect already captured by the capitalist and monopolist, and that it will be available for the use of the colonists only when it has been squeezed and sucked dry of most of its wealth." Bryden again used nearly the same end phrase in his last paragraph:

> I believe as much as any one in the expansion of British South Africa. But I have, and have always had, the gravest doubts whether such an expansion under the rule of Mr. Rhodes and his monopolist crew would not in the long run do infinite harm to South Africa as a whole.
> The Chiefs Khama, Sebele, and Bathoen, as was stated last week, are just now in England for the purpose of preventing their countries from being seized and sucked dry by Mr. Rhodes and his "ring." (5 October 1895: 435-436)

A very similar unsigned article, "Khama and the Chartered Company," appeared in the *Saturday Review* on 26 October 1895 (536-537).

The Anglo-African novel of empire grew out of a specific call for direct appropriation or control through settlement for agricultural or mineral resources in "the great and fertile continent of Africa to be no longer kept wantonly sealed, but made available as the scene of European enterprise" (Livingstone, *Zambesi* 2)–and of course, perhaps not as an intentional afterthought, that the "happiness," "prosperity," "freedom," and "the blessings of the Gospel" will result for the African tribes. This was the missionary's largely humane agenda. But when that evening at the Anglo-African Writers' Club Bryden accused "Rhodes and the monopolists" of trying to seize and suck dry the land of native tribes, he voiced a dissent to a colonial ideal that Cecil Rhodes, if not Lionel Décle, had imbibed from John Ruskin, one of the most influential professors at Oxford. There is no more direct expression of imperialism than that offered by the enormously admired and influential Slade Professor of Art at Oxford University. Ruskin articulated *the* quintessential statement of British imperialism, "ripe with sinister idealism" (Monsman, *Schreiner* 2-3). His editors, Cook and Wedderburn, said Ruskin described this passage from *Lectures on Art* (1873) "as 'the most pregnant and essential' of all his teaching":

> There is a destiny now possible to us–the highest ever set before a nation to be accepted or refused. We are still undegenerate in race; a race mingled of the best northern blood. We are not yet dissolute in temper, but still have the firmness to govern, and the grace to obey.... Within the last few years we have had the laws of natural science opened to us with a rapidity which has been blinding by its brightness; and means of transit and communication given to us, which have made but one kingdom of the habitable globe. One kingdom;–but who is to be its king? Is there to be no king in it, ... or will you, youths of England, make your country again a royal throne of kings; a sceptred isle, for all the world a source of light, a centre of peace?

English global hegemony would be built on a "pure" aristocratic Anglo-Saxon bloodline. Ruskin's "race" of "best northern blood," for the moment "still undegenerate," connects with a broad fear of contamination, especially by darker races. Perhaps Alfred Tennyson's jilted and bitter young man of *Maud* (1855) had been influenced by such ideology–he who was tempted to "take some savage woman" but recoiled at the bestiality of being "mated with a squalid savage," siring offspring "with narrow foreheads, vacant of our glorious gains" (90).

Somewhat later Bram Stoker's *Dracula* (1897) and H. G. Wells's *War of the Worlds* (1898) took up this theme fictionally when England's vision of hereditary entitlement was challenged by a foreign invasion of blood-draining predators. In the opening pages of Wells's novel, the Martian observers of mankind are malevolent spies; but man, the arrogant observer of the protozoans (ironically, his ultimate savior), is the noble scientist. For Wells, privileging the terrestrial perspective resembles ethnocentric British imperialism, implying that the Martians, the technologically superior invaders, are only the British themselves in another guise. When Wells described the Martian attack upon London, center of the British empire, he allegorized the vulnerability of imperial ambitions, as a reminder to his countrymen that imperial rule upheld by force of arms may be challenged by the very progress it embodies. The salvation of London's citizens was owing to the Martians' progress in eliminating disease, thus also extinguishing their immunity to those insignificant bacilli. What the British in Bryden's image do to Africa's inhabitants through Rhodes–captured, "squeezed and sucked dry"–Stoker's or Wells's vampires do fictionally. Just before these novels, Mitford's *Sign of the Spider* (1896) featured a vampiric arachnid that drains its prey, another image of ethnocentric values that victimize by means of enforced customs, institutions, and laws.

Ruskin, the Anglo-African Writers' Club's *éminence grise*, elaborates:

> There are the two *oriflammes* [golden flames]; which shall we plant on the farthest islands,–the one that floats in heavenly fire, or that hangs heavy with foul tissue of terrestrial gold? There is indeed a course of beneficent glory open to us, such as never was yet offered to any poor group of mortal souls. But it must be–it *is* with us, now, "Reign or Die." And if it shall be said of this country, "*Fece per viltate, il gran rifiuto*,"[5] that refusal of the crown will be, of all yet recorded in history, the shamefullest and most untimely. And this is what she [England] must either do, or perish: she must found colonies as fast and as far as she is able, formed of her most energetic and worthiest men;–seizing every piece of fruitful waste ground she can set her foot on, and there teaching these her colonists that their chief virtue is to be fidelity to their country, and that their first aim is to be to advance the power of England by land and sea.

Here we have the dominant metropole and its unresisting periphery. Although possession of "fruitful waste ground" sounds almost like an ecological obligation, the reality of underutilization was quite different. Those rain-fed grazing areas are not "waste" but used by nomadic herders. To dispossess these pastoralists of their land would be to ruin them. Yet, says Ruskin:

---

5. Dante, *Inferno*, 3:59-60: "I saw and recognized the shade of him / Who made, through cowardice, the great refusal."

> The England who is to be mistress of half the earth, cannot remain herself a heap of cinders, trampled by contending and miserable crowds; she must yet again become the England she was once, and in all beautiful ways, . . . polluted by no unholy clouds, . . . she must guide the human arts, and gather the divine knowledge, of distant nations, transformed from savageness to manhood, and redeemed from despairing into peace. (20: 41-43)

Ruskin would consign industrial pollution to foreign soil, replacing it with an ideal of "arts" and "knowledge" regenerated for the British at home and abroad by empire. One may wish to compare the above quotations with another passage from Ruskin's *The Crown of Wild Olive* ([1866] 1906: 185).

Cecil Rhodes wrote his agenda as a young man of twenty-three, just before he left for Africa to become the greatest nineteenth-century political figure on that continent, after whom the territory of Rhodesia was named. If Rhodes had not elsewhere acknowledged indebtedness to Ruskin, his use of "seize" and "duty" would certainly have established an influence. In what has been entitled "Rhodes's 'Confession of Faith'" (1877), he wrote:

> I contend that we are the finest race in the world and that the more of the world we inhabit the better it is for the human race. Just fancy those parts that are at present inhabited by the most despicable specimens of human beings, what an alteration there would be if they were brought under Anglo-Saxon influence; look again at the extra employment a new country added to our dominions gives. I contend that every acre added to our territory means, in the future, birth to some more of the English race who otherwise would not be brought into existence. Added to this, the absorption of the greater portion of the world under our rule simply means the end of all wars. . . .
>
> Why should we not form a secret Society with but one object, the furtherance of the British Empire and the bringing of the whole uncivilised world under British rule, for the recovery of the United States, for the making the Anglo-Saxon race but one Empire? What a dream; but yet it is probable, it is possible . . . . Africa is still lying ready for us; it is our duty to take it. It is our duty to seize every opportunity of acquiring more territory. (Flint 200)

Ruskin was the theorist, Rhodes the practitioner. Perhaps neither set out to warp and deprave his given portion of history, to create a ruthless and cruel empire controlled solely by notions of blood purity and racial heredity.

In contrast with Ruskinian urbanity or Rhodesian crudity of direct appropriation, there was another ideal, one of cooperation, voiced by Bryden and Schreiner but best encapsulated by John Buchan in hindsight. Novelist and political figure, Buchan had accepted an invitation from Lord Alfred Milner, the colonial administrator, to go with him to South Africa. Milner's quest for British influence in Africa was reflected in Buchan's highly idealistic hopes for empire:

> Those were the days when a vision of what the Empire might be made dawned upon certain minds with almost the force of a revelation. . . . It was an inspiration for youth to realise the magnitude of its material heritage, and to think how it might be turned to spiritual issues. Milner, like most imperialists of that day, believed in imperial federation. . . . I dreamed of a world-wide brotherhood with the background of a common race and creed, consecrated to the service of peace; Britain enriching the rest out of her culture and traditions, and the spirit of the Dominions like a strong wind freshening the stuffiness of the old lands. I saw in the Empire a means of giving to the congested masses at home open country instead of a blind alley. I saw hope for a new afflatus in art and literature and thought. Our creed was not based on antagonism to any other people. It was humanitarian and international; we believed that we were laying the basis of a federation of the world. As for the native races under our rule, we had a high conscientiousness; Milner and Rhodes had a far-sighted native policy. The "white man's burden" is now an almost meaningless phrase; then it involved a new philosophy of politics, and an ethical standard, serious and surely not ignoble. (Buchan, *Memory* 124-25).

Buchan contrasts Africa's "scents, sights and sounds" to London's "dull mercantile" tone and its "vulgar display of wealth, and a *rastaquouère* craze for luxury. I began to have an ugly fear that the Empire might decay at the heart" (127-28). But the irony is that if the idea of empire had been less idealistic and more realistic, then cynically self-enriching liars would not have been able to manipulate the naive and single-minded belief in a cooperative international world. Nor would the blundering created by colonial ransacking of resources and a failure to recognize and honor cultural differences have led to Buchan's dawning realization "that the Empire might decay at the heart." A power in the land's historic and material possession by its inhabitants created anxiety about the Empire's future. In the colonies exploitation was paradoxically mixed with appreciation of African spirituality; in the metropole humanitarian views were often neutralized by profit-driven financial schemes. This debate on colonial affairs pivoted between the fantasy of a harmonious empire and a violent capitalistic and Western venture that incited black resistance. Precisely here lies the central dilemma of the imperial debate–either idealistic assimilation or hypocritical victimization. Britain's "most energetic and worthiest men" were offered incorruptible devotion to duty and the chance to make the kind of world they aspired to inhabit–or they must resist the siren song of hope, of idealism, of over-much faith in those around them and of a mission to spread the British gospel of light to all the dark places of the earth.

Invited speakers at later gatherings of the Anglo-African club comprised such luminaries as Conan Doyle, whose first story, "The Mystery of the Sassassa Valley," was set in Southern Africa– appearing the same month that his first professional article came out in the *British Medical Journal*, both in September 1879; afterwards, as a young physician Doyle had worked as medical officer on a ship going to west Africa, becoming gravely ill with typhoid. Invited in 1897 to speak, Doyle replied on 15 June: "I have, as you know, been idling for a long time and so I contemplate a hard winter's work, which can only be done by cutting off all festive occasions however tempting. I am none the less very much flattered that the Anglo-African club should have wished to have me as their guest" (Reznikoff 883). A few years later, on the brink of the Anglo-Boer war in which Doyle would serve as medical officer in South Africa, Haggard wrote (in the hand of a secretary, signed by Haggard) to Greville Matheson, Secretary of the Anglo-African Writers' Club on 18 April 1899: "I enclose Conan Doyle's answer. Perhaps you could see, or write to him & try to make some arrangement. I enclose cheque for my share of the Grand Hotel account" (Hart 6602). *The North Otago Times* reported on 27 November 1899 that "Dr. Conan Doyle, the well known author, was on Monday night the principal guest of the evening at a dinner of the Anglo-African Writers' Club at the Grand Hotel, London, where he observed that "violence would be a sign of weakness," and cautioned against "the bullying of a small Power by a large one," referring to President Kruger of the dissident Transvaal (4).

Another notable was Rudyard Kipling in May of 1898. Kipling, so the newspaper reported, was introduced by Haggard as a visionary of empire: "There was more in the idea of empire than that of trade, and the poet and idealist had a nobler conception of empire than the trader, and none was better qualified to give expression to that conception than their friend Mr. Kipling, who realized as few had realized the Divine right of a great civilizing race such as ours." Kipling praised the "strong men who were working for our Empire," who "had to deal with an agricultural simplicity which objected to the very elements of civilization–to simple precautions against the spread of disease among their sheep, against rinderpest, objected to railways and to roads of all kinds. (Laughter.)" ("Anglo," 17 May 1898: 11; also *The New York Times* 11 June 1898: BR385; *African Review* 21 May 1898: 311-313). Haggard's old boss, Henry Bulwer, the lieutenant Governor of Natal, later its governor and special commissioner for Zulu affairs, brought as his guest the future film-maker, Charles Ken, to this talk (Archives, Hertfordshire).

At the next meeting, on 20 June 1898, Haggard chaired a dinner of the club at which he and Ex-Chief Justice J. G. Kotzé both gave speeches. Haggard recalled with nostalgia riding the judicial circuit with Kotzé, a native Boer appointed judge soon after the Transvaal had been annexed:

> I looked at him, and I said, "Well, if a person can become a Judge at that age I will take to the trade myself." . . . Well, in the course of our various voyagings–and in those days it was really a case of voyagings, because we travelled together through many

and many a mile of veld, dragged by oxen–as you may imagine, I became well acquainted with your guest of to-night. I saw him in every relation. I saw him on the Bench, executing the duties of his office; I saw him in private life; I saw him, I remember, sitting on the legs of a drunken usher while I was in the post of honour on his head. (Laughter.) I saw him stuck up to his chin in a Transvaal swamp; and, by the way, gentlemen, I think that perhaps it might be said that he is stuck in another Transvaal swamp now. (Cheers.) I had the honour then of pulling him out, and I only wish I could have the honour of pulling him out now. (Cheers.)

Haggard then turned to the uproar caused by President Paul Kruger's recent unconstitutional dismissal of him as chief justice. Kipling, Haggard remarked, would have attended this dinner but for a family funeral, so he sent instead "some lines which he wrote out for me." After jokes about whose muse inspired this effort, signed "Vrede" ("Peace" in Afrikaans), Haggard quotes two of them: "May there be no moaning at the Bar, / When I put out Kotzé." Haggard added: "All of you have read it in the Press. They have talked of him as a devil. Well, if Mr. Kotzé is a devil, all I have got to say is that a certain place loses much of its terror. (Laughter.) They have talked of him as mad. If he is mad, all I have to say is that I hope my own sanity will go the same way, because he is the most brilliant lunatic whom I have ever met. (Hear, hear.)" (*African Review* 476).

After a very lucid account of how affairs in the Transvaal were spinning out of control towards near-dictatorial subordination of the judicial branch by the executive, Kotzé challenged the members of the Anglo-African club, who, he said, "hold a great and, let me add, a very responsible position," to put forth their influence "by aiding the independent Press of South Africa in supporting us in fighting for a liberal and broad Constitution–a Constitution based upon the people's will; and when I say the people I include the new-comer [i.e. British] as well as the old population." Kotzé even unwittingly all but introduced the speaker some months hence: "A very able and right hon. gentleman, Mr. Bryce, has said in his very admirable and able book on South Africa that the Transvaal is in a condition of unrest. I regret to say that there is a great deal of truth in that remark." The former Chief Justice concluded by recalling that the young Haggard "was as good a cook as he was a shot, and how delightful it was to sit over their evening meal discussing their good old whisky and roast snipe on toast prepared by their Chairman" (*African Review* 25 June 1898: 477-18).

At its December meeting in 1898, chaired as usual by Haggard, the group was addressed by James Bryce (now honorary President of the club), one of Britain's most intelligent statesmen, whose *Impressions of South Africa* (1897) had recently appeared. *The London Times* summarized his remarks that evening:

> It might be asked what literary men could do for the colonies, and what the colonies could do for literary men. . . . There still existed in England an ignorance of colonial society and of the conditions of colonial life, and he thought literature could remove that ignorance. Literature might make people in England understand the deep and peculiar charm that South Africa had for all who lived in it, and also make them understand its difficulties. (Hear, hear.) The chief difficulty which beset South Africa was the difficulty of race, but that was a difficulty which would ultimately give way under tact and judgment. (Hear, hear.). . . .
> As to the question of what the colonies might do for literary men, he thought they might give them new fields, new topics, new subjects which were very welcome now that the old fields had been tilled and crops reaped from them over and over again . . . When the soil of the old country had been exhausted, there were abundant fields in the outlying portions of the Empire. The works of Rudyard Kipling, Thomas Pringle, Olive Schreiner, Mr. Scully, and Mr. Bryden, and the brilliant romances of the chairman [Haggard], were instances of what the study of new conditions might do in the way of stimulating and developing the force of the writer's thought, and he did not think it was idle to suppose that the time might come when the literary activity of the colonies themselves might be far more abundant than it was at present. (*Times* 22 December 1898: 8).

Bryce said these twin ideals of dispelling British ignorance of colonial life and of igniting "the literary activity of the colonies themselves" were tasks that writers such as Haggard already had initiated. Bryce's promise of "new fields, new topics, new subjects" is not unlike Buchan's youthful "hope for a new afflatus in art and literature." Given the club's political sympathies with "the Divine right of a great civilizing race such as ours," Bryce is not sowing here in the depleted British imagination any budding awareness of the unacceptable ethnocentricity of adjudging cultures superior or inferior based on divergent customs or technology; nor was he foreseeing any burst of writing by black Africans describing in their own distinctive voices the circumstances of their lives. But "new fields, new topics, new subjects" *did* include African spirituality as an antidote to the Empire's materialism.

Bryce also observed "that his first impressions of South Africa–formed before he went there–were derived from missionary narratives read in his youth, and partly from the brilliant descriptions of their Chairman"–Haggard (*New York Times* BR23). If one applies Bryce's analysis of the British colonial writers' role to Mitford–his name is not mentioned by Bryce, most likely because he avoided the limelight of interviews (much loved by Haggard) and book-signings (Scully's promotional forte)–his Zulu-Ndebele novels go in the direction of Bryce's "new fields, new topics, new subjects" by leading "the people at home" to see "the difficulty of race" in imperial Africa. This was a time of cultural exchange as well as intense conflict within a shifting balance of power among indigenous African communities themselves and between them and European adventurers, traders, and settlers. But after the Zulu and Matabele Wars (in 1879 and 1893), this see-saw of negotiation between races and disparate economic systems was supplanted in southern Africa by a monolithic industrial economy. Mitford, recollecting the once-mighty Ndebele empire (the current terms in the nineteenth-century were Matabele/Matabeleland) that had collapsed, presents Mzilikazi (or Umzilikazi) as a ruler standing by concurrence of events in the crossfire of past and present. Eurocentric power and a world economy destroyed indigenous social and cultural traditions and expunged African self-determination and a sense of historic identity and national consciousness.

Typical of its topical political interest was a meeting of 17 October 1899 at the outbreak of the Anglo-Boer War. Haggard warmly asserted that at the retrocession of the Transvaal England had deserted "loyal Englishmen" and is "now, in 1899, reaping the fruits of 1881." That evening's speaker also suggested that "the curse of the slave was in the Dutchman in South Africa–he did not work, and he was one of the most unhappy people in the world, inasmuch as his leaders were not educated" (*Times*: 6). On 27 March 1900 the speaker seconded Haggard's sentiments by saying that "if blame attached to any one in connexion with the present war in broad justice it attached not so much to the Boers of the Transvaal and the Free State as to the weakness of British policy during the quarter of a century which preceded the war." A dinner of 12 November 1900 extolled the exploits of the scout Major Frederick Burnham, an American, recently returned from the front with praise from Field Marshal Frederick Roberts. Another guest was A. G. Hales, an Australian, who "regretted that Mr. Winston Churchill was not present, because he hated hitting a man behind his back," but nevertheless he thwacked him. Churchill had accused Hale of belittling the courage of the officer corps whereas Hale had criticized its training: "That had been his contention all through, and in twisting his statement, Mr. Winston Churchill had shown the imagination for which his family had ever been remarkable. (Laughter.)" (*Daily News* 13 November 1900: 5). Hale, who had proposed to the War Office to command in South Africa a corps mounted on camels, instead had to settle for becoming Special Correspondent of the *Daily News.* One of the most (inadvertently) amusing comments was made on the post-war Boers by the then-President of the club, Sir Walter Peace: "The first need of South Africa was a class of people who would convert the authorities of the Dutch Reformed Church to a better conception of the principles and practice of Christianity" (*Times* 15 October 1902: 12). This comment would certainly have met with Mitford's approval inasmuch as the self-righteous citizens of Barabastadt described in *The Weird of Deadly Hollow* (1891) were in need of just this.

      The Anglo-African Writers' Club, its topics and its speakers, became a filter by which the alien "other" on the periphery was construed. If for some Africans colonialism initially had provided profitable access to far-flung markets, the settlers in consequence of local competition used their clout in the metropole to turn nebulous self-seeking into a seizure of tribal lands and their instruments of production, a logical if deplorable manifestation of opportunistic capitalism. One probably should not conjecture that, free from the political push-and-shove of the far flung territories, such urban centers of empire were ostensibly "neutral" ground. Certainly in a number of stories and novels by Haggard and others, especially Mitford, the dual English/African setting suggests that the principal character has engaged African culture and, by the final outcome, either been able to accommodate his European self to the Other (rarely with contentment and a clear conscience, more likely with no conscience whatsoever) or must repress that Other entirely. The nineteenth century recognized on some subliminal level that this Other they controlled and feared was within themselves. From Stevenson's Mr. Hyde, Wilde's *Picture of Dorian Gray* (1890),Wells's Morlocks in *The Time Machine* (1895), Stoker's Dracula, these fearful fictional doubles feed directly into the political suppression of the indigenous populations under imperial rule. W. C. Scully, one of the members of the Anglo-African Writers' Club, wrote a powerful polemic in *Kafir Stories* (1895) entitled "Kellson's Nemesis." Revisiting Mary Shelley's allegory of creation, Scully describes the outcome of Kellson's adultery: "The face that the prisoner's reminded him of, and that he could not localise, was his own" (85). Like Victor Frankenstein, Kellson has created a horror–because this son was bi-racial–that he is too weak to accept. Only his suicide can close the loop of sin, no other escape remains. Both Frankenstein's creature and Kellson's "half-caste" son are their repressed selves; the double's guilt is really a reflection of their own sin.

One evening in June1900 at a meeting of the Anglo-African club, the members discussed the tensions of the current Anglo-Boer War and its future settlement–in particular, whether English should be the official language in the colonies (*Times* 19 June 1900: 11). Language (spoken or written) can never be taken as innocent of social perceptions, mental attitudes, and ambitions; it serves political objectives, change, and historical transformation not only in the functional realm of capitalism and the international corporate world, but in the aesthetic and intellectual arenas as well. Chaired by H. Rider Haggard and attended by Mitford, this discussion must have been a prime instance of how language could be used to create a political reality. Every speaker's experiences and ideas of the world are delineated and conveyed by a communal language; and this linguistic construct is pliable and vulnerable to biased and ideological interpretations that frame its discursive meanings. The totalizing effect on settlers and indigenes alike of such an imperially-controlled standard assists the geopolitical construction of a British myth–of white settler superiority, heroic military self-image, religious truth, or whatever–evolving as the needs arise to "explain" conquests, insurrections, and disasters. Six months later at the December meeting of the club, language was again suggested as a prime political tool. Then a Rhodesian visitor not only "advocated the official use of the English tongue in all affairs in South Africa" but added (ominously in hindsight) that an official language promoted the solidarity of "race feeling" (*Times* 18 December 1900: 10).

Clearly the definition of imperial English as a civilizing force over against the "many languages and dialects" (Bryce) of Africans and Boers who embodied "an agricultural simplicity which objected to the very elements of civilization"(Kipling) casts light on a theoretical truism: a tightly centralized language policy deriving from the metropole tends to marginalize the linguistic and cultural background of the local populations. The stronger social group has the power to impose its official interpretation on the groups it dominates, refusing to recognize the narrative authority of the dominated and, usually, being unable to envisage a point of view other than its own. Yet among those *initiating* an international or African English not subservient to empire is Miford. While utilizing the language of colonial occupation to tell Untúswa's story in *The King's Assegai* (1894), Mitford, like African novelists Sol Plaatje or Chinua Achebe afterwards, melds English with "Africanisms" in daily use, idiomatic turns of phrase, songs, proverbs, and even changes of the meanings of words to match localized African concepts–as for example Untúswa's "My father" idiom, a form of respectful address among Africans or by blacks to whites, authentic for the pre-colonial and colonial eras. Because all events can be retold and every fact recast, what Haggard and Mitford wrote becomes a part of that reality, as constitutive of understanding as the archival "facts" themselves. Neither Haggard nor any of his contemporaries in the Grand Hotel would have been comfortable with this level of theorization; yet the political disorder that exists today in post-colonial Africa is largely the product, not entirely of pre-colonial governance systems, but of nineteenth century jingoism about "great civilizing races such as ours," formulaically uttered in the Anglo-African club or deliberate lies, as Plaatje says of the Boers, of peaceful coexistence in the name of religious freedom. Language–the voices of paramount chefs, traders, soldiers, teachers, missionaries, adventurers, indigenes–were indeed among the most powerful instruments in resisting or creating new political realities–not least that of the British Empire.

James Bryce observed in *Impressions of South Africa* that "the conditions that have been described as unfavorable to literary production are not necessarily permanent, and there is no reason why the Europeans of South Africa should not in due time emulate their kinsfolk at home or in North America in literary or artistic fertility. The material for imaginative work, whether in poetry or prose, lies ready to their hand." His linguistic observation may be even more significant:

> The Kafirs, now divided into many tribes and speaking many languages and dialects, will lose their present tribal organization, their languages, their distinctive habits. Whether some sort of native *lingua Franca* [a jumble of different languages] will spring up, or whether they will all come to speak English, is doubtful; but probably in the long run English will prevail and become the common speech of the southern half of the continent. They will also lose their heathenism (though many superstitions will survive), and will become, in name at least, Christians. Thus they will form to a far greater extent than now a homogeneous mass pervaded by the same ideas and customs... When, perhaps in the twenty-first century, the native population has reached the point of progress we have been imagining, the position may be for both races a grave or even a perilous one, if the feeling and behaviour of the whites continue to be what they are now. (401)

Olive Schreiner also echoes this ideal of a universal English language:

> We do not dream of our language that it shall forcibly destroy the word's speeches and all they contain, reigning in solitary grandeur, but, as gold in a ring binds into one circle rare gems of every kind and some of infinitely greater beauty than itself, so we dream that our speech being common may bind together and bring into one those treasures of thought and knowledge which the peoples of earth have produced, its highest function being that of making the treasures of all accessible to all. . . . We look for the spread of our language, not because it is of necessity the finest and most complex and expressive instrument of thought, though, after our instinct for freedom, it is the noblest outgrowth of our race, . . . but because in this tongue will be preached the most valuable lesson humanity has yet to learn; because, wherever a people has come into contact with it, it has meant for them freedom and advance. (Schreiner, *Thoughts* 355-56)

This ideal turns back upon the use of language to create a political reality–will the new international English discussed by Bryce, Schreiner, Mitford and Haggard represent a hegemonic imperialism or will it somehow stand alongside of African tongues in a dialogic way? Any imperfect integration of an "other" into an adopted cultural language creates psychological handicaps. Native speakers who forfeit their mother tongues are alienated from their origins. Gustavo Firmat reports that "one of the most disabling forms of low-self-esteem arises from the conviction that one cannot speak one's native language well enough, the shattering sense of inferiority that arises, not when words fail you, but when you fail them" (175). And from a revolutionary Guinean political leader who defied colonial rule: "To be ourselves once again, to be in harmony with ourselves," writes Ahmed Sékou Touré, "it is essential that we express ourselves in our own languages" (Corbett 9). The assimilationist ideal of multiple tongues within a unifying English language is betrayed at its source by the guileful script of imperial greed that preceded it; mutual trust broken between native and colonial voices, all outcomes that would have encouraged a multiplicity of tongues became illusory.

§

In most venues the colonial "script" allowed the imperialist to establish control over the Africans by framing intrusion with deceit. Thus in H. Rider Haggard's *King Solomon's Mines* (1885) when the hunters beg to be pardoned for mistaking the trio of adventurers as merely mortal rather than the gods they say they are, Allan Quatermain's "imperial smile" is so self-aware that Haggard must have intended a deliberately ironic scene:

> "It is granted," I said, with an imperial smile. "Nay, ye shall know the truth. We come from another world, though we are men such as ye; we come," I went on, "from the biggest star that shines at night."
> "Oh! oh!" groaned the chorus of astonished aborigines.
> "Yes," I went on, "we do indeed"; and I again smiled benignly as I uttered that amazing lie. "We come to stay with you a little while, and bless you by our sojourn. Ye will see, O friends, that I have prepared myself by learning your language."
> "It is so, it is so," said the chorus.
> "Only, my lord," put in the old gentleman, "thou hast learnt it very badly." (112)

Is Quatermain's smile only the gracious royal awarding of a petition– or is it the knowing smirk of imperial duplicity? Clearly Quatermain's assertion of truth-telling covers a most outrageous prevarication that disguises the adventurers' basic intentions. Of course, the old induna's observation on Quatermain's linguistic attainments amusingly opens the door a crack on imperial fallibility. Later, just before Captain Good hoodwinks the tribe with the prediction of an eclipse, Quatermain calls out: "Look, chiefs and people and women, and see if the white men from the stars keep their word, or if they be but empty liars!" King Ignosi, clearly aware that Quatermain is an adept liar in at least two languages, declares with merely the barest soupçon of barbed puffery that "English 'gentlemen' tell no lies"

(157, 151). Such self-misrepresentation discredited the imperial enterprise and made it difficult for idealists to maintain faith in its political future.

John Buchan's *A Lodge in the Wilderness* (1906) is a searching philosophical analysis of the political basis of imperialism at a time when that idea was undergoing serious challenge. He modernizes Ruskin's call to an imperial rule not as an "obscene empire of mammon" but a recovery of the arts and social capital lost to globalizing industrialization, the scenes set on the African premises of a "patriotic" millionaire very much like Cecil Rhodes (1906: 1-19). Buchan cannibalized text from an unfinished novel, "The Mountain" (1905), for this new project. Although he was born too late for the Anglo-African club, Buchan's fictive month-long conversation among seventeen carefully chosen British men and women, set in a opulent villa in Kenya and interspersed with sightseeing and hunting episodes, is a forum very much like that of the Anglo-African Writers' Club–almost its philosophic continuation. Like the club, this imaginary gathering was not a "debating society" (38) but an organized group that met for a common purpose–to unpack and reshape empire as a new form of imagined place with "a new language" (98). Hermann Wittenberg has convincingly demonstrated that Buchan's landscape is not that of Kenya but of a "very specific place" in South Africa "east of Pietersburg (now Polokwane) in Limpopo province" (8-10). During this symposium, one of the women describes her famous relative, Sir Charles Weston, who, she had discovered upon his death, kept two diaries–thirty volumes of his actual dry-as-dust political life and a shorter account of a fantasy life as a Byzantine emperor. Reflecting a public and private "double life" (275) not unlike the Jekyll/Hyde doppelgänger so close to the Victorian heart, these two diaries overlap for a period of time in Sir Charles's life with contrastingly parallel passages; that is, though the "entries correspond" (279) they describe reciprocal and radically different events. Because we "have in our breasts odds and ends of strange souls" (271)–this, a nod to E. B. Tylor's anthropological notion of savage "survivals" –Sir Charles's "clash of opposites" (271) between the real and the exotic also lies "at the bottom of our new conception of empire" (274) and is "an allegory and true of us all" (272).

Whether or not Buchan's classic study is envisioning Tylor's savage "survivals" as able to reanimate contemporary society, Buchan appears both to have anticipated the modernist's fantasy of Africa as the locale for a recovery of spiritual vitality and to have foreshadowed T. S. Eliot's interpretation of modernism's handing of myth as "a continuous parallel between contemporaneity and antiquity" ("Ulysses" 177-178). Previously, in *Lodge in the Wilderness* London had been described as the "imperial center of gravity" (122-123, 95); that is, the source of power that provides the will to act. In London, Sir Charles assumed the role of a minor prophet and "cried 'Ichabod' to the future of Israel" (273)–that is, he bemoaned the loss of glory in the world of political liberalism. But for Sir Charles it is clear that the metropolitan center secretly needed the ambitions of imperialism and its challenge to "create a new earth" (282), a phrase used by Buchan several times elsewhere, apart from Sir Charles's fantasy. The Charles on London's inglorious and jejune stage cannot be reconciled with the role of Charles as a Byzantine emperor.

If Buchan and such predecessors as Mitford or Haggard did not wholly escape British stereotypes of what Africans were believed to be, they considered their psychic powers, lost to the more-evolved colonizers, to be culturally desirable. The Anglo-African felt that wonder and mystery were undermined by modes of rationalistic thought and sensed that African spirituality might address the moral and intellectual decline of British culture, particularly dubiety about traditional Christian answers to the ultimates of life and death. Missionaries believed that the supernatural, paranormal, and occult practices connected with necromancy were all darkly superstitious, but others within the empire approved of animistic attitudes, such as ancestor veneration, that seemingly endowed Africans with psychic powers. Although the missionaries brought the Bible to Africa, their acculturative enterprise became a two-way street when the imperialists appropriated indigenous philosophies and spiritualistic sentiments–along with their territories. As part of this hybridization of colonial culture and discreet subversion of ideologies of empire, gender, and race, several of these writers achieved something like a dual European Christian/African animistic posture. They superimposed the symbols, rituals, and holistic experience of African spiritualism–never institutionalized as in Western religious practices–upon all those imported Bibles handed out by the missionaries. The irony is that while metropolitan centers exported an unquestioned "essentiality of western civilization" (if one may invoke such a controversial concept)–its values of human rights and dignity, free enterprise, democracy and self-determination–African beliefs about supernatural powers and the spiritual world shifted Western theism's center of gravity. For some, rationalistic monism yielded to strangely intermixed qualities of good and bad, light and dark, life and death, a dualistic embeddedness of one's own primitive self in the blood of earth.

Until recently regarded in most quarters as old-fashioned writers who pandered to imperial stereotypes, Mitford's and Haggard's reputations have been nurtured among literary critics, select but few. Although a number of Haggard's novels have never been out of print since their first publication, a problem with Mitford's legacy is that although copies of his novels are in many libraries, in recent decades none was in print until recently. The reasons for this oversight are not far to seek:— First: like H. Rider Haggard's fantasies of exoticism and magic that fell afoul of patronizing attitudes towards work grounded in the popular culture, Mitford's writing is mistakenly considered naive historical fiction, a popular genre unworthy of scholarly analysis. However, both Haggard's and Mitford's novels are anything but dry antiquarian costume histories enacting some stilted reanimation of the past; rather, they were imaginatively forged by events that unfolded in the recent arena of their personal experiences. Ultimately, the role of their romances involves not just the facts of imperial activity, of what happened, but raises the critical issue of the imperial lesson and shows why one still cares to read about the past for the sake of the present.

Second: after the catastrophes and costs of the Boer War (not to mention the unsustainable economics of a metastasizing empire during World War I) and with few people still possessing first-hand memories of the frontier wars and pre-colonial inhabitants, there was an appreciable lessening of popular interest within the United Kingdom about current events in South Africa. Moreover, by 1900 maps that only a few decades earlier had spelled out "Unknown Interior" now confidently marked, even in the equatorial regions, rivers and swamps, railways and canals, oases and colonial capitals. The unknown had been largely tamed and the exotic adventure novel of Africa was losing its functional footing. As interest in pioneer life waned within the broader culture, global industrialization made the freedom of adventures on frontier veldts and farms quaint in comparison to an urban existence beset by crushing social and physical circumstances. Haggard's and Mitford's stories became redolent of yesteryear, sagas all dead and done with that no longer competed in the public consciousness with more-urgent cosmopolitan conflicts and tragedies.

Third: modernism also burdened with new political baggage the old ideas of what makes a hero. Romantic tales of resolute pluck were balanced now by an awareness of the arrogance of Eurocentrism and its harm to African nations and cultures. Already even during Victoria's reign, which encompassed the glory days of empire, both occasionally within the colonies and certainly within Britain, the ideological seeds of an imperial break-up were germinating. Perhaps the "values-fade" of those older aristocratic-chivalric virtues that the English once relished in literature received their quietus by the malevolent and twisted sort of national "honor" and "progress" endorsed in the following century by Nazis and Communists.

But what is still "of quality and fabric" in the fiction of Mitford, Haggard, and others that no thoughtful person could ignore is that they portrayed with authentic local color the sudden changes wrought by the British empire upon traditional, indigenous ways of life in South Africa. Mitford's novels, especially, describe authoritatively the peculiarities of specific regions, characters and scenery that possess factual content. On the level of national events his works follow history and chronology fairly closely and contain authentic details that he probably gathered from first-hand sources, such as the frontiersman Johan Colenbrander, an "old friend" (*Ames*, v)–much as Haggard used Andrew Lang for ethnographic authenticity to forestall racist stereotypes and drew upon Fred Fynney for details of tribal character and ritual. Supporting Mitford's factuality is the oddity that when A. T. Bryant's *Olden Times in Zululand and Natal* (1929) quoted a "native informant" about a detail in Ndebele history, Leonard Thompson in the *Oxford History of South Africa* (1969) cited this passage in Bryant's book as an example of authentic African oral tradition. The amusing thing is that Bryant's "native informant" is a character in one of Mitford's novels, and if Bryant did not borrow this from Mitford, then both men must be borrowing it from some still-unknown third source. In negotiating the contract for his eerie doppelgänger tale, *The White Hand and the Black* (1907), Mitford wrote to his literary agent that the publisher must agree "not to alter or suppress any word, either of the copy, title page, or of the spelling of words or names of a technical or indigenous character, but to issue the book exactly as he receives it" (Monsman, *Haggard* 279).

Mitford was only too acutely aware of large-scale changes moving across the traditionally pastoral horizon of 1890s South Africa's eastern Cape Colony. Railroads, telegraph, international commerce, economic pressures–all united to create a deleterious social flux, pushing the Africans from the land into urban bondage. Confronted with an 1890s colonial African society in flux, Mitford's professed fictional objective is to document an authentic but "vanishing" history. As he remarked in *The Gun-Runner*:

> If our narrative deals with history, it is with a vanishing page of the same; and as such we look to it to interest the reader, if only as a sidelight upon the remarkable military power and ultimate downfall of the finest and most intelligent race of savages in the world–now, thanks to the "beneficent" policy of England, crushed and "civilized" out of all recognition. (vi)

Similar sentiments are expressed in the preface to H. Rider Haggard's *Child of Storm*. To write of the past–or of a vanishing present–may be to infuse it with nostalgia, but it need be no more fictionally inaccurate as to the meanings of action or event than any historical memoir or chronicle of former days.

Few Anglo-African writers have told their tales better or with more fidelity to life than Mitford, who combined suspense with a grasp of colonial traditions and vicissitudes. In comparison to the mythic world of Haggard, Mitford presents a more contemporary, realistic Africa, though certainly not as severely drab as Olive Schreiner's. Perhaps because Mitford more frequently writes of the Eastern Cape Colony, rather than of Rhodesia (so-named then) or of the far interior–his Ndebele-Zulu quartet and *The Sign of the Spider* (1896) being among the exceptions–he stresses the ordinary social realities of colonial existence: neighbors, mounted police, and towns with Westernized blacks, bicycles, trams, judges and banks. His narratives are launched with leisurely attention to tone and feel, sometimes with such domestic reverberations as the employment of the New Woman in *Averno* (1913) or urban tedium in *Sign of the Spider*; then their plots tighten toward lightning-paced dramatic action. R.W. Jones suggests that "as one of the first to transform personal colonial experience into fiction," Mitford's "long descriptive passages are an intimate and accurate record of the hazards and hardships and casual incidents of frontier life, and of the daily habits and customs of colonists and tribesmen. As such they are invaluable source material for the social historian. The passage of time may revive interest in them as contemporary historical novels" (*Dictionary of South African Biography* 3: 619). These "descriptive passages" are a necessary grounding of the exotic within the familiar, establishing interpretive parameters, and recognizing the complementarity of reality and fantasy. Zulus and other tribes are not sensationalized, except occasionally as with the blood-drinkers in *Gerard Ridgley* (1894) or the cannibal orgies in *Sign of the Spider* or *The King's Assegai*.

Another admirable feature is Mitford's period adventure heroes, exemplary Victorians with a desire to explore both unknown physical territory and the *terra incognita* of the spirit world–dual journeys from the known into the unknown, from the unexplored geographic expanses of the world ripe for colonization into the mysterious preternatural rites of South Africa that offered new occult possibilities. Of course, the psychological interiority of nineteenth-century romance, even the ironies of Joseph Conrad's "An Outpost of Progress" (1897), never went so far as the strategic unreliability of Vladimir Nabokov's "Terra Incognita" (1931) in which the physical and mental worlds cannot be distinguished and even lucidity turns out to be just another illusion. But in no small measure Mitford's fiction contributed to an emerging aesthetic indebted thematically and intellectually to "the primitive," in the spirit of anthropologists E. B. Tylor and J. G. Frazier. The Latin poet Horace said that the task of the fine arts was to instruct and to entertain. Polemicizing, propagandizing, and proselytizing are aesthetically ill at ease with an artistic vision; but narratives of human interactions that blend imagination with respect for known facts is a fine art. Because of his experiences, Mitford was exceptionally responsive to what today we call "third space"or border thresholds. Writers living on the border have a firsthand opportunity to instruct and enliven by detailing the processes of cultural interchange. In more than forty novels, Mitford explored several geographical and psychic "spaces" of encounter between the British and tribal inhabitants–the Xhosas (or amaXhosa) on the Cape's Eastern frontier; the Zulus in what is now KwaZulu-Natal; and the Matabeles (or Amandebele) in what was then called Rhodesia, now Zimbabwe.

Finally, there is also a sophisticated narrative interface between the voices of his historical figures and imaginary characters, the opinions of the author, and his readers' responses. The primacy of raw data, of facts speaking for themselves, is an illusion. The living novelist must speak for those facts and supply the connections of an intellectual context; and the reader must judge those interpretations in the light of what else may be known. Since novels never emerge into historical reality except as aesthetic artifacts, their pragmatic meanings are only such as readers other than their authors take them (perhaps too gullibly) to be. The sayings or doings of the fictional characters cannot be correlated unequivocally with any authorial opinion; rather, the reader is encouraged to search behind the masks of character, to see through the social or moral ambiguities of settler and savage alike–whether sentimental fantasies, half-truths, noble lies, inconsistencies or lunacy–for the elusive authorial viewpoint. The text never says entirely what the reader thinks it says. Writers often introduce settlers such as Lyndall in *The Story of an African Farm* (1883) or Lorraine in *The Gun-Runner*, Africans such as Sapazani in *Forging the Blades* (1908), Jeekie in *The Yellow God* (1908) and John Laputa in Buchan's *Prester John* (1910)–all of whom may be dubious characters. Neither role models nor virtuous leaders, they yet simultaneously serve as the alter ego and mouthpiece for the authors' concerns and opinions. Certainly this is the case with Mitford's slayer Untúswa, who treats the "inferior and conquered" race of Barolong ironworkers as mere animals (*Induna's Wife* 24) and he has little horror at Umzilikazi's brutal, cold-blooded punishments. Although Untúswa and Lalusini are both entirely imaginary, through their eyes the reader is given a significantly new set of explanations and insights into the back of the tribal mind. Understandably, when an author such as Mitford actually participated as a settler and journalist in the imperial enterprise, the reader supposes his historical figures are cast to reflect the empire's political biases. But the challenge is that Mitford expected his readers to see past ethnic speakers who by British standards may have glaring moral faults yet nevertheless serve as mouthpieces for a legitimate ideology. Behind the actions and ambiguities of wizards or rebellious chiefs Mitford's readers are expected to find credible ideas and facts.

Possibly Mitford's most notable instance is found in *Renshaw Fanning's Quest* (1894) in which he writes that the land's "riches lying waste for ages in this remote solitude must at length yield to the grasping hand of their predestined owner–Man" (243). This may be an absurdity the author expected would remain unrecognized, inasmuch as the image pandered to Anglo-political ideology; and yet of course the Bush*man*, whom every "grasping" settler described as looking like an ape, is indeed a man long predating the English*man*. That readers disregard this inhabitant of the "waste" proves they are unseeing, their visionlessness being *au fond* Mitford's ironic attack on racism. Among all these fictional voices, ideas overlap lightly or deeply and may be confused or connected with each other, even sometimes giving rise to meanings-by-contrariety, as in *Renshaw Fanning*; yet when one responds apperceptively to the ways syntactic patterns and visual effects work, one moves slowly from a faintly-felt sense of the author's voice toward a more clearly-defined structure of his ideas and feelings. Not only in the more expository or editorial interludes of his discourse, as for example in *The Induna's Wife,* but also behind his rendering of tribal and colonial minds Mitford's distinctive authorial voice reveals itself in the suggestive patterns, structures, and ironies of the cultural and historical situations. The effects of syntax and diction, the patterns of imagery and action, the play of thoughts against thoughts, all signify that the would-be interpreter who reads unproblematically arrives at reductive interpretations. In making sense of Mitford, the mistake would be to miss the causative reality of events by reducing his texts entirely to limiting contemporary issues, such as "the colonial mentality," "victimization," "Eurocentrism," "gendered viewpoints," "authorial control," "oppressive power relationships"–all implicates of the readers' European background, surely. But the indigenes are equally agents who negotiate cultural values encompassing race, territoriality, gender, history and nationality.

After the disintegration of the Zulu *ancien régime*, the liberal members of the Anglo-African Writers' Club had looked forward to justice, literacy, medicine, modern communications, and relative prosperity, all under a new Anglophone dispensation. That delusion of a Europeanized Africa now stands in stark contrast to the post-colonial reality of today's stumbling giant. What was important about the Anglo-African Writers' Club was not its endorsement of empire, progressive or regressive as remarks may have been, but the twin ideals suggested by Bryce of dispelling British ignorance of colonial life and of igniting "the literary activity of the colonies" through "new fields, new topics, new subjects." This principle of artistic creativity, of what is "new" or fresh or innovative in literature, constituted the club's significance–new values and new subjects, certainly, but more radically the creation of literature, hitherto an under-practiced artistic genre in colonial society, introduced a new and subversive component into imperial discourse. It brought the language of obliqueness, subtle subversion, rather than mere journalistic attack or support for any explicit ideology. Such new literature from geographically diverse lands is contextual and capitalizes on less-familiar materials, uncovering forgotten roots and utilizing little-heard ideas, perhaps from oral sources. Many Anglo-African writers established an ironic distance between themselves and chauvinistic imperialism, their voices relevant even today for their fictional presentation of conflict and culture to the readership they addressed. Mitford's late-nineteenth-century "now" and his African "there" become in hindsight more interesting in our new century than when his novels were first written–our experience of reading him is constructed both out of his interpretation of historical forces then and also out of our composite knowledge now from the intervening years since then. Mitford's work, and that of his compatriots, curiously has become *more* significant in hindsight than in the heyday of its earlier popular success.

CHAPTER 2
A PROFILE OF BERTRAM MITFORD

When James Bryce spoke to the Anglo-African Writers' Club he "observed that his first impressions of South Africa–formed before he went there–were derived from missionary narratives read in his youth, and partly from the brilliant descriptions of their Chairman. What had impressed him in Mr. Haggard was his perception of what might be heroic in the character of a native, and he believed that was a point they ought to bring out more" (*New York Times* BR23). Bertram Mitford had been in attendance that evening and may have wondered why Bryce, who suggests Africans have a capacity for self-determination if not immobilized by globalizing capitalism, omitted mentioning his sagas about Mzilikazi's Ndebele nation-state arising from diverse elements yet unified by the character of larger-than-life leaders. Mitford is always mentioned in passing as an Anglo-African writer, yet not until Michael Lieven's essay ever discussed in his own right. Lieven argues that Mitford's fictions are "of interest as a cross-road of various discourses in late nineteenth-century popular imperialism," citing Martin Green in *Dreams of Adventure, Deeds of Empire* (1979), who saw adventure tales as "the energizing myth of English Imperialism" (Lieven 1; Green 3).

Originally a successful writer of popular fiction, Mitord's nineteenth-century "period adventures" presumably today would cause a contemporary mass audience to shy away–from a style too weighty, descriptions that slow down the pace of the action, and unfamiliar social conventions. But with a small step of the historical imagination, the mature reader discovers in Mitford whole dimensions beyond the escapist pleasure of "what next" to which he probably owed his first popularity. When one hears phrases such as "the timeless criteria of canonical literature" one supposes that the speaker is not thinking of the high romance of empire; however, all of Mitford's novels based on his first-hand observations analyze historical events and synthesize its human responses. If that sort of historical interpretation is a criterion of canonicity, then it could require letting go of previous value judgments of recognized artistic value–that chimerical boundary between popular and high-brow, *here* but not *there*, *now* but not *then*.

Between 1889 and 1914 Mitford wrote many short stories and more than forty novels, various ones going through multiple editions, sold in Great Britain, the United States, and in the colonies through George Bell's Indian and Colonial Library. They were widely reviewed in journals, magazines, and newspapers, and taken up by circulating libraries and train station newsagents. Most of Mitford's fiction is set in southern Africa. As documented by a multitude of reviews cited in "Opinions of the Press" (*Golden Face* i-iii), the popularity of Mitford's African novels in this "comparatively new field of fiction" (*Enquire Within*)–as also James Bryce described it–lay in their appeal to the modern "rising generation" (*Gentlewoman*) which afterwards supported the expansion and resisted the decline of empire. Mitford's masculine themes of a "wild outdoor life" (*Westminster Review*; similarly, *Scotsman, Observer*, &c), of a "romantic love-story" (*Westminster Review*; similarly, *Figaro, Irish Society, Scottish Leader*, &c), of adventure (*Westminster Review* and dozens more), of "inter-racial warfare" (*Daily Telegraph*; similarly, *Cape Times*, &c), and of colonial conditions and manners (*South Africa*, &c) all fed the ideal of a "high destiny"as outlined by Ruskin for England's "most energetic and worthiest men."

One aesthetic standard reviewers used to judge Mitford's fiction included its local color realism (*Evening News, Scottish Leader, Irish Society, Morning Post, Spectator* &c); the *Daily Telegraph* deemed that such narrative realism crossed genre lines into "travel" writing, presumably in the tradition of Speke, Burton, Livingstone, and Stanley. Reviewers stressed Mitford's "long and personal association with the scenes and types of character he depicts" (*Evening News*; similarly, *Daily Chronicle, Athenæum, Westminster Gazette*, &c). Not only did the verisimilitude of the fictional roles (*Vanity Fair*) in which "characters can be locally recognized" make Mitford's novels effective representations of human experience (*South African Review*; similarly, *Academy, Daily Chronicle*, &c) , but for the *Leeds Mercury* in 1894 the novel under review described earlier Zulu fighting and was "of peculiar interest just now" because the British were then fighting the Ndebele. Moreover, a streak of exoticism in Mitford's narratives replaced "the tamer features of the ordinary novel" (*Speaker*; similarly *Athenæum*), although his fiction did treat of both the "wild and 'tame' parts of South Africa" (*Pall Mall Gazette*).

Finally, Mitford's "crisp vigorous style" (*Gentlewoman*; or *Sunday Times*, &c) reflected the gendered character of his masculine writing–direct, bold, economical–a quality also of successful empire building. This he shared in common with Haggard's *King Solomon's Mines* (1885), in which Allan Quatermain speaks of his plain and "blunt way of writing" without "any pretence to the grand literary flights and flourishes which I see in novels" (vi). As far back as Mitford's earliest novel, his narrative was "full of virility and animation" (*Natal Mercury*). Some of the more-genteel reviewers censured both Haggard and Mitford for a bloody sensationalism and an inelegantly crude style, although as Joshua Reynolds would have remarked, those are the notional defects of the narratives' strongest qualities. Several journals in comparing Mitford to H. Rider Haggard had noted that Mitford's "terror" was "the real thing" (*War Office Times*; similarly *Literary Opinion*, *South Africa*, &c). Among Mitford's novels, the half-dozen discussed here will clearly be considered minor classics when they are rediscovered, especially the Zulu tales that are studies in kingship, of the conduct of men in power or struggling for power, and the climactic fall of the Zulu kingdom that involved not merely the nation itself but, as in Mitford's tales and Haggard's *Nada the Lily* (1892), the whole world of which they were a part.

Like H. Rider Haggard, Mitford wrote his novels rapidly. At the expense of a fashionable belletristic or "literary" style, Mitford sought something of the storyteller's spontaneity, causing one reviewer to grump that "the author drives his pen along with clever contempt for every natural obstacle. Result, a fatal crudity, which extends even to the style" (*Sketch* 8). But this is not to say he wrote carelessly. In a presentation copy of the *Sign of the Spider,* Mitford apparently purged this volume of those illustrations he detested and made more than a dozen proofreading corrections, most in blue pencil and a few in graphite. The expertise of emendations such as the Zulu word, *Izímu,* as well as other place-specific words, leaves no doubt but that they are a product of the author's care. And again like H. Rider Haggard, Mitford also made his literary reputation in his first publications; but like Haggard his fiction had the ill luck to encounter a reception without understanding, certainly if the puffery of his reviewers is any touchstone. The exoticism of his subjects–the vivid battles, betrayals, and sublime loves–did indeed bring his readers into satisfying contact with emotion, imagination, and the unknown, but also caused his profounder intentions to be overlooked as mere adventure–then and now. Mitford and Haggard may be more original than our contemporary preconditioned responses lead us to expect. The bookseller Robert Temple asserts that Mitford's work is "full of excellent idiomatic speech giving a far better impression of how educated people spoke at the time than is found in most novels" (Temple, *Heath Hover*).

The general notion that adventure fiction is simply a detestation or distrust of the domestic Victorian novel aimed at an increasingly female readership can not explain the initial popularity or durability of these hair-raising romances. Aristotle himself had deemed the homespun taste for tales of the fireside, of deeds that made men miserable or happy–that is, the happenings of the plot– essential to the nature of imitative art and the source of its intellectual pleasure. Mitford's distinctive stylistic trait–readable and dramatic storylines that seem almost to keep the action rising in every chapter– parallels popular forms. But the charm and fascination of Mitford's novels always had to do fully as much with his character-driven plots, his understanding of both the vicissitudes of the settlers' daily lives and the exotic aspects of African cultures and customs, as with his subtly complex, compellingly-paced wild adventures in which the stakes are high and the danger escalates toward a resolution abounding in peril. To lose sight of these frontier stories popular with previous generations is to lose not only the simpler scenes of humor and suffering inherent in the African settler experience, but also to miss in the widest sense of Aristotle's *mythos* those elements in the narratives that embrace the complexities and consequences of being human–and in that there is nothing parochial.

Both Mitford and Haggard began their fiction-writing careers as political observers–Mitford as a journalist and Haggard by writing on Zulu-white relations. Neither had attended a university but both enlisted in the Colonial Civil Service. Both belonged to the British gentry and both their mothers were by birth from the ruling class of British-Indians.[6] Moreover, prior to the Civil Service, Mitford had been a stock farmer; Haggard, subsequent to his Civil Service, had been an ostrich rancher. Yet Mitford, despite his evident qualities, never achieved Haggard's enormous popularity and is now neglected. In *The White Hand and the Black* (1907), Mitford invents a war dance at a kraal with more than a bit of applicability to real-life histories: "The boy's face flushed with delight. He had read plentifully about this sort of thing–in fact such reading had largely to do with bringing him out to the country at all. Now he was going to see it–to see the real thing" (*White Hand* 205). The resident magistrate suggests to the young man "you might add to your pay by knocking up a description of it for one of the home magazines–or even two" (208)–precisely as Haggard had done in his first essays. But with typical Mitford irony, this dance turns real and the young trooper is "barbarously butchered. Then into his poor bleeding, mutilated body these fiends drove their assegais again and again, anointing themselves with the blood, in some instances even licking it" (279). Wishful thinking about the burgeoning career of Mitford's chief competitor in later years, one is tempted to speculate–except that Mitford himself had included just such a dance description in the conclusion of *Through the Zulu Country* (1883) which he clearly reused here in this novel as Haggard had reused "The Zulu War-Dance" (1877) in *King Solomon's Mines*. Thus the murdered young trooper is as much the shadowed double of

---

6. Ella Doveton, Haggard's mother, was the daughter of "a prominent member of the Bombay branch of the East Indian Civil Service, and thus it came to pass that his elder daughter, Ella, spent much of her girlhood in India, a country in which she took the keenest interest during all her life, and for which she cherished a warm affection" (E. Haggard, *Life and its Author* 3).

a callow Mitford as of his erstwhile literary nemesis. Finally, once back at the metropolitan center of empire, both men belonged to the Anglo-African Writers' Club and shared the same literary agent, A. P. Watt.

The meaning of Mitford's or Haggard's novels–their implicit notion that service to the empire is a noble duty, for example–has been ironized for us by our lens of self-conscious knowingness and the temporal distancing of history. One now asks how, consciously or subconsciously, these writers disavowed the popular imperial agenda of economic and military coercion or anticipated its future collapse? But beyond the fascination of political exegesis there is also in Mitford's fiction an aesthetic-moral significance. In synopsis, the action in a Mitford story perhaps seems like that in more-ordinary thrillers; however, apart from his skill at dramatizing generic events in fresh and effective ways, the value of his fiction lies in its instantiation of an authorial perspective born of truly exceptional life experiences, an innovative "Catholic existentialism" that acquiesces to the tragic circumstances of life with shame and outrage but that, through the instrumentality of forgiving others, confers *upon oneself* pardon and peace. In this, Mitford and his fictional personae seem to belong somewhere between the nineteenth-century preoccupations of Søren Kierkegaard and the twentieth-century crisis theology of Karl Barth–if not the renovated paganism of Albert Camus. Mitford's novels acquiesce to a world neither rational nor quite irrational; but through the forgiving and awakening heart certain characters find love–others abandon hope, such as the protagonist of *The Gun-Runner* (1893), who falls into an abyss of hate, instigating tribal attacks upon his countrymen to revenge the death of his beloved.

Mitford's family heritage was in civil service, not merely administrative or soldierly tasks but including biological observations that embodied the sort of scientific explorations akin to those which sent Darwin across oceans on *The Beagle*. This is the philosophy of Tennyson's "Ulysses," Odysseus, who represents the exemplary Victorian's desire to explore unknown territories. Like Ithaca, the island of England had become too small to hold one "roaming with a hungry heart." Surprisingly, Mitford's private life has not been widely documented. Prior to this research only sketchy information had been reported–scarcely comprising a few short paragraphs, since each perfunctory entry merely repeated the others. Even reliable fundamental statistics and answers were missing: Where was he born? Where and for what periods did he hold Civil Service appointments in Africa? Did he marry? When? And what children did he have? Such new data as can be meticulously uncovered at the present time for the incidents in Mitford's life are presented here, but no collection of letters or diaries and family papers has as yet surfaced. Many of his personal relationships continue to be puzzling and open-ended. Although it seems likely that this absence of biographical facts will in some measure persist, yet the key to Mitford's vivid descriptions of colonial encounters with otherness seems firmly rooted in his ancestry and youth. A concise biographical account of Mitford is indispensable because of the light it sheds on the origins of his colonial mind-set and on the imperial adventure genre in the hands of Haggard and others. Mitford was born 13 June 1855 in Bath, England, the sixth of nine children of Edward Ledwich Osbaldeston-Mitford (1811-1912) and his first wife, Janet Bailey (c. 1821-1896). Bertram's father Edward (with or without the hyphen in his surname, but with "Lord"–after 1895–preceding and F.R.G.S. following) had been born in the picturesque village of Mitford, a parish in the county division of Morpeth, Northumberland, where the family had lived for over 900 years on an estate given by William the Conqueror to Sir Richard Bertram for his military support in the campaigns of 1066. Bertrams intermarried with Mitfords, living first in Mitford Castle (its ruins at present are a "scheduled monument" legally sheltered, situated a knoll overlooking the Wansbeck river, opposite the Norman Church of St. Mary Magdalene) and later behind the ruined castle in the Old Manor House, itself now also a vestige. Edward is recorded as "of Mitford Hall," the stately mansion in Northumberland, and "of Hunmanby Hall," Yorkshire. Much earlier, in the time of Robert Mitford (1612-1674), this line had branched from that which produced the "Mitford sisters," those scandalous ornaments to the era of Evelyn Waugh's "Bright Young Things"(*Burke's Landed Gentry*). In his sole novel, *The Arab's*

Pledge–a Tale of Marocco in 1830 (1867), Edward describes in his Preface this tale as "written more than five-and-twenty years ago, after a residence of six years in Marocco" (iii). Something of Bertram's future concerns may be glimpsed here: this romance does not attempt to compete with the novel of domestic Victorian realism; rather, it aims to enlarge the reader's grasp of a distant colonial world of exotic "Maroqueen customs" by telling a tale based on bona fide "tragical facts, which occurred at the time" of Edward's residence of "six years" on the scene (32). Racial strife, racial amity: these will be Bertram's themes as well. This tale's final spectacle of an insane penitential self-immolation on a pyre has just that grotesquerie of Bertram's climatic scenes as well. Edward must have returned from Morocco to Northumberland only to leave shortly for Ceylon by what surely was the most unique route anyone hitherto had taken, which he described and illustrated with original sketches in *A Land-March from England to Ceylon Forty Years Ago* (1884). Its full title clarifies this adventurous undertaking: "through Dalmatia, Montenegro, Turkey, Asia Minor, Syria, Palestine, Assyria, Persia, Afghanistan, Scinde, and India, of which 7000 miles [were] on horseback." Although Mitford does not mention Austen Henry Layard, his traveling companion, Layard in his *A Popular Account of Discoveries at Nineveh* (1854) also tells how he, aged twenty-two, and Mitford, then twenty-eight and more fluent in Arabic, covered this distance from England to Hamadan during the autumn of 1839 and winter of 1840, visiting the ruins of the ancient seats of civilization, "equally careless of comfort and unmindful of danger"(Layard, *Popular Account* 1: 1; *Adventures* 1: 7, 275). Both young men intended to seek a career in Ceylon, but in Persia at Hamadan, Layard chose archaeology over the civil service; Mitford continued on to Ceylon alone.

Once there, Edward Mitford seems to have developed a naturalist's fascination with the birds of the island. J. E. Tennent in *Ceylon* (1860) mentions his indebtedness to "Mr. Mitford, of the Ceylon Civil Service . . . for many valuable notes relative to the birds of the island" and quotes Mitford's description of the Devil-Bird, not an owl but a hawk: "I never heard it until I came to Kornegalle, where it haunts the rocky hill at the back of Government-House." Its cry is "the most appalling that can be imagined, and scarcely to be heard without shuddering; I can only compare it to a boy in torture, whose screams are being stopped by being strangled" (Tennent 1: 2). Even Darwin in the seventh chapter of his *Variation of Animals and Plants under Domestication* (1868) cites Mitford's study of a feral Ceylonese rooster that "visits solitary farms and ravishes" the domestic hens; Darwin retreats from this faintly ludicrous image to observe that the hybrids produced are "quite sterile" so "this species, then, may in all probability be rejected as one of the primitive stocks of the domestic fowl" (1:246). When Edward wasn't stalking rapist roosters, he wrote plays in verse, publishing *Poems: Dramatic and Lyrical* (1869). On 1 November 1911 *The London Times* reported that King George V sent a message of congratulations to Edward on his 100th birthday, and on 16 May 1912 it reported a kingly message of sympathy on his death two days previously. Lords and Ladies, General Staff Officers, Members of Parliament, and family including Bertram, attended the funeral on the 17th conducted by five clergymen in "Mitford Church," Northumberland (*London Times*, 18 May 1912: 11). At the time of Edward's death his widow and *relict* (Edward's second wife) was Ella Elizabeth Osbaldeston-Mitford of Sunniside, Morden, Surrey. The gross value of his personal estate at decease was £8,495 ("Grant" 12 November 1912).[7]

Bertram, our current subject, was Edward and Janet's fourth son, incorrectly thought to have been born in Ceylon. All the other children except Bertram and his sister Sybil, indeed, were born in Ceylon (today Sri Lanka). Edward Mitford presumably was on the staff of the Ceylon Civil Service when in 1844 he married Janet, daughter of the Reverend Benjamin Bailey (1791-1853). Bertram's maternal grandfather, remembered as the Archdeacon of Ceylon, initially had been sent in 1816-1817 by the Church Missionary Society, sponsored by the Anglicans, to the "Syrian" Christians amid

---

7. The relative value of this estate currently as given on internet monetary-conversion sites is skewed by variables, but it appears to be about four or five times a typical middle-upper class annual income.

the lush hills and lakes of Kottayam, India, on the Arabian sea. Bailey's translations of English texts–certainly the Gospels, but one also may conjecture such likely works as *Pilgrim's Progress*–may have served an evangelical purpose; but they worked equally well in spreading a Western socio-cultural orientation toward rights and liberty which, it may be suggested, contained the seeds of the British empire's eventual dissolution. Whether Edward Mitford wanted his sons to benefit from the Britishness of an English education, avoiding their acquiring the Anglo-Indian "chi-chi" accent that carried the social stigma of mixed blood and thwarted professional opportunities, or whether it was a matter of access to schools, several sons were educated in England. One elder brother, Edward (1853-1948), and one younger brother, William (b. 1858), later became clergymen in the Church of England. Edward attended Winchester and St. John's College, Cambridge, taking his B.A. in 1875, then served as vicar of Hunmanby, 1888-1919, and rector of Acrise, Kent, 1919-1923. William attended Durham University and afterwards was installed as rector at St. Peter's, Ickburgh, Norfolk. His brother Bertram later stayed at the Ickburgh Rectory on at least one occasion in March 1905. St. Peter's comported well with the family background–in the Early English style with intricately-carved gargoyles flanking the nave.

At the age of five young Bertram had been a "scholar" along with older siblings Frances, Edith, and Edward, living in a Kent household headed by Robert and Alicia Beevor in Ramsgate on St. Lawrence Street. Mitford's youthful educational circumstances were like Kipling's, with an enforced separation from his parents, although in 1862 his sister, Sybil Emma Mitford, was born in this district of Thanet, suggesting that Bertram's mother was nearby at least some of this time. At or after the age of eight he then attended the Royal Naval School in New Cross, Kent, which at modest cost principally educated upwards of 210 sons of impecunious naval and marine officers. Its curriculum qualified students "for the university, naval or military service" ("Royal Naval School" *Cruchley*). Fittingly, it had a large swimming pool, which perhaps added to the number of Mitford's future recreations: "shooting, fishing, bicycling, walking, in early life mountain climbing, swimming when available, reading other people's novels"("Mitford" *Who Was Who*). Later, as a fifteen-year-old, Bertram is numbered among those enrolled at St. John's College, Sussex, a school for 300 boys about a mile north of the small market town of Hurstpierpoint. In Bertram's time the school's Head Master was Edward Clarke Love, D.D. He seems to have finished his secondary schooling at Hurstpierpoint College, also in west Sussex. Either before sailing to the Cape Colony or during visits back to England, Bertram apparently lodged at Tivoli, a borough of Cheltenham, Gloucestershire, with his younger brother William, who was an undergraduate at Durham University. One may speculate that the reason Mitford did not pursue a university course of study but went to South Africa with the less ambitious intention of raising animals on a farm was his conversion to Catholicism. Perhaps the most evident instance of Mitford's Catholic leanings may be a covertly autobiographical exchange in *The Weird of Deadly Hollow* (1891). "You are a Catholic, are you not?" asks the young woman, adding "It is a grand old creed." The protagonist replies:

> "I was not brought up in it, I assure you. Very much to the contrary. When I was eighteen I began to discover that it was about the most infamously slandered creed extant, and that, I suppose, to my contrarious spirit constituted an attraction, and I began to study the whole question. When I was twenty-one I told my father I intended to enter the Catholic Church. He flew into a great rage, and vowed that the day I did so he would turn me out of doors. I was as good as my word, for I entered it without further delay, and he was as good as his, for he did turn me out of doors also without further delay." (Mitford, *Weird* 144-45)

A large number of the novels contain discreet references to Catholicism, such as the heroic Jesuit in *The White Shield*. But in keeping with a paucity of biographical data, Mitford is not mentioned either in W. J. Gordon-Gorman's *Converts to Rome* (1910), nor in Madeleine Beard's *Faith and Fortune* (1997), nor does his name appear in the index of Joseph Pearce's *Literary Converts* (2000); only the *Catholic Who's Who and Yearbook* has a cursory entry.

Evidently, the Mitfords had a large branch of the family well-established in South Africa when Bertram first arrived in 1874 with the intention of stock farming. His family connection came about in this fashion: The sister of Bertram's grandfather, Robert (1780-1818), Anna Maria Mitford, born in 1782, married Miles Bowker, a Wiltshire farmer. After the British occupied the Cape, Miles led a party of settlers who sailed from Portsmouth, England, in January of 1820 for the Cape Colony, ultimately landing in Algoa Bay. These impoverished "1820 Settlers" were sent inland to create a buffer between the Xhosas, who had been chased by the British from this area, and the Colony. With his wife and nine children--his tenth child, Anna Maria Bowker was born on board the "Weymouth" while lying at anchor in Table Bay--Miles settled in the Eastern Cape, where his eleventh child James Henry was born. R. M. Ballantyne's *The Settler and the Savage* (1877) fictionally chronicles this episode, including lion hunting and fighting Xhosas by

> four brothers named Bowker. There were originally seven brothers of this family, who afterwads played a prominent part in the affairs of the colony. One of these Bowkers was noted for wearing a very tall white hat, in which, being of a literary turn of mind, he delighted to carry old letters and newspapers. From this circumstance his hat became know as "the post-office." (365-74)

Miles became one of the founders there of the wool industry. Bertram perhaps apprenticed himself to learn the family trade, much as Kenrick Holt in *A Veldt Vendetta* (1903) began a new career in the Cape Colony at East London. A rare first-person narrator among Mitford's fictional protagonists, Holt alludes in the novel's last paragraph to Bertram Mitford (unnamed but recognizable) as his friend. This "settler country" of the Eastern frontier was/is a turbulent, diverse region–from its sultry coast to the often snow-clad Katberg and Amatola Mountains it is both arid and desolate, as well as lushly green and forested, one of the most fertile regions in South Africa--in which the English built forts to maintain peace. The strongest of these bastions of imperial pacification was Fort Beaufort that once weathered an offensive by a full Xhosa *impi* (army). Possibly

Mitford's first job was not stock farming but ranging and guarding the Eastern Cape frontier. The Hurstpierpoint College register indicates Mitford had migrated to South Africa and "Joined Cape Mounted Police." This unit may have been the famed Frontier Armed and Mounted Police (FAMP).

One of Mitford's finest novels, *The King's Assegai*, is dedicated to "Colonel James Henry Bowker, sometime commandant of the Cape Frontier Armed and Mounted Police, and Governor's Agent for Basutoland, whose wide knowledge of the South African native character and whose sympathy with all that is best in it are surpassed by none." As the eleventh and final child of Miles and Anna Bowker, born in 1822 on their farm "Olive Burn" in the Eastern Cape Colony ("burn" is the Scots word for "stream"), Colonel Bowker was Mitford's second cousin. Bowker never married but we can assume that he must have taken a fatherly interest in the twenty-year-old Bertram. As a "convinced expansionist," not only did Bowker fight in the Seventh and Eighth Kaffir Wars, but afterwards was appointed inspector, then commandant, and finally commanding officer of the FAMP. He also was designated High Commissioner's agent in Basutoland (now Lesotho) and directed the expedition to annex the diamond fields of Griqualand West. In 1872 he led a punitive expedition against the amaHlubi and their chief, Langalibalele–Bishop Colenso decried this as a dishonestly expedient campaign but the colonists rallied to it–and in 1879 he led the suppression of Moorosi's Rebellion.

Oddly, Bowker is co-author with Roland Trimen of *South-African Butterflies: A Monograph of the Extra-Tropical Species* (1887-89). Trimen writes there:

> Colonel Bowker's debut as a votary of entomology took place in Kaffraria twenty-seven years ago. . . . The fine collection of native butterflies in the South-African museum owes the greater part of its treasures to his exertions,–no less than forty new species, and one most remarkable new genus (Deloneura). . . . The gift of specimens has been immeasurably enhanced in value by his copious notes on the haunts and habits of the insects, their distribution in South Africa, and their earlier stages. (Trimen 1: vii-xiv)

If Bertram did not inherit his observant naturalist's eye from his father Edward, then surely it was a Bowker gene. The Commandant of the FAMP in Mitford's *Harley Greenoak's Charge* (1906) is clearly a portrait of Colonel James. There a recent recruit is described by the sub-inspector as a "very black-hued Kafir" who is "rather a pet of the Commandant's; helps him to find new sorts of butterflies and creeping things that the old man is dead nuts on collecting" (177). This naturalist-warrior cousin prompted Mitford's wonderfully bizarre scene of the Commandant awaiting a massive dawn attack of assegai-wielding warriors while calmly examining a lizard in a pickle-bottle by the light of "a pale, wrack-swept moon, . . . his thoughts running about equally on the work in front, and the latest 'specimen' he had captured" (202; 204). At the novel's end Mitford echoes his cousin's move from what Trimen called the "productive region" of Kaffraria "to his fruitful labours in Basutoland, Griqualand West, Natal, and Zululand" (Trimen 1: vii-ix): "'There's some talk of giving him Basutoland.' 'Oh, well, that's not so bad. The fine old chap'll have lots of time to hunt butterflies and lizards up there'" (352).

In 1878 Bertram apparently either forsook arms or family sheep in order to enter the Colonial Civil Service of the Cape of Good Hope, assigned as a clerk to Fort Beaufort (probably the Fort Lamport in several of his novels) and to border outposts. Both the localities and the principal southeastern chiefs and *indunas* (headmen) in his fiction are portrayed from first-hand experience. Since Mitford was not a senior official appointed from London, only the voluminous unindexed Colonial Office records in the South African National Archives and its depositories may provide a basic outline of his postings: such sources as the Cape Civil Service Lists, the Cape General Directory, the Imperial Calendar, Civil Service Year Books, Government Gazettes and original Colonial Office correspondence. No application or correspondence between Mitford and the Colonial Office pertaining to positions or transfers has yet been found. We do know Mitford was registered in 1878 as a voter in the Karoo village of Tarkastad in the electoral division of Queenstown that included

Fort Beaufort. At this time, not far from Tarkastad, the Cape Colony and the Xhosas were engaged in the Ninth Border War.

The reporter for the *Eastern Daily Press* (Norwich) did his homework by reading Mitford's non-fiction publication, *Through the Zulu Country* (1883): "He was personally acquainted with King Cetewayo, John Dunn, and many of the Zulu chiefs. After the war of 1879 he travelled over the battlefields of Zululand collecting material for his literary work. The insight thus gained into Zulu life and character proved invaluable in the graphic descriptions so familiar to the many readers of his books" ("Death" *Eastern Press*, 4). Mitford's visit to Zululand occurred in 1881-82, after which he says he embarked on "the homeward-bound mail steamer, having trodden South African soil for the last time" (Mitford, *Zulu Country* 305). Actually he returned to the Eastern Cape in 1886 to try his luck with newspaper ownership; and later at least once he visited Cape Town in the spring-summer of 1898-99. However, Mitford may not have been a government official beyond 1880, inasmuch as he is described on the title page as "Late of the Cape Civil Service." Mitford's recurrent suggestions in his later novels that Africans have the fullest protection of British law, the magistrates bending over backwards to give them the benefit, is undoubtedly an echo of his own administrative observations. His further implication that under legal protection blacks become more aggressive, that access to justice empowers their resistance, may be an early and inchoate hypothesis for the end of colonialism.

Underlying Mitford's role as empire writer is his early poetry and journalism–the latter notably beginning with a 14 December 1886 announcement of his proprietorship in the *East London Advertiser* (East London, SA) "offering this journal to the public under new auspices." This South African paper was founded in 1879 by Thomas Goodwin. For this period between 1886-88 Mitford became its proprietor; Goodwin resumed control in April 1888 only to oversee the paper's liquidation in May. Hitherto little has been published on this news medium of Mitford that preceded his empire romances, but it is apparent he and his editor saw the role of the *Advertiser* as gadfly, provocative and intensely antagonistic towards colonial shortsightedness and pretensions, whether of race, religion, politics, or bourgeois getting and spending. Prior to 14 December 1886 social articles and regular reports on the local Literary Society in the *Advertiser* do not mention Mitford. But on that date this appears:

> In offering this journal to the public under new auspices we propose to preface the present issue with a few introductory remarks. We shall not commence with the thread-bare and timeworn fiction relative to the disinterested, noble and high-and-lofty-all-round mission of the press and its conductors, nor insult our readers' intelligences by springing upon them any inflated balderdash of the kind. Nor shall we pretend that we are moved by exalted yearnings after the regeneration of the human race and so forth.... No; our mission is to enlighten our fellow creatures to the utmost of our ability, but not for nothing.... We, for our part, shall do our utmost to give our readers their full money's worth, and shall look to them, not merely for continued, but ... greatly increased support. An independent judgement combined with due regard for the principles of fair play will form the basis of our programme, and while refusing to be bound by any narrow considerations or trammels of party in dealing with the political questions of the day, we shall at the same time give our careful attention to the interests of our friends and fellow-townsmen. And here we take the opportunity of declaring that the line we mean to pursue as conductors of public opinion, so far as our influence may reach, will be a bold and decided line, firmly believing as we do that by this course we shall best serve the interests of our readers, our friends and our supporters, and last, but not least, of ourselves.

This is undoubtedly when Mitford took over the proprietorship of the paper. Though the style is generally consistent, even for shorter local-flavor news items, the tone and pace of the articles differs from the preceding editions. There is on the part of the editorials outspoken opinion as well as reportage. Also the writing is more pithy and barbed; and there may be underlying humor, be it tongue in cheek or outright poking fun.

A prominent advertisement on the back page of the 31 December 1886 edition of the new *Advertiser*, owned by "Mr. Mitford," touted it as "a Valuable Advertising Medium for Business

Men" but concluded with: "It is the aim of this paper to become something more than a mere local record." Only the National Library in Cape Town has complete copies dating from 1879 to 1888. A breakdown of the layout of the paper, both in content and arrangement, indicates that this noble news-organ was published twice a week on Tuesdays and Fridays, four pages per edition, of which the middle two were taken up with news (sometimes lifted from other papers such as the *Cape Times*, the *Eastern Cape Herald*, or the *Natal Mercury*) and the remaining half with advertising. As with all the older newspapers, the layout is in strict columns with few headlines to differentiate the changes of articles and requires more diligence than skimming allows. According to an unwritten journalistic policy prevailing at the time, the names of reporters and correspondents are never divulged which means that one cannot say which news articles in the *Advertiser*, if any, Mitford wrote. In one of the preceding editions a few months prior, the previous editor takes another newspaper to task for daring to divulge in one of its articles the names of a reporter and editor of a rival newspaper.

Mitford himself did not stay in South Africa very long after taking control of the journal. He departed East London on 16 December 1886 on board the *Melrose* via the coastal ports of Port Elizabeth and possibly Mossel Bay for Cape Town, connecting there with the *Pembroke Castle* which left for London on the afternoon of 22 December 1886. He apparently was traveling alone, without his bride Zima, neé Ebden, whom he had married in London in 1886 but whose family resided at the Cape. His name only is listed for December in the shipping news of the *Cape Times*. Because Zima's previous divorce at the suit of her husband for adultery with Blennerhasset Blennerhasset, a medical officer, had been reported by *The London Times* in lurid detail, she either hid in England to avoid her family or remained in Africa for additional solace. The latter possibility is reasonable, given that Zima's Aunt, Martha Ebden, married Charles Davidson Bell, the Surveyor General of the Cape Colony, who was also an artist of note and who designed the Cape Triangular stamp. She had a scandalous affair with one Lestock Wilson Stewart–a surgeon in the Madras Army. (The Ebden ladies apparently had a weakness for medical men with extraordinary given names.) On 4 February 1887 the *Advertiser* reported: "We hope shortly to give our readers the promised English letters. By last mail we heard that Mr. Mitford had reached Madeira."[8] Mitford's series of "English Letters" covered British parliamentary events, social events and the odd local "strange but true" story.

A name associated with the *Advertiser* is that of "Bettington," as on 18 April 1887: "A dinner for 46 gentlemen at the Buffalo Hotel.... Mr Goodall proposed a toast to the Press. East London had the reputation of having an impartial press. As a rule they did not get all the credit they deserved. The East London newspapers took high rank amongst the other papers of the Colony. Mr. Hebbes of the *Despatch* and Mr. Bettington of the *Advertiser* acknowledged the compliment." There is a later reference to an R.A. Bettington attending a fancy dress ball as a "Knight of Malta" on 12 July 1887. The local editor of the *Advertiser* was thus probably Colonel Rowland Arthur Albemarle Bettington who came to the Colony in 1872 and joined Bowker's Rovers (a cavalry unit of irregulars under the command of Mitford's second cousin) during the wars of 1877-78 (Wright 60). Among the Cape Colony volunteer units in this Ninth War (the Gaika-Galeka War) on the Eastern Cape frontier, Bowker's Rovers was under Commandant Bertram E. Bowker at King Williamstown, a corps of seventy-four mounted rangers from Graaff Reinet and Somerset East, young men of education and property with a roving commission. As the first volunteers at the front (17

---

8. Shipping news of 4 January 1887 in the *Times* of London says: "The Pembroke Castle left the Downs [where ships gathered either to go up or down the English Channel] today for London"; and on 17 January advertises the fact that the Pembroke Castle will be returning to the Cape from London on 2 February and from Dartmouth on the 4th. Mitford thus arrived in England in time to write and mail the first English Letter which came out in the *Advertiser* on 25 February 1887 with the heading, "Our English Letter (from our own)." With a few exceptions here and there this feature appeared every Tuesday. Often they are lengthy, taking up two or two and a half columns. Probably *all* the English Letters were written by Mitford himself and posted, rather than telegraphed, as often the letter bears a date about a month prior to publishing.

September) after the Rising, they were exposed to hardships in the field such as lack of forage for their horses, food for themselves, and sleeping half-frozen at night without tents. This Bettington has a further link to the Bowker family. In *Women of South Africa* one finds:

> "Bettington, (Mrs.) Fanny. Wife of Colonel R.A. Bettington, who served in the Kaffir Wars of 1877 and 1878, also through the Boer War. Born at Oakwell, near Grahamstown, Cape Colony. Daughter of the Hon. Bertram Egerton Bowker. Educated at home. Her husband was imprisoned as one of the Reform Committee after the Jameson Raid. Her four eldest sons fought in the Boer War, and two of her sons (Vere and Rowland) during the Zulu Rebellion of 1906. Favourite Recreation, Entomology and Botany. Five Sons–Claude; Vere; Egerton; Rowland; and Aylmer. Residence, Santa Clara, Princess Place, Parktown, Johannesburg, Transvaal."[9]

Thus Mitford's cousin who commanded cavalry unit was also Bettington's father-in-law.

In the *Advertiser* for April 20, 1887 nine stanzas of doggerel entitled "Rovers" is republished:

> That our contemporary has felt the martial glow is shown by the following verses published by him in 1877.
>
> Rovers
> Rover round and burly
> Rover lank and lean
> You were very early
> In the breach I wean
>
> Rovers are you tired now?
> Rovers, come away!
> Rovers, will you hire now
> For a crown a day?

---

9. *The Register of S. Andrew's College, Grahamstown: 1855-1902* (Capetown, etc: Juta, 1902) gives his address for two of these sons at the College as "Col. R. A. Bettington, Rand Club, Johannesburg."

> Rover, was the battle-field
> All that you could ask!
> Was it a rare cattle-field
> Underneath a mask?...

We know that Mitford's first recognized publication was *Our Arms in Zululand* (1881), an epic poem of "the three great battles of the Zulu War" well below par as serious literature and one that conflictedly portrayed the Zulu *impi* as "the very pick and flower, / Of warrior Zululand" and "a maddened host, / Drunken with British blood." One wonders if this early doggeral may be Mitford's; the sixth stanza might reflect his efforts at a verse-writing carrier:

> 'Tis but part and parcel
> Of the craft and cant,
> Making universal
> Hash of all we want.

There is another reference to Bowker's Rovers during the Gaika war of 1878 under "Every Day Topics" in the 1 July 1887 issue of the *Advertiser*.

One cannot say for sure whether Mitford's was the opinion concerning "that ghastly Jubilee Ode of Tennyson" (29 April 1887). Nor should one suppose that in the *Advertiser* on 17 September 1887 Mitford did more than endorse after the fact the view in "Every Day Topics" that "the *Star* ought to know better than to publish" a line from H. Rider Haggard giving permission "to use the name of the heroine" Ayesha in *She* for a new waltz the *Star* was printing. The request was simply for the sake of advertisement: "It's astonishing to what length of sycophany people will go now-a-days." There also was obviously great disrespect for the publishing fraternity on the part of Bettington and Mitford, given "Barabbas at Fault," a sarcastic piece about a frustrated writer and "the sapient idiots who guard the portals of literature." The poet copied out Milton's *Samson Agonistes*. "Then he submitted it to the confraternity of Barabbas, under the title 'Like a Giant Refreshed' [Psalm 78: 66] and calmly sat down and awaited his revenge. It came. So did the M.S. – rejected of course. Not that the trick was detected, oh no!" The publishers' rejections are amusing and the manuscript is finally lost altogether: "These worthies, however, were not devoid of all sense of the fitness of things, for by way of fulfilling the eternal law of compensation, they obligingly returned . . . other authors' MSs instead. How they arranged matters with the said 'other authors' is not known–never will be known in all human probability." Whether the paper's Proprietor or Editor wrote the piece, both probably endorsed its sentiments. The rejected poet may again have an autobiographical significance for Mitford. This satire also reminds one strongly of H. Rider Haggard's *Mr. Meeson's Will* (1888), an amusing and bizarre novel about a publishing firm in which the publisher's last will is tattooed on a woman's body, transforming her into a textual commodity at variance with her selfhood (141-42).

Mitford's satiric description of dignitaries at Westminster Abbey on the Queen's Jubilee visit in "Our English Letter" appeared on 30 August 1887:

> One of the most comical pictures ever offered to the gaze of the jest-loving, is a photograph stuck up in many shop windows. It represents the group of dignitaries, who ecclesiasticized the Queen's Jubilee visit to Westminster Abbey, and thus sanctioned the saturnalia which desecrated a venerable church. These Right Reverends, Very Reverends and Rather Reverends, having arrayed themselves in copes in honour of the Queen of Queens (in other churches these vestments are worn in honour of the King of Kings, and their Right Rev. lordships don't like it), were evidently so pleased with the result that they started off in a body to the photographer's, like the newly fledged B.A., on being invested with the snowy fur. . . . But all the copes appear to be slipping off their wearers, one of whom is both shoulders through his, like a silkworm moth half out of its cocoon and looks the very picture of distress. These vestments, by the way, are now laid by in lavender until it shall graciously please the Sovereign– or some other Sovereign–to come and be worshipped at Westminster Abbey once more.

Mitford is implicitly contrasting formal Anglicanism and its priests with African animism and its witch doctors in full regalia of animal bones and entrails.

Very little more is known about Mitford's stint as proprietor of the *Advertiser*. After little more than a year the last edition under Mitford's proprietorship ends with a farewell from the editor, presumably Bettington, since he says that he has lived in East London for the past twelve years. In the same edition under local news the following appears: "Captain Bettington's resignation appears in the Government Gazette dating from 1st March (1888)." Perhaps as the *Advertiser* folded, Bettington resigned his Commission to seek fresh woods and pastures new. When the *Advertiser* came into Mitford's hands he had pledged journalistic independence. Now the editor or proprietor asserted in his adieu, "HAIL AND FAREWELL" (21 February 1888): "if getting into the numerous rows and setting the town generally by the ears be allowed to count for anything we certainly may claim to have kept our promise." The *Advertiser* had rubbed criticism into its readers as if they were spiced beef: "The 'rubbing in' process has been impartially distributed to young and old, big and little; from the Premier in his chair of office to the newly emancipated schoolboy in his first masher collar. . . . If we have done any of you some little good and turned you from the error of your ways, you're welcome to the service and we ask for no thanks; if some of you feel sore and bear malice it can't be helped, we shant say we're sorry, for probably it served you right." But having already published his travelogue of the Zululand battlefields and some poetry, Mitford at this juncture seems to have settled finally on a fiction-writing career: "In the latter year he took seriously to literature as a profession" ("Mitford" *Anglo-African Who's Who*).

At what point Mitford met his future wife, we do not know; but in 1886 at Brighton, Sussex, he married Zima Helen Ebden ("Louisa" in the 1891 census, a distorted homophone one supposes), daughter of the wealthy Alfred Ebden, a prominent surname in the southern suburbs of Cape Town. Her unusual forename–a matronymic, her mother was Decima Zima Grimley–may be a diminutive of Simon. Zima had been born at Port Elizabeth in the

Cape Colony, 23 September 1854; she died in 1915 the year after her husband. Zima's *first* marriage had been in 1874 at barely twenty years of age to Alexander Gentle, some fourteen years her senior, a Scottish-born retail businessman and son of a clergyman in northern Scotland. That first marriage had been solemnized at Christ Church in the Parish of Paddington, Middlesex. Zima's divorce was at the suit of her husband, who managed the Chamber of Commerce in Singapore, a British businessman's trade association barely relevant to the concerns of non-native speakers of English there. Zima's similarity to the heroine Aurelle in Mitford's late novel *Seaford's Snake* (1912), who begins an affair when her husband is absent, presents an echo. However, unlike Alex Gentle, Seaford responds subtly to his wife's growing infidelity, and thereby forfends the promised end. As a consequence of Zima's divorce proceedings, her mother paid a visit to England in 1882-1883 (running up expenses of £640). Zima's divorce was owing to her affair around 1882 in Singapore with an Irish surgeon and widower serving in the Royal Army Medical Corps: Blennerhassett Montgomerie T. Blennerhassett (1849-1926). Montgomerie had a daughter, Venice Maud (b. 1876), in the same age cohort as Zima's girls. Faced with mounting proof that when Alex was absent Monty habitually had relations with Zima at Bellevue, her home in Singapore, and that also in July of 1882 they "committed adultery" at the Bathing Pavilion at MacRitchie Reservoir four miles north of the city, Zima amended her legal response after six months of flat denial to a declaration that the Petitioner had condoned the adultery, if any, of the Respondent. But in light of the affidavits, her extenuation was discredited and custody of her son and daughters was awarded to Alex. Of the three children that Zima and Alex Gentle lost in infancy or childhood, only Eric Grant (1880-1889), who died in Amersham, Buckinghamshire, is so far identified (Archives, Kew).

The Times on 4 April 1884 reported on Zima's divorce proceedings in humiliatingly public detail: "a suit by Alexander Gentle for the dissolution of his marriage with Zima Helen Gentle whose maiden name was Ebden, on the ground of her adultery with Blennerhassett Montgomery Blennerhassett." Zima was defended by

"Mr. M'Intyre, Q. C." who in 1887, during the rampage of Jack the Ripper, gained notoriety by defending a Whitechapel murderer who had poured nitric acid down a woman's throat. Londoners were told:

> In 1882 Mr. Blennerhassett, who was an army surgeon in charge of a military hospital at Singapore, made the acquaintance of the petitioner and the respondent, and Mr. Gentle invited him to his house; but the petitioner soon saw reason to think that there was more intimacy than was becoming between the respondent and the co-respondent. Blennerhassett hung about Mrs. Gentle's carriage at public places, and at a ball he and she made themselves remarkable by conversing together in corners. Mr. Gentle remonstrated with his wife; but she showed temper and alleged that she only acted as other ladies did at Singapore. Mr. Blennerhassett he called "a blackguard" on the promenade at Singapore, as the co-respondent stood close to Mrs. Gentle's carriage, and told him not to speak to that lady again. The co-respondent replied that he would until forbidden to do so by Mrs. Gentle. In August, 1882, after several denials, Mrs. Gentle admitted to her husband that Blennerhassett had been in the habit of paying her frequent surreptitious visits, and that they had several times committed adultery. . . . She asked her husband to forgive her. He refused to do so or to cohabit with her again. She came to England and joined her mother. Mr. Gentle, being in London in October, 1883, she and her mother had an interview with him at his hotel. On that occasion the petitioner and the respondent, at Mrs. Gentle's request, had a few minutes private conversation in a room by themselves. In three days after she wrote to him a penitent letter, in which she spoke of her sin and of her love for her husband and children, and again implored his forgiveness, but he refused to put an end to the divorce proceedings which had then been instituted. This was Mr. Gentle's account of the matter. He distinctly swore that he never had condoned the adultery. Both the respondent and the co-respondent denied the adultery, and the respondent pleaded condonation. . . . The jury found that the respondent and the co-respondent had committed adultery, and that there had been no condonation. (3)

Zima's penitence undoubtedly sprang solely from her desperation over custody of the children. The divorce decree was dated 3 April 1884.

The registration for her subsequent marriage to Mitford on March 9, 1886 describes her as "the divorced wife of Alexander Gentle" and gives the residence for both of them at the time of marriage as 60 Regency Square, Brighton, possibly a resort rooming house. Their ages then were both thirty-one years and Mitford is listed as a "bachelor" and a "gentleman" by profession. They were married in the Register Office in Brighton with no family witnesses. Mitford's Catholicism may explain why he married the divorced Zima in a civil service. At that time, Zima had a son and two daughters, Zima Helen Gentle and Winifred Ebden Gentle, from her first marriage.[10] Bertram and Zima's daughter Yseulte Helen was born in Kensington, London in 1888. Mitford's 1902 *Word of the Sorceress* was tenderly dedicated to the fourteen-year-old Yseulte: "*Nkosazana o'zandhla zimhlope...* ("Little Chieftainess, whose hands are white. . ."). By 1891 the Mitfords were living at 84 Westbourne Park Road, Paddington, a district in London of substantial three story homes, where their son Rowland was born on 17 June of that year.[11] In those days Bertram described his occupation rather melodramatically, or with a sense of self-irony, as a "*Littérateur*" of independent means. From June of 1895 forward, his other London addresses included: 21 John Street, Bedford Row; 61 Seymour Street, Hyde Park (1896); 15 Blandford Street, Portman Square (1899); 28 and, then, 11 Addison Mansions, West Kensington (from 1901 to 1907)–here also at Addison Mansions in later years Agatha Christie kept a business flat–and finally, for several years until his death, Mitford's address was 5 Furzeham Road, West Drayton (Monsman, *Haggard* 276). It is quite possible that during the 1895-1901 period of frequent address changes the Mitfords traveled abroad intermittently; no record exists

---

10. Entries of marriage for Alexander Gentle (22 October 1874, No.145) and Bertram Mitford (9 March 1886, No. 149), General Register Office, England. In 1885 Zima's father believed her to be married already to Mitford; her address then: Bertram Mitford, Esq., 50 St. James Street, London, S. W. (Archives, Pretoria 203).

11. Entry of birth for Roland Bertram Mitford (17 June 1891, No. 146), General Register Office, England; "Births," *London Times*, 19 June 1891:1. "Roland" is spelled without the "w" on the entry of birth.

of them in the 1901 British census when they may have been in the United States where *War and Arcadia* (1901) is set–*Golden Face* (1892) may have been the product of an earlier trip to the Black Hills of South Dakota. Mitford's London agent was the firm of A. P. Watt & Son, which presided over publishing's first and largest literary agency and led the trade in fiction. Describing the "pre-eminently useful institution" of the "Literary Agent," Mitford wrote Watt in a testimonial letter of 31 August 1898 from Kenilworth, one of Cape Town's prime residential areas in the southern suburbs: "Speaking from experience I can only say–as a friend of mine said when he had learnt to ride a bicycle–I don't know how I got along all that time without one. More particularly does this hold good of a writer like myself, the very exigencies of whose especial line of fiction necessitate prolonged sojourns in far countries" (Monsman 286 n.34).[12] The bicycle is a frequent image in Mitford's later novels; by 1890 the "safety" bicycle, with chain-and-sprocket thrust and same-sized wheels, had become popular.

The 1891 contract that Watt negotiated on behalf of Mitford for an edition of two thousand copies of *The Weird of Deadly Hollow* paid him "one shilling per each and every thirteen copies sold for each shilling of the published price." His 1896 contract for *The Sign of the Spider*–arithmetically more straightforward–was ten percent of the selling price up to two thousand copies, fifteen percent for each copy over and above that number, with an £80 advance upon publication. Later in 1899 he received for *John Ames* sixteen and two-thirds percent of the price on the first five thousand copies; eight pence for copies over and above that number, with an advance of £150. At the last minute he retitled this novel on the contract, crossing out the possibly puzzling Bantu title, *The Umlimo* (Monsman 276). Copies generally sold for 3/6, suggesting that with the better publishers Mitford may have cleared an initial £50-150 in

---

12. Although the A. P. Watt & Company records are entirely of a business nature, they do supply Mitford's addresses. Watt was also H. Rider Haggard's literary agent; Haggard wrote Watt that "since the year 1885 some thousands of letters must have passed between us to say nothing of countless interviews" (*Letters to Watt* 81).

the first six months. Perhaps Mitford's novels also had run serially before book publication; unpropitiously, his splendid *The White Hand and the Black* was sold for a flat-rate of £150 to John Long, Ltd., Mitford complaining (30 November 1906) to Watt that Long was "not a first rate firm" and expressing a fear Long might bowdlerize cultural details of tribal life. Such residual royalties as his contracts produced diminished steadily. During the First World War, Yseulte (fulfilling her legendary name by nursing at the Red Cross hospital "Oaklands" in Somerset) received one of Watt's infrequent royalty payments for 5/10. Her brother Rowland, who may have been in the armed services, is not mentioned in this correspondence; Yseulte clearly was the only one who negotiated with Watt for marketing new editions.

Broadly speaking, Mitford's fictional interest in the settlers in southern Africa covers *three* geographical areas of historical conflict between the British and the tribal inhabitants–Xhosas on the Eastern Cape frontier in nine wars (actually beginning with the Boers in 1779) until 1879; the Matabeles in Rhodes's War of 1893 with its subsequent Ndebele-Shona insurrections of 1896-97; and the Zulus in Zululand in the Anglo-War of 1879 and the Bambatha Rising in Natal-Zululand of 1904-06, the last African military resistance to colonization in South Africa until the nationalist militancy in Rhodesia in that began in December1972. The first of the three geographical-historical areas was that of the Eastern frontier adjoining Xhosa territories, an area inland from East London to which the "1820 settlers" came, among them relatives of Mitford, originally called British Kaffraria. During the Ninth Frontier War, this was the operational area of Bowkers Rovers and the Frontier Armed and Mounted Police, from which Mitford took numerous details of African conflict as background for his romance-plots. The second area is that of his Zimbabwe novels with a background of Ndebele history, which are centered around Lobengúla's defeat by Cecil Rhodes and the Ndebele-Shona insurrection of 1896-97. The third area, Zululand, was the setting for the opening and ending of Mitford's quartet of stories about the Zulu warrior Untúswa from his teens "in the early stages of the Amandebili migration" (*The King's Assegai* 248) through to the downfall of King Dingane. Mitford also set novels here during both the Anglo-Zulu War and the Bambatha Rising.

The conflict in the Transvaal of the British with the Boers in the war of 1899-1902 is represented only by a single novel, *Aletta* (1900). In this war small commandos of old men and boys staved off the enormous resources of the British empire, spelling the beginning of the empire's decline. The period during which Mitford composed these narratives was the era prior to national union that proved a watershed in the emergence of a unified South Africa in 1912. Just to round out categories, a half-dozen or so of Mitford's novels, although overlapping with other groups, have a pronounced supernatural theme. Mitford's preference for rational, empirical data does not run counter to curiosity and open-mindedness, but it does contrast with Haggard's strong disposition to believe in spiritualistic-mystical phenomena. Also, there are another half-dozen non-African novels, such as *The Sirdar's Oath* (1904), originally entitled *Raynier, Political Agent*, with settings in Central Asia, Switzerland, the United States, or the South Seas. Mitford also wrote short stories, all of which have been waiting a century or more to be rediscovered. Many writers of popular fiction from the 1870s through to the Second World War sold stories (or even novels for serialization) to British newspaper syndicates. A. P. Watt's literary agency negotiated the sale of several Mitford stories to the Northern Newspaper Syndicate for publication in provincial gazettes–such as "The Left Behind" (contract, 15 November 1899) and "The Gojela's Third Wife" (publication possibly 5 November 1900)–as well as to *The Graphic*, which competed with the famous *Illustrated London News* for the same middle-class readership, with "The Dilemma of Verna Halse" (published 11 May 1907) and "An Island of Eden" (published 19 October 1907). Yet another story, "The Umpunga Skull" (contract 5 January 1907) appeared in Cassell & Co.'s "new magazine," perhaps the old *Cassell's Family Magazine*, now retitled without "*Family*." "A Veldt Vendetta" appeared in *The Windsor Magazine* (1895); curiously, as late as 1903 it reappeared in expanded book form with the identical title. Terms of Mitford's contracts for short stories ran £7.17.6 per 2,500-word story, slightly less if Mitford wanted to sell two stories at the same time, or £3.3.0 per thousand words in another outlet. One suspects that "Maxted's Temptation" (1910) in the journal of the Natal Mounted Police, *The Nongqui,* may have served as seed-ground for the climactic battles in *A Dual Resurrection* (1910) (Kearney 42). The stories in *The Graphic* and *The Windsor* are the *données* for later novels. Each presents characters confronting dangers; and around these predicaments the novels weave more-complex webs of motivation and action. Mitford thus begins with character in crisis and then capitalizes on the novel's fuller exploration of regional setting, customs, and particularly themes of motivation and character.

The Ndebele-Zulu tales, though fictional, are laced with authentic but arcane historical facts that only appeared well after his novels in later documented accounts. Mitford himself had traveled in what is now Zimbabwe and his friendship with the legendary frontiersman Johan Colenbrander, to whom he dedicated *John Ames*, provided him with original data. He originally met Colenbrander during his battlefield tour of Zululand in 1882 as he described it in *Through the Zulu Country* (1883). One Sunday outside the trading store at Inyoni two white men and a black servant on horseback dismounted:

> The new arrival is introduced to me as "Mr. Colenbrander," and I find myself shaking hands with a pleasant-looking man of about thirty, every inch the frontiersman, with dark beard and bronzed complexion, and dressed in buckskin suit, with riding boots and spurs; a revolver in its holster is slung round him, and a formidable clasp knife hangs from his belt. The removal of his hat displays a deep scar over the temple several inches in length, pointing to what must have been a very awkward and dangerous wound; it is in fact the result of a blow from a battle axe received during an intertribal foray some months previously. (190)

Mitford and Colenbrander then traveled to visit the white Zulu chief, John Dunn, in the Umgoye mountains, exploring the battlefield of Gingindhlovu on the way. The morning after arriving at Dunn's, Colenbrander departed, but not before inviting Mitford "to join him in a sea-cow [hippopotamus] shooting expedition in the winter," graciously declined: "though if ever I did launch out into that particular branch of venerie, I should not wish for a better companion" (198). Fluent in Zulu, Colenbrander had served as interpreter for Rhodes in talks to end hostilities in 1893 and to gather intelligence for him at Lobengúla's kraal. In "Rhodesia in 1890," H. F. Hoste recalled that "Colenbrander was trading at Lobengúla's kraal and in very amiable relations with the chief and the Matabele indunas as a consequence of which the Company offered him an appointment as their representative in Matabeleland. In this capacity he kept Rhodes, and the Column, informed of events there" ("Colenbrander," *People Directory,*). In 1910 Colenbrander was "busy on material for a book on his life which Bertram Mitford, the English novelist, planned to write," but a friend of Colenbrander "who had the manuscript for the book on Johan's life, had mislaid the thing and it was never seen again" (Bulpin 340). It is likely that Mitford's darker alter ego, the fictional Lorraine, owed much to Colenbrander's lore. Lorraine, who first appears in the Zulu War novel, *The Gun-Runner* (1893), makes a later appearance in the Matapos impersonating the "Voice" of the god of the Matabele.

Mitford does not seem to have given many interviews or cultivated the limelight, worse luck for his sales. In 1896 the *Eastern Daily Press* reported:

> Mr. Bertram Mitford, the author of "The Sign of the Spider," is a quick writer. He says that he "can turn out a 320 page novel in two months, if in the vein." He works best in the morning, all day long in winter, but never at night. A firm believer in outdoor exercise, he is a great walker. Twenty-three years ago he went to South Africa, and during his long stay there became personally acquainted with Cetewayo and all the prominent Zulu chiefs and leading men who engineered the Kaffir war of 1877, on the Cape border. Most of them figure in his South African novels. Mr. Mitford, before he turned his attention to fiction, had a very varied experience. He was at one time engaged in stock-farming, and he has held several Government posts. He is the third son of Mr. Osbaldeston Mitford, of Mitford Castle, Northumberland. ("About Men and Women" 8)

Mitford's annual output fluctuated between one to three novels, exclusive of short stories. This career total of more than forty novels suggests that he made words his *métier* and by them he created a steady income stream. However, his nineteenth-century titles currently on the first-edition market are more plentiful than the twentieth-century ones, suggesting smaller press-runs in the later years.

Needless to say, Mitford, like his father, was also a Fellow of the Royal Geographical Society, the origins of which lay in the exploration of Africa. Founded in 1830, it later sent Richard Burton and J. H. Speke to discover the source of the Nile. Mitford, proposed by his friend Arthur Montefiore, was elected on 28 April 1890 while residing at the Junior Athenaeum Club, Piccadilly. Montefiore was a committed trout fisherman and a writer of exploration literature, including biographies of David Livingstone and Sir Henry Stanley; he witnessed Mitford's contract with Sutton, Drowley for *The Weird of Deadly Hollow*. In the Society's Archives is a portrait of "B. Mitford" by Maull and Fox, Piccadilly, photographers to the Royal family–a small-framed, alert and wiry man with a bushy mustache and clean-cut features. Although there is at least one other "B. Mitford" on the fellows' membership list, the picture is probably *not* General Bertram R. Mitford, a relative. The common Piccadilly address for both Mitford the author and the photographers, *floruit* 1879-1908, also suggests the sitter is our Bertram. In its obituary, the *Eastern Daily Press* reported that "Mr. Mitford was a keen sportsman, and in search of adventure and information had traveled in America and India, and was very well acquainted with the Alpine districts of Switzerland, having as far back as the eighties made a successful ascent of the Matterhorn" (4).

In addition to membership in the Royal Geographical Soceity and his affiliation with the Anglo-African Writers' Club, Mitford also was a member of the Junior Athenaeum, the New Vagabond Club, the elite Wigwam Club, and the posh Savage Club, chaired by G. A. Henty ("Mitford" *Who Was Who*; Muddock; Norgate and Wykes; Leach). This last had been founded in 1857 and remains at present one of the most unusual clubs for men of the arts, bohemian journalists, and adventurers; they refer to each other as "Brother Savage." At a typical dinner of 7 June 1893 the Savages entertained W. M. Stanley, recently returned from the "Dark Continent"; an earlier dinner in 1885, just before Mitford arrived back in London, welcomed a returning group of journalists who had suffered massive casualties from the Mahdi's Dervish hordes as General Gordon fought his way up the Nile Valley. Mitford's Junior Athenæum Club occupied the London mansion of the late Duke of Newcastle, Piccadilly West. Its roster included members of Parliament, of the universities and fellows of learned and scientific societies. One meeting (that may or may not be fantasy) followed a lecture at the Royal Institution–the discussion topic, "The End of Books," suggesting gramophone recordings will replace books (Uzanne 51). Mitford seems to have stayed at this club on occasion, perhaps when his family was out of town or to avoid interruptions when finishing a novel. We are told that Mitford's New Vagabonds "in their club capacity do nothing else but dine. Periodically in the season they assemble together, the gentler sex at times included amongst them, and invite into their midst some other lady or gentleman, or both, who have won laurels in the fields of art and literature, and then there are compliments and happy speeches till the home-going time arrives" (Leach 3: 159). One such visitor was Arthur Conan Doyle; on that same evening or another Fred G. Abberline, the police office in charge of the Jack the Ripper murders, attended. Finally, Mitford was a member of the Wigwam Club–one such club by that name was on the South Platte River, Colorado, with fishing for rainbow trout, and another was in London of which George Samuel Jealous, journalist and short story writer, was Secretary. Perhaps Mitford's club life could have been a way of regaining some of the insider status lost by his religious conversion or, more likely, he simply was fond of bourbon and cigars.

Certainly in the final years of Bertram and Zima's marriage, an estrangement had set in. On 20 November and again on 29 November 1912, Zima, writing from 60 Brompton Square, London, S.W., presses Mitford to sign a power of attorney joining her in a tangled lawsuit against several heirs and executors of her father's will. Mitford's reply, 3 December 1912, from 5 Furzeham Road, West Drayton, is harsh, probably not entirely because old Ebden clearly favored the daughters of Zima's first marriage: "I have looked through the Will and find there is no reason whatever why I should touch the affair with the tip of the tongs–my children's interests in it are so remote, and absolutely in the clouds that I don't care to join in any litigation concerning it whatever. As far as I am concerned I am afraid you must fight it out among yourselves and I decline to put my name to any document connected with it. Bertram Mitford." No salutation, no closing, and "my," not "our," children. Indeed, in a postscript Mitford even manages to cast an aspersion on his deceased father-in-law: "the whole thing is so obscurely–not to say slovenly drawn–as to be the reverse of creditable to the attorneys who drew it and the Testator who signed it." In the 20 November letter he added a postscript that he was enclosing a "Cheque for this week" (Monsman 284). As reported in the *Eastern Daily Press*, Mitford died on 4 October 1914 at Cowfold, Sussex (4).[13] His death certificate cited the causes as "cirrhosis of the liver" and "dropsy," that is, edema, probably here a symptom of liver failure. The most prevalent agent of cirrhosis might also explain his separation from Zima, though viral hepatitis also shares a final common pathway with alcoholic liver disease. His funeral was nearby at West Grinstead on 8 October in the churchyard of the Shrine Church of Our Lady of Consolation. He lies beside his wife Zima, who died the following year, both in unmarked grave-plots numbers seven and eight according to Church records; and also by his son Rowland, buried there in 1932, aged 40.[14] As a

---

13. Grant of Administration for the estate of Bertram Mitford, Probate Registry (Family Division of the High Court of Justice), 24 March 1915.

14. The Rector states: "I am able to confirm that Bertram Mitford was indeed buried here at West Grinstead. There is an entry in our Graveyard Records showing that he was buried in plot no. 7; that he was aged 46 [*sic*; 5 or 6 may look alike] when he died in 1914. There is also a Zima Mitford (plot no. 8) . . . and a Rowland Mitford buried here in 1932, aged 40. . . . There are no records of memorial stones and . . . I have never come across a stone bearing the name Mitford" (Monsman 288 n. 67). There is no civil death record for Rowland (or Roland) Mitford for 1932, which suggests that either he died abroad, with his body brought home for burial, or

place of pilgrimage, the shrine may have appealed to him as a haven of meditation and spiritual strength. The earlier house of the parish priest had been used to hide clerics traveling between London and France during the Tudor persecution of Roman Catholics who refused to attend Anglican services. *The London Times* reported that Mitford "aged 55, of Cowfold, Sussex, at one time of Mitford Castle, Northumberland, and of Hunmanby Hall, Yorks, afterwards in the Cape Colony Civil Service, author of numerous novels and descriptive stories," died intestate and left "unsettled property" of £2,196 ("Grant" 29 March 1915: 11). In March 1915 "Zima Helen Mitford his lawful widow and *relict*" had also "died without having taken upon herself the administration of his estate," which thus devolved upon and became vested in the twenty-seven year-old "Yseulte Helen Mitford of 7 Bedford Gardens, Campden Hill, Middlesex, spinster, natural and lawful daughter and one of the next of kin" ("Grant" 24 March 1915). When Zima died on 11 March 1915 at 31 Bedford Gardens, Kensington, London, she was sixty years, five months of age, survived by her four children and attended by Yseulte at her death.[15] Later registers of British marriages (up to 1948) do not reference Yseulte; however, after the deaths of her half sisters (Winifred died in 1931 and Zima Helen in September 1941), while residing in the medieval-renaissance village of Caldarola in the Marche region of Italy, she began to receive (or did not receive, owing to the Second World War) interest on capital left by her grandfather (Archives, Pretoria 204-5). According to a note in what the Mitfords call "The Brown Book" of family records, she died in July 1969 (Archives, West Sussex).

---

that his family failed to register the death. Fiona Mitford reports Roland married Marion Huntoun, born 1891, of Springfield, Massachusetts. Passenger records and ship's manifest indicate "Roland B. Mitford" of Great Britain, last resident in Paris, France, aged 32 and unmarried, arrived at New York on 7 February 1923 aboard the *Olympic* of the White Star and Dominion Lines (sister ship to the *Titanic*) from Southampton.

PART II

PRE-COLONIAL *IMPERIA*

CHAPTER 3
SHIELD AND ASSEGAI: WARRIORS

Part II, Pre-colonial *Imperia*, considers H. Rider Haggard's *Nada the Lily* (1892) and Bertram Mitford's *The King's Assegai* (1894) as a mix of ostensibly factual biography with fictional speculation: "faction," as it is sometimes called. The authors of these accounts of the dynastic founders of the Zulu and Ndebele regimes took the bare bones of what was known historically about Shaka, Mzilikazi, and their chief indunas, and they lived inside those historical figures until they really became alive in the authors' imaginations. The dialogue that propels the narratives of what these warriors thought and felt meshes with a background chronology of events fixed by first-hand sources and research. Of course, such documentary material often derives from imperial sources and reflects a covert white colonial construction of Zulu-Ndebele culture, as noted by Armstrong, Chrisman, Hamilton, Katz, Low, McClintock, Wylie and others. But it is less the historical and political truth of events and circumstances that constitutes the narrative achievement of these novelists than two other accomplishments: first, it is their authorial voices assessing the imperialist's destiny as laid down by Ruskin, as applied to literature by Bryce, and as recollected and redefined by Buchan–voices behind and within their narratives of tribal and colonial interactions variously ironic or elusive or polemical. And secondly, it is what has been called the "disquieting vitality" of their "mythopoeic" vision (Lewis, 1045), those deeply embedded mythoi of socially powerful narratives–echoes of fundamental things at the roots of human reality such as life-death-rebirth, sacrifice, the loss of grace, the struggle with natural or supernatural forces.

§

H. Rider Haggard never went to Oxford or any other university. Squire Haggard, his father, shipped him out to the east-African colony of Natal in company with Sir Henry Bulwer, the newly named Lieutenant-Governor, to get him away from Lilly Jackson with whom he had become infatuated. When Sir Henry took over his administrative duties in Natal from General Sir Garnet Wolseley, the General observed in his diary (28 August 1875) that Bulwer's "only staff consists of a leggy youth not long I should say from school who seems the picture of weakness and dullness"–none other than Rider himself! Perhaps poetically dreamy by nature, Haggard quickly found his focus in Africa. Acquiring a knowledge of the Zulu people, he was recruited to negotiate with tribal chiefs. Then during the Zulu War of 1879 he was a cavalry officer garrisoned at Pretoria; and some years later, his first book was a prescient political analysis of Zulu-European politics. While others attended Oxford and Cambridge, Haggard had been one of a small party that took over the Boer (Dutch) republic of the Transvaal–with its gold and its diamonds–in the name of Queen Victoria. He personally hoisted the Union Jack over Pretoria and, as he recalled,"when the late Sir Melmoth Osborn grew nervous in reading the proclamation"–they were standing in front of an armed, ominously silent crowd of Dutchmen–"I took it from his hand and finished the business" (*Private Diaries* 33-34, 111). Certain of the Boers who did not appreciate British intervention (ostensibly designed to head off a Zulu invasion) intended to ambush the party on its return to Natal; but because Haggard talked the group into taking the brilliantly-lit moonlight route across a ridge rather than through a valley, they avoided certain death. Some years later when the British government returned the Transvaal to the Boers, Haggard was living on the Natal-Transvaal border and wisely decided to return to the safety of England with his wife (not Lilly) and young child–to do what, he hardly knew. Law seemed a possibility; but the incredible success of his *King Solomon's Mines* (1885) followed by *She: A History of Adventure* (1887) decreed otherwise.

Although his inamorata Lilly had broken his heart by marrying someone else while he was managing the Transvaal justice system, the echo of her name and traumatic loss perhaps hovers about his novel *Nada the Lily* (1892). Serially published in *The London Illustrated News* before Longmans, Green brought it out in book form (twice published, twice remunerated), *Nada* came out a decade after Haggard's permanent return to England and at the height of his literary popularity. Haggard's character Allan Quatermain, the most famous imperial adventurer in fiction, appears in this novel as the person to whom Nada's story is told. Many readers had first encountered Quatermain in Haggard's *King Solomon's Mines* (1885), and continued to read of his adventures in other novels, both before *Nada* appeared and long afterwards. Quatermain is a blunt, unpolished hunter and trader of ivory. His fictional role seems to undercut or at least to critique the imperial agenda of foreign rule and tribal dispossession. A "gentleman" not unlike Rider himself, Haggard's alter ego subjects British assumptions, practices, and jingoistic persiflage to a practical common sense founded on a direct experience of Africans, a perspective uncontaminated by crassly self-serving political myths.

Though not as well known as Haggard's *King Solomon's Mines* or *She*, *Nada the Lily* is a historical romance that recounts the bloody reign, assassination, and aftermath of the greatest African ruler of the nineteenth century, the Zulu chief Shaka. Probably the origin of *Nada* lay in the remark of Haggard's friend, the folklorist and anthropologist Andrew Lang, two years before its serial publication: "How delicious a novel *all* Zulu, without a white face in it, would be!" (Cohen 187). Not long after Lang's comment on an "*all* Zulu" story, Haggard in *Allan's Wife and Other Tales* (1889) described "a record of events wherein Mr. Quatermain was not personally concerned–a Zulu novel, the story of which was told to him by the hero many years after the tragedy had occurred"(13-14). Here also in *Nada*, Haggard introduces his famous character, the warrior Umslopogaas, whose love for Nada, the "lily" of the Zulus, is doomed. The character of Umslopogaas is based on M'hlopekazi, a son of Mswazi, King of Swaziland, "a tall, thin, fierce-faced fellow with a great hole above the left temple over which the skin pulsated, that he had come by in some battle. He said that he had killed ten men in single combat, of whom the first was a chief called Shive, always making use of a battle-axe" (Haggard, *Days* 1: 75-76).

The overwhelming bulk of literary work in and on Africa has been produced in the twentieth century and concerns colonial and post-colonial issues. Haggard's romance is notable in that–although written by an Englishman–it has a *pre*-colonial setting, was written well before the greatest proportion of African fiction (it antedated Sol Plaatje's *Mhudi*, 1930, the first novel in English written by an *indigenous* South African, by nearly forty years), and derives from the author's first-hand experience and his use of primary source material. It thus takes a prominent place among literary works with African settings, of interest to the fields of pre-colonial-colonial studies, gender studies, cultural anthropology, nineteenth-century British fiction, and fantasy literature. As to fantasy, *Nada* is historically based; but Zulu ritual and magic are also a significant component of the indigenous narrator's presentation. Quite simply, Haggard's is the *first* popular history of the Zulu empire. Andrew Lang called Haggard's vision of Zulu life, love, and history "the epic of a dying people" (Ellis 136). Quatermain hears the story of Nada from Mopo, an assassin of Shaka, in the wake of a rare Natal snow-storm, not long before the outbreak of the Zulu War in 1879. This War is invoked in the novel's first sentence because it was a critical point in African history, an event that forever changed Zulu cultural formations. The time and the teller in this narrative framework thus set up a dramatic contrast between the pre-colonial life of the inhabitants and their lives in the impending colonial era. The snow that covers the ground, like the white hand and blind eye of Mopo, perhaps suggests fiery emotions that have been frozen in the receding past–almost as if the drink of water that Mopo gave to the boy Shaka in the opening chapter has precipitated and iced at the moment of Mopo's story-telling, when Shaka's dying prediction of the white man's advent is about to be fulfilled.

Today *Nada* is perhaps something of a lost masterpiece; but what made it such an audacious undertaking in 1892 was that Haggard redirected his imaginative and literary interests to African auto-biography/biography–a genre outside both scientific ethnography and the secure objective focus of reportorial writing, yet very much unlike such popular adventure tales as those of G. A. Henty or R. M.

Ballantyne that echoed Victorian conventions, those intrepid English with "brave hearts and stout arms" over against the Africans' "wild and passionate uproar." An amusing and instructive comparison with Ballantyne's *The Gorilla Hunters* (1861) shows how vastly more aware a writer such as Haggard has become. In Ballantyne's novel, a trader observes that "all the nigger tribes in Africa are sunk in gross and cruel superstitions" (78); and there is no scene or comment here or elsewhere to offset this slur. Moreover, in this exotic terrain, Ballantyne's dialogue and digressions keep reverting back to topics more suitable to London's West End theater district; likewise, his actions and images are not always organically related to his plot but are isolated in a geographical no-man's-land devoid of particularization (the shooting of gorillas becomes, thankfully, subordinate to events of slave-trading). Were one to compare Ballantyne's potted landscapes–"The forest out of which we had emerged bordered an extensive plain, which was dotted here and there with scattered groups of trees, which gave to the country an exceedingly rich aspect,"and so on–with any of Haggard's similar vistas, the difference would be conspicuous. When one of Ballantyne's characters steps on a deadly black mamba that the narrator immediately shoots, the viper is described as a "black snake . . . of a very venomous kind, whose bite is said to be fatal." This commentary has all the earmarks of a second-hand account–no species name, no bionomic or zoological details. And surrounding this event we are treated to pious sentiments about the performance of a very British "all-wise Creator" in times of danger (298; 392-93). No wonder Olive Schreiner in her preface to *The Story of an African Farm* spoke so scathingly of those who wrote of Africa from the viewpoint of Piccadilly Circus, and not merely because her literary realism was out of sympathy with the adventure-romance genre.

Haggard's novel was so creatively daring that his fellow Anglo-African author, Bertram Mitford, was inspired to write a parallel account of the Ndebele ruler Mzilikazi, *The King's Assegai* (1894). Mitford then went on to produce three more chronologically successive novels on Ndebele-Zulu history–*The White Shield* (1895), *The Induna's Wife* (1898), and *The Word of the Sorceress* (1902).

Undoubtedly, *Nada* originally had been envisioned as a "stand-alone" narrative of the Zulu state under Shaka and his successor, but after Mitford's tetralogy Haggard seems to have decided on a similar quartet of novels. So, several decades after Mopo's story, Haggard followed it with *Marie* (1912), *Child of Storm* (1913), and *Finished* (1917)–an epic history of fact and legend about the rise and fall of the Shakan dynasty. In *Nada* Haggard's account of Shaka is, as its dedication and preface impress upon the reader, carefully documented. As a multi-voiced Zulu epic, Haggard has found a new way of handling tribal history in which, even though seemingly constrained by the ideologically restricted parameters of colonial fiction, he struggles to replace European stereotypes with depictions of Zulu cultural practices that go beyond cursory colonized presentations.

But the relationship of Mopo the story-teller to Quatermain the listener is considerably more problematic than in ethnographic interviews, since both the teller (Mopo) and the auditor (Quaterman) are of the author's own creation. Haggard as novelist invents the life story that Mopo tells–which simultaneously opens to view Shaka's biography. Haggard is thus the sole mediator between colonial and tribal cultures, inventing scenes, selecting data, emplotting or embedding isolated events in a chronological order, and giving narrative form and linguistic style to Mopo and Shaka–all of this shaped by his sense of audience and market. It is very easy to suspect that a political, even propagandistic, function might contaminate the blurred distinction between fictional and biographical data while narrating Shaka's life. Studies after *Nada*, such as A.T. Bryant's *Olden Times in Zululand and Natal* (1927) and recent works by John Wright, Julian Cobbing, and Dan Wylie have mitigated the more-lurid deeds of Shaka. Nevertheless, the history of the brutal Ugandan "king," Idi Amin, the subject of a novel by Giles Foden (1998) dramatized in the recent film "The Last King of Scotland" (2006), upholds the likelihood of a murderous political paranoia in practice. As seen from the viewpoint of the dictator's personal physician, who only emerges from his association scarred and compromised, Amin's personality in this film seems almost a contemporary reworking of Haggard's psychologizing of the Zulu king and his doctor, Mopo.

Haggard's putative "salvage" mode of Victorian ethnography, as much focused on recovering traditional life-ways as on analyzing the dynamics of cultures in flux, has earned him and other Anglo-African writers such as Mitford the academy's scorn–Mitford had described his fiction as dealing with "a vanishing page" of Zulu history (*The Gun-Runner* 26). Haggard and Mitford are reproached for perpetuating a sentimental and unreal perspective on African society as it existed prior to imperial incursions. Such attempts to portray the pre-European "essence" of ethnic culture are said to cover up the central overwhelming fact in the 1890s of the imperial presence–the author's ideological stance in his manipulations, selectivity, and appropriation of lives not his own. Early adventurer-traders who described Shaka in the last years of his reign, Nathaniel Isaacs in *Travels* (1836) and Henry Francis Fynn in his various writings (collected by James Stuart as Fynn's *Diary*, posthumously published in1950), created an image of Shaka as demonic and the Zulu kingdom as a genocidal society. Certainly Mopo seems aghast at Shaka's killing of the Langeni and at Dingaan's massacre of the Boers. Possibly more influential were the views of Haggard's mentor, Sir Theophilus Shepstone, administrator of native policy in Natal, to whom *Nada* is dedicated. Shepstone supported indirect British rule through a strong indigenous leader and defended the nobility of Zulu life. Mopo even echoed Shepstone's forecast of vengeance for acts of violence (v, 203). Haggard also kept abreast of data from the "field" when in England. He sent for approval before publication a draft of *Child of Storm* (1913) to James Stuart (1868-1942), an official in the Natal colonial civil service from the 1890s until the early years of the twentieth century. Although Stuart's publications both in Zulu and on Zulu orthography, proverbs, and his *History of the Zulu Rebellion* (1906) appeared well after the appearance of *Nada*, he did begin early in his career to transcribe interviews with hundreds of Zulus who remembered Shakan times, now published as *The James Stuart Archive* (1976).

To claim that Haggard's earlier "nostalgic" (if that's what it was) history of a pre-colonial Africa should obscure such contemporary issues as consortium mining and railways, labor migrancy, land dispossession and urban slums reduces itself to this: Anglo-African novelists must not write about any "poetic," "mythic," or past "bloodstained grandeur"; they must confine themselves to the immediate modernizations of tribal culture in their day. Of course, many fine writers of that period did; W. C. Scully comes to mind. But Haggard marched to the throbbing beat of a tribal war-drum–he believed the English, fixated on mere wealth from Africa, could learn much, both from the earlier warrior virtues and from an African oneness with the land, its cattle and crops, the wind and the moon. Current ethnographers strive for "uncolonized," "multi-textual" narratives of ethnic life while at the same time recognizing that divergent concepts of African and Western identity, behavior, ideology, and history put into question such goals as "truth," "objectivity," or "reality." So, is Mopo's tale merely Haggard's sentimental nostalgia for an outdated image of Africa and the cliché of its noble savages (now defeated) that placed little or nothing of the imperial enterprise at risk of criticism? Or does Mopo effectively document what is about to be lost by the Zulus in a sudden and overwhelming transition to a debilitating and sterile imperial rule?

Certainly Haggard was not oblivious to the deleterious effects of empire. In his dedication to *Child of Storm* (1912), he wrote:

> I learned [the lore of Africa] by personal observation in the 'seventies, or from the lips of the great [Sir Theophilus] Shepstone, my chief and friend, and from my colleagues [Sir Melmoth] Osborn, [Fred] Fynney [chief interpreter on Sir Theophilus Shepstone's staff, inspector of Natal native schools and former border agent], [Lieutenant-Colonel Sir Marshal] Clarke and others, every one of them long since "gone down." Perhaps it may be as well that this is so, at any rate in the case of one who desires to write of the Zulus as a reigning nation, which now they have ceased to be, and to try to show them as they were, in all their superstitious madness and bloodstained grandeur. Yet then they had virtues as well as vices. To serve their Country in arms, to die for it and for the King; such was

> their primitive ideal. If they were fierce they were loyal, and feared neither wounds nor doom; if they listened to the dark redes of the witch-doctor, the trumpet-call of duty sounded still louder in their ears; if, chanting their terrible "Ingoma," at the King's bidding they went forth to slay unsparingly, at least they were not mean or vulgar. From those who continually must face the last great issues of life or death meanness and vulgarity are far removed. These qualities belong to the safe and crowded haunts of civilised men, not to the kraals of Bantu savages, where, at any rate of old, they might be sought in vain. Now everything is changed, or so I hear, and doubtless in the balance this is best. Still we may wonder what are the thoughts that pass through the mind of some ancient warrior of Chaka's or Dingaan's time, as he suns himself crouched on the ground, for example, where once stood the royal kraal, Duguza, and watches men and women of the Zulu blood passing homeward from the cities or the mines, bemused, some of them, with the white man's smuggled liquor, grotesque with the white man's cast-off garments, hiding, perhaps, in their blankets examples of the white man's doubtful photographs–and then shuts his sunken eyes and remembers the plumed and kilted regiments making that same ground shake as, with a thunder of salute, line upon line, company upon company, they rushed out to battle. (v-vii)

Similarly, when Mitford spoke of recording a "vanishing page," he concluded his ethnographic appraisal with the ironic observation that "now, thanks to the 'beneficent' policy of England," the Zulus have been "crushed and 'civilised' out of all existence" (*Gun-Runner* vi). Many might not agree with Haggard's judgment that "doubtless in the balance this is best." He undoubtedly is thinking of the justification of British rule he put into Mopo's mouth in chapter nineteen of *Nada*, which begins: "the white man holds the land, he goes to and fro about his business of peace where impis ran forth to kill . . ." (157). Yet Haggard's reluctant assessment suggests that, weighed in the balance, British and Zulus both have virtues as well as vices–and no matter how he feels, neither he nor all Zululand's witch-doctors can keep at bay the inevitable losses or gains in the clash of cultures.

Can one ever pronounce with formal infallibility upon whether the evidence that Haggard selects for his picture of Shaka overtly or subliminally reflects racist attitudes that artfully justify imperial conquest? The recent upsurge of identity politics considers shared group oppression to be not only the basis for political critique and action but allows only group members to speak for their society because outsiders do not share the community's collective experience. Yet this understandable desire for self-representation may encourage a politics of exclusion and *ex cathedra* privilege that will not acknowledge the co-relations and connections within all historical experience. Any intense application of logic to historical evidence, if carried too far, may cast doubt on its validity, an outcome that reminds one of Richard Whately's satiric point in "Historic Doubts Relative to Napoleon Bonaparte" (1819) in which he demonstrated that no evidence either for a miracle or for the existence of Napoleon is unassailable; the existence of both can be questioned–or not. One's sense of the "reliability" of Mopo's narrating voice hinges on how much one is drawn toward the imaginative, mythic, and mystical as over against politicizing or circumscribing preoccupations with "colonialism," "racism," or "cultural imperialism." The reader gets beyond reductive or doctrinaire reactions if he/she recognizes how Haggard cedes control of Mopo's narrative to multiple historical tethers–how he uses documentary data, such as Shaka's many innovations in military and social life; tribal stories, myths, legends, songs, and oral histories; missionary treatises on indigenous religious beliefs; extended quotations by historical speakers; ethnographic data; employs indigenous narrative styles and proverbs ("the climber at last falls with the tree, and in the end the swimmer is borne away by the stream"); and includes variant versions of episodes or, at least, of interpretations (as, for example, Shaka as a "colossal genius and most evil man," a wild beast nevertheless loved by his people).

Interestingly, the novel's titular figure is Nada, not Shaka, a clue that Haggard either is more concerned with her significance than that of Shaka or that he sees her as somehow inclusive of Shaka's *res gestae*. And since Nada is not a historical figure (her prototype probably was sketched in David Leslie's retelling of a local legend[16]),

---

16. Leslie's record of the legend of the doomed lovers is taken up by Haggard at the point where the young chief, having been smelled out as a witch, was surrounded at his kraal by the king's slayers; he and his beloved then flee.

her significance is more likely mystical than political–an expression of *fin-de-siècle* otherworldliness and anxieties. In England's increasingly industrial culture of the late 1880s, in which science and technology threatened belief in religious faith, there was a resurgent interest in spiritualism–in séances, spirit voices, and ghostly materializations–in part owing to tales from England's colonies, particularly Africa. Skepticism held that most displays of supernatural effects were either psychogenic, pharmacological, or trickery; but it also left some sensational events open to further speculation. Mitford and others may have regarded spiritual "forces" much as his contemporary, H. Rider Haggard, did when recalling the ghostly materialization of an attractive girl at a séance:

> To this day I wonder whether the whole thing was illusion, or, if not, what it can have been. Of one thing I am certain–that spirits, as we understand the term, had nothing to do with the matter. On the other hand I do not believe that it was a case of trickery; rather I am inclined to think that certain forces with which we are at present unacquainted were set loose that produced phenomena which, perhaps, had their real origin in our own minds, but nevertheless were true phenomena. (*Days* 1: 39).

The explanation of the spectralized girl is in some way natural because her "real origin" lies in the evanescent sense-perceptions of "our own minds."

Such events were reported and probed by the respected Society for Psychical Research, founded at Trinity College, Cambridge to study hypnotic, psychic, and spiritualistic events. Its membership reads like a scientific *Who's Who* and even included Haggard's close friend Andrew Lang. Along with interest in telekinesis, hypnotic trance, clairvoyance, and pre-death visions, evolutionary speculation took place. Janet Oppenheim notes the current supposition "that evolutionary change had actually eliminated certain faculties, like telepathy, from conscious human control, thereby depriving modern man of some prowess/powers enjoyed by

---

Haggard's varied borrowings from Leslie include: 73; 44-57; 85-91; 279-84.

his remote ancestors" (269). Haggard's circle believed that ancestor worship endowed Africans with psychic powers. Finding realism inadequate and inspired by this deconstruction of the authority of rationalistic states, authors of late nineteenth-century romances often portrayed women who possessed psychic gifts.

Broadly, Haggard's eponymous Nada-figure belongs to a traditional iconography of love like Psyche in Apuleius's *Metamorphoses* and is a "new Venus" who has arisen not from the sea but from earth. However, in specific late nineteenth-century symbolism Nada seems an echo of the mystical word for "sound" in Sanskrit, "*Nada,*" popularlized in H. P. Blavatsky's *The Voice of the Silence* (1889), a collection of theosophical teachings from yogis in the East. William James in *Varieties of Religious Experience* (1902) quotes Blavatsky:

> "He who would hear the voice of Nada, 'the Soundless Sound,' and comprehend it, he has to learn the nature of Dhâranâ [i.e., intense concentration]. . . . When to himself his form appears unreal, as do on waking all the forms he sees in dreams; when he has ceased to hear the many, he may discern the ONE–the inner sound which kills the outer. . . . For then the soul will hear, and will remember. And then to the inner ear will speak THE VOICE OF SILENCE. . . . And now thy *Self* is lost in SELF, *thyself* unto THYSELF, merged in that SELF from which thou first didst radiate. . . . Behold! thou hast become the Light, thou hast become the Sound, thou art thy Master and thy God. Thou art THYSELF the object of thy search: the VOICE unbroken, that resounds throughout eternities, exempt from change, from sin exempt, the seven sounds in one, the VOICE OF THE SILENCE. . . ." These words, if they do not awaken laughter as you receive them, probably stir chords within you which music and language touch in common. Music gives us ontological messages which non-musical criticism is unable to contradict, though it may laugh at our foolishness in minding them. There is a verge of the mind which these things haunt; and whispers therefrom mingle with the operations of our understanding, even as the waters of the infinite ocean send their waves to break among the pebbles that lie upon our shores. (421)

Thus James on Blavatsky on the significance of *"Nada."* Nada embodies that transformative beauty, a whisper of which brings sorrow and the recognition of man's enduring exile.

May one add that the figure of Nada in the novel represents precisely the problem of what we can know objectively and of what we cannot? She is, possibly, the figurative embodiment *in* her novel *of* her novel's problem with historiography, with the endless succession of subjective perceptions that negates the objective truth of every past account. This is not to say that in narrating the events of Shaka's life Haggard was unmindful of the classical-humanist emphasis upon man's control through reason over his circumstances or of the countervailing Christian-medieval concept that history affirms a divine pattern of justice. Mopo, like Quatermain, seems to make fateful choices–this allows Haggard to contemplate a possible rewriting of Zulu history from the point of view of what might have been, had Umslopogaas replaced his father Shaka. But yet this humanism is mingled with its apparent opposite:

> "We think that we can shape our fate, but it is fate that shapes us, and nothing befalls except fate will it. All things are a great pattern, my father, drawn by the hand of the Umkulunkulu upon the cup whence he drinks the water of his wisdom; and our lives, and what we do, and what we do not do, are but a little bit of the pattern, which is so big that only the eyes of Him who is above, the Umkulunkulu, can see it all. Even Chaka, the slayer of men, and all those he slew, are but as a tiny grain of dust in the greatness of that pattern. How, then, can we be wise, my father, who are but the tools of wisdom? how can we build who are but pebbles in a wall? how can we give life who are babes in the womb of fate? or how can we slay who are but spears in the hands of the slayer?"

William James in his discussion of Blavatsky notes that mystical literature frequently uses self-contradictory phrases, such as "dazzling obscurity," "whispering silence," "teeming desert," which suggest that mystical truth is less conceptual than "musical." Such antithetical qualities define the enigmatic figure of Nada (not to mention also the singing voice here of the *Inkosazana-y-Zulu*), who is both an ideal of immortal perfection yet is also the goddess of the reproductive energies of the earth: "all men, white and black, seek that which is beautiful, and when at last they find it, then it passes swiftly away, or, perchance, it is their death."

The most problematic scenes in Haggard's novel involve the tale of Galazi the wolf, the only part of this drama not directly inspired by African sources of history, legend or folk story; thus its mythic significance for Haggard's purpose is all the more critical. Whatever the boundaries of its practice may have been, Galazi's homoeroticism or romantic friendship with Umslopogaas seems equivalent to what some scholars suspect was the latent homosexuality of Shaka, who defined manliness in terms of sexual abstinence from women. In a world where what Nada represents cannot be had, what will take its place? Here the mountain cave strongly suggests a womb/tomb, inasmuch as this is the cave Umslopogaas and Galazi cohabit, centered in the lap of the "the old stone Witch who sits up aloft there forever waiting for the world to die"(101)–and in which Galazi discovers a corpse and in which Nada will perish. In *King Solomon's Mines* there was a similarly portentous cave of diamonds presided over by the old witch Gagool. Galazi has reclaimed from this cave the body of an old woman's son (she is a refracted image of the stone Witch, as is the "aged woman" who later guides Nada to Umslopogaas) in order to win from her a phallic African club: "It was great and knotty, black as iron that had been smoked in the fire, and shod with metal that was worn smooth with smiting" (97; Callaway 166-68). Galazi becomes her son reborn, resexualized. His retrieval of the body, the supreme ordeal of a heroic quest as it were, required that he kill the king and queen of the wolf-people guarding the cave. The recovered corpse teaches him the wisdom of the old witch–that he and Umslopogaas will become kings of the ghost-Wolves who in a former life had been cannibals.

When Galazi dons the skin of the dog-wolf (male and male) and Umslopogaas that of the she-wolf (male and female), they become in the moonlight the new leaders of the ravaging wolf pack. This is both an echo of the bear-shirt of the berserker warrior and a direct instance of werewolf shape-shifting. Haggard's friendship with

Andrew Lang undoubtedly led to his connection of the ravening hunts of cannibal-wolves with myths associating death and fertility, as suggested in several Zulu festivals. Blood and its violent shedding embodies those creative energies of fertility in the land that turn the wintery and concealing darkness of the tomb back upon a renewal of life and plenitude. The flesh (*sarkos*)-eating (*phagein*) "devouring hunger" (108) of the cannibal-ghosts defines the cave in the lap of the Witch as a sarcophagas (*sarkos*+*phagein*) and drives the process of destruction and regeneration, for in this cave Umslopogaas is healed. From the fertile darkness of the tomb as womb, held in gestation like seeds in the earth, comes reborn life. Other mythic overtones are the 363 wolves lead by Galazi and Umslopogaas (the number of days in the annual cycle) and the 51 challengers for the axe that precede Umslopogaas (the number of weeks in the year).

Galazi's death-dealing club, like the moon-shaped axe Umslopogaas wins, are symbols of death–not just for others but for themselves as well. To own the mythic club or axe ultimately will be fatal to the bearer. Here lies the novel's deep paradox: to deal out death is to be subject to death, but to die is to be reborn. Death is the portal to life. One might ask what the waiting Witch who surveys the world's ceaselessly interacting antinomies of generation and decay will do when the world itself dies, when the seasonal and human processes come to an end? That, of course, involves the doppelgänger of the witch, the *Inkosazana-y-Zulu* who appears three times to Mopo in the novel–once in a dream of divine judgment pronounced upon Shaka; again in her Song of the end of Peoples by which she announces Mopo will kill Shaka when next she appears; and finally, shortly thereafter, when she rides in on a storm with a flaming spear and commands Shaka's death. The Witch is associated with the darkness as the Queen is with light; but moon and sun, winter and summer, horror and justice are dialectically interfused elements. Similarly, Umslopogaas as Slaughterer and Nada the Lily are the anthithetical sides, the dark and light doubles of an ambiguous, twofold identity. This duality or *prima facie* opposition is basic to myths of the seasonal cycles, such as the summer and winter phases of Dionysus or Persephone. The death of nature in the winter is personified in the hunter as wolf and devourer; but the flowers of spring and summer are personified by the return of the child of the earth from the madness of slaughter and the underworld (Pater, *Greek Studies* 42-49; 109-110).

In Haggard's earlier novel, *King Solomon's Mines* (1885), Twala the king was undoubtedly based on his detestation of king Lobengúla, the historical ruler of the Ndebele after Mzilikazi, who had murdered one of Haggard's loyal retainers together with a whole peace delegation. In *Nada* this savage-kingly role belongs to Shaka, who kills his way to complete insanity. But the blood-madness of Shaka may be a form of Galazi's and Umslopogaas' dark hematomania. Fynney's account says: "Tyaka's character appears to have been one which was an enigma even to the Zulus themselves, for, as one of his old indunas once explained to me....'He was a strange man; nay, a *silwana* (a wild animal), but we Zulus loved him for all that'" (Fynney 1: 9). This quotation of the "old induna" reappears in *Nada* when Umslopogaas learns that he is the son of Shaka: "'*Wow*! who would have guessed that I was the son of that *Silwana*, of that hyæna man? Perhaps it is for this reason that, like Galazi, I love the company of wolves'"(242). Shaka is a *silwana*, a wild beast of bloody slaughter, a wolf like his son. Recently, such theorists as Konrad Lorenz, Walter Burkert, René Girard, and Maurice Bloch have explored violence in ritual and myth. The postcolonial rendering of African races as imperial victims requiring protection may instead be replaced by an understanding of indigenous practices designed to resist colonization rather than to be exploited by it. Intragroup bloodshed was felt necessary to assure survival in the outer world; and as illogical as such slaughter may be, for the participants its ritual enactment lifted it above rational questioning. Bloodshed effectuated the intervention of the sacred–those tribal ancestors and gods–into human affairs. The rejuvenated dialectic between ancestral spirits and tribal members reaffirmed the life-giving power-relationships of the tribal episteme and sustained the balance between animals and humans, young and old, male and female, sacred and profane, good and evil, friend and enemy. The Witch of the mountain and the Goddess of heaven may together represent mystical balance; but as mortals, Umslopogaas and Nada, within the temporal limits of their lives, cannot reach such an ultimate synthesis: "THOU art THYSELF the object of thy search."

§

Joseph Conrad once observed that "Fiction is history, human history, or it is nothing. But it is also more than that; it stands on firmer ground, being based on the reality of forms and the observation of social phenomena, whereas history is based on documents, and the reading of print and handwriting–on second-hand impression. Thus fiction is nearer truth. But let that pass. A historian may be an artist too, and a novelist is a historian, the preserver, the keeper, the expounder, of human experience"(Conrad, "James" 20-21). A simple point and logically irrefutable, but its truth demands a progressive updating of our notions of canonical inclusion. Certainly there was nothing second-hand in Mitford's South African experiences of which he wrote–he spoke Zulu, served with the frontier mounted police, labored on farms, owned a newspaper, and as a military historian placed battlefield archaeology in the context of local oral testimony. Although Mitford's successive plots might be said to repeat "formulæ of success," he nevertheless deploys his incidents not unlike a musical composer who has a favorite set of related chord types or a painter evoking a stylistic or thematic center–with the quickening power and breadth of lived experience, the only hallmark of art. With a small step of the historical imagination, the mature reader discovers in Mitford's "period adventures" whole dimensions beyond the escapist pleasure of "what next" to which as novelist he probably owed his first popularity. Even back then the artificial distinction between high-brow social realism and popular adventure fiction suggested negative assessments of his work. Also from the 1920s onwards Mitford's upper class values clashed with a populist resentment at the unequal distribution of wealth and with a growing distrust of foreign influences–even the aristocratic heritage of Edgar Rice Burrough's Tarzan is erased from popular celluloid adaptations. But currently Mitford can be appreciated in the hindsight of the intervening years, allowing his novels to be read as more allusive and prescient than when they were first published. A fresh critical re-evaluation focusing on the range of Mitford's contributions to the high romance of Africa would show the importance of this author, often mentioned, less often read.

Because Mitford had experienced both traditional Africa and its modern industrial transformation, his object was to visualize the old kingdoms before their conquest and subjugation, particularly in contrast to the Eurocentric Africa that emerged in the wake of the Zulu War. If the cultural imperialism of pulpits and crass commercialism of newspapers often inhibited the emergence of authentic African voices, Mitford articulated the social, economic and political undertows within his African experience without jingoistic rhetoric. In short, he recognized (and we may also include fellow Anglo-African Club members Haggard and Scully) that when descriptions of specific events by groups with opposed interests and visions conflict, these versions reflect a broader social struggle to enforce a partisan view. Mitford as contrarian links the settlers' struggles to the history of the blacks themselves, humanizing Africans in an era of European chauvinism. Just as seeing eyes define objects from two intersecting angles, so Mitford leads his readers to visualize "the colonies" through the eyes of both the settler and the indigene. There, at that cultural intersection or zone of contact, Mitford's readers look past the public respectability of amoral imperialism or the bloodshed of the old Zulu kingdom to the terror and pity of humanity's quest for survival and love on both sides.

The King's Assegai is the first of a quartet of tales about the Ndebele and Zulu nations as narrated by the warrior Untúswa in his great old age. As a richly detailed fictional life story by this warrior, whose military exploits were equaled only by his unbounded gift for survival, Mitford's first volume is all the more plausible because for many years he had honed his flair for observation and characterization through first-hand experience in the frontier mounted police, on farms, and as a journal owner. Like a seasoned anthropologist deciphering cultural codes or a psychic assessing how reordered consciousness engenders prescience or a historian tracing an arc of events from past to present, Mitford is out to understand, not to vilify or sanctify, the Ndebele nation and its volatile and cunning king, whose name, it has been alleged, meant Path of Blood. The Ndebele-Zulu belong to the Nguni peoples of South Africa (which also includes the Xhosa and Swazi) who, at the time Mitford wrote this novel in 1894, had been overrun by the Europeans–the Zulus by British troops in the war of 1879 and the Ndebele by the British South African Company under Cecil Rhodes in 1893. The period covered by *The King's Assegai*, however, begins and ends much earlier in the century, opening in the early 1820s with the *Mfecane*, a Zulu word meaning "hammering" or "crushing." The *Mfecane* denotes those largely internecine conflicts–although recent conjecture appends external socio-political stimuli, even "dendro-climatological" changes–out of which emerged both the Zulu empire controlled by its warrior-chief Shaka and the Ndebele nation–the particular focus of this novel–led by Shaka's quondam general Umzilikazi.

As narrated by the Tswana writer and journalist, Sol Plaatje, in his political novel of 1930, *Mhudi*, Umzilikazi's people swept north and west from Natal in the early 1820s, they were forced to move several times afterwards and eventually were dispersed throughout a wide territory, carving out a center in present-day Zimbabwe (4-5). Plaatje was a Barolong, one of the Bechuana tribes crushed by the Ndebele in the 1830s. The figure of Untúswa in Mitford's novel depicts a pre-colonial Ndebele warrior, one whose nation subjugates Bechuanas and Shona tribes just as later in the century the British colonized the Ndebele themselves at the point of a gun. In later novels Mitford implies the British rationalized that 1893 conquest in the same way that here in this narrative he reports the Ndebele's view of their "crushing"–as an inherent right of the more powerful to seize space from weaker tribes "whose only destiny was to serve the all-powerful Amazulu" (9). The received wisdom today about Mitford as a romancer of empire is that he wrote rapidly and was popular for presenting an image of Ndebele and British nationality that he and his readers should have known was not the whole truth but in which nevertheless they very much wanted to believe. The reality is that Mitford challenges his readers' reluctance to admit how colonization, both Ndebele and British alike, is constructed upon an ingrained habit of refusing to acknowledge underlying greed, injustice, and horror. When a Ndebele asks a white adventurer in a later Mitford novel: "What is that which is most desired by all white men, *Nkose*?" his answer is "Gold," to which the Ndebele replies: *"Yeh-bo, Nkose,* and by black ones, too, if with it they can buy cattle and wives"(*Blanchland* 88). Below the ostensible adventure surface of Mitford's novels lie acute observations of power relationships; Mitford was not blind to the dark side of the British empire's civilizing mission nor, contrawise, to indigenous strengths, even during the mass displacements of state-formation. Certainly no one can accuse Mitford of paving the way for Professor Trevor-Roper's comment on African history as entirely "the history of Europeans in Africa."[17] Not only does this pronouncement overlook supra-Saharan records as well as sub-Saharan histories by literate Europeans and Africans (Sol Plaatje, to name only one of the latter), but it fatuously discounts indigenous "orature" (*oris* mouth, speech or "auriture" *auris* ear; analogous to "literature" *litterae* letters): myths and tales and riddles, songs (*izingoma*), praise-poems (*isibongo*), and proverbs (*izaga*).

Mitford was a sophisticated, complex novelist; but then as now such critical recognition eluded him (sales of his novels, of course, were brisk). Back then the false antithesis of serious social realism as the high-brow alternative to popular adventure fiction produced distorted assessments; today there is the additional chilling notion, as noted, that any novelist who is not tribally African cannot "speak for" the indigene. This would place such a *persona* as Untúswa fictionally off-limits because, as in H. Rider Haggard's epic saga *Nada the Lily* (1892), Mitford's retelling of battles actual or imagined required that he place himself in a tribal mind and speak

---

17. One of the most outrageous (and widely reported) historiographic statements on Africa was that of Hugh Trevor-Roper in a BBC television lecture, broadcast November 1963: "Perhaps in the future, there will be some African history to teach. But at present there is none. There is only the history of Europeans in Africa. The rest is darkness" (*King's Assegai* [2007] ix n. 2).

with cultural authority in a pre-colonial "voice." But given the total absence in the 1890s of indigenous African novelists–although unheralded oral storytellers abounded–what was to be done? If one's past is to be known but one is unable to write about oneself, then the language of others communicates those events and defines one's emotional and intellectual meanings–this much readers might grant Trevor-Roper.

To transcribe the stories of Zulu tellers became the task of missionary-ethnographers like Henry Callaway, whose *Nursery Tales, Traditions, and Histories of the Zulu* (published in installments, 1866-68) was printed in parallel columns of English and Zulu. My personal copy, once given by the South African-born son of a missionary, H. F. Ellenberger (*"un des plus grands historiens de la psychiatrie et des la psychanalyse"*) to Henri Ey (*"le grand psychiatre français"*), suggests that within tribal orature there exists mythic imagery, latent motivations and meanings, dreams and taboos–all conveyed within a traditional Zulu folk form. In a later novel, Mitford has a "rough and ready prosaic trader in the Zulu" begin with the necessary empiricism of direct experience in response to an Anglo-African girl's query about whether learning the language is easy: "To tell the truth I don't know whether it is or not. I didn't *learn* it, myself. I sort of absorbed it. But I can tell you it makes all the difference in the world if you can talk with them and understand them or not. If you can I can't imagine any people more easy to get on with." Then to her father he adds:

> "I don't mean to say they're perfect, no one is, but make the best of them. To begin with, learn the language. . . . I knew a man once . . . who had gone stone blind late in life. . . . He had got hold of the Bible in Zulu, done up by missionaries of course, and began putting all sorts of grammar cases to me. I own he fairly stumped me. I told him I didn't know anything of Biblical Zulu– had always found that in use at the kraals good enough."
> (*Frontier Mystery* 17-24).

His (and behind this character, Mitford's) contrast is not only between an indigenous oral language and the documentation of that language in the Latin alphabet of the *Ibhayibheli Elingcweele* (selections first translated into Zulu in 1848, New Testament in 1865, complete text in 1883) but also between lived experience and Western mores funneled into Zulu words, the latter a blind-man's game.

Admittedly, in the first two novels of Mitford's tetralogy, written after the 1893 British conquest of the Ndebele but before their Rising against imperial rule in 1896–that is, when all resistance to European supremacy seemed passed and the stereotype of the bloodthirsty warrior had modulated into an unthreatening trope of the "noble savage"–Mitford's nostalgia-tinged admiration for the more heroic times and peoples might be discounted as sentimentality. But the figurative blindness of Mitford's countrymen toward the patterned, coherent life of the Ndebele prior to the arrival of the Europeans became a subtext, as his epilogue to the second novel in the series, *The White Shield* (1895) implies. Untúswa's story underlines "the boundless stupidity of certain Britons of the denser sort, who in official or private capacity could move among such for a greater or lesser period of time, and yet bring away no more of an impression than that of a lot of 'blacks' who wore precious little clothing and were not eager to learn the arts of 'civilization.'" This is even more emphatically stated in the conclusion to *The Induna's Wife* (1898). There Mitford implicitly decries evolutionary racial ideas and supports a relativist and functionalist social interpretation when he inveighs against "one hard-and-fast point of view, and that point of view the British" (*White Shield* 301; *Induna's Wife* 299). The stylistic archaisms are in Mitford's "homiletic register." That Mitford should protest this shortsighted and insular ignorance of indigenous cultural formations and the "race feeling" inherent in the pejorative stereotype of semi-naked and subservient natives argues that if there is any likelihood of rescuing forgotten autochthonous voices from colonial texts, it certainly might include *The King's Assegai*: "The incidents and recollections which would cluster round that beautifully-made dark-handled spear could not fail to be copious as well as passing strange. Then, in his pleasant and flowing Zulu voice–*the* voice *par excellence* for narrative purposes–the old man began: 'I am

Untúswa . . ." (6). The success of Mitford's endeavor depends upon his ability to portray the consciousness of that "flowing Zulu voice" – *in English*, the language of the conqueror.

The King's Assegai takes as its epic "argument" a people led out of captivity and a nation founded in a new land. The analogue is the children of Israel led by Moses, the same that the South African Boer settlers and even American colonists applied to themselves. Mitford celebrates this Ndebele heroic sense of destiny, their spontaneous love of war (his romanticized image of the warrior may be taken *cum grano salis*), their bravery in face of death, their courteous Zulu manners, their staunch loyalty to their chief (*inkosi ebunene*, "a sympathetic and kind king," a phrase that Mitford may or may not have heard spoken). Also he admired the new social stability emerging in the eastern Transvaal from the disorder of the times, recognizing explicitly the outwitting of Shaka and the multiple alliances built by Umzilikazi. In addition he has Untúswa argue that Umzilikazi was not gratuitously sanguinary: his scorched-earth policy created a security zone that ensured no pursuit and also discouraged local resistance. Finally the Ndebele are admirably free from the corruption of the West's cunning and ruthless craving for limitless materialistic wealth, nor have they been debased by participation in such cruelties as cannibalism or, by inference, of the slave trade. Whatever acts particular individuals may have committed, such admiration is possible because Mitford is not inclined to see the pragmatism of the Ndebele *in the aggregate* as any more heinous than the opportunism of British or Boer settlers.

Analysis of Mitford's novel could begin with what its title might imply. An "assegai," an Arabic word for the tree used to make shafts for spears, is a weapon of the Nguni peoples, a traditional symbol of military conquest, of warrior status, and of the chief's authority in matters of order, law, and justice. The shorter-style assegai described in novel's opening pages was invented by Shaka. With a longer, broader, and heavier blade for use as a stabbing weapon in close combat, it supplemented the traditional handful of lighter and longer throwing assegais also carried by fighters. This Shakan assegai was also the soldier's sole knife for slaughtering cattle, hunting, and even shaving. Umzilikatzi's assegai, like the scepter that invests European monarchs with royal authority, is closely connected to the power of his "word" as king. Throughout the novel, the king's ex-officio"word" is one of promise or declaration or judgment, but very unlike the speech of commoners. J. W. Colenso remarks in *Ten Weeks in Natal* (1855): "It is remarkable that in the Kafir language there is no word for *command*, although in no people is the exercise of authority more common and the sense of it stronger. The chief's 'word'—*iliZwi*—is his command" (121). When the missionary William Sykes told the king that his people needed to be able to read God's word, Mzilikazi responded, "I tell my people my own words." Sykes replied that God had spoken in his Bible to all men, an exchange that provoked multiple and increasingly loud roars of laughter from the king and his attendants.[18] Mitford, alert to cultural comparisons, knew that the king's assegai as a physical symbol of his inviolable "word" was not unlike the temporal sword of steel and the spiritual sword of the Word that the Bishop of Rome held above the nations. And such biblical imagery as "Where the word of a king is, there is power: and who may say unto him, What doest thou?" (Ecclesiastes 8:4) or "the sword of the word" or "a sword of mouths" would have been deeply ingrained through his Catholicism.[19] In the novel, Masuka drops his "words slowly and as the cuts of assegais"; also "Even as a spear, too, did the bitter derision of the King's voice cut" (132, 232).

The precipitating incident for *The King's Assegai* comes from an encounter during Mitford's trip to the Zululand battlefields shortly after the war that ended at Ulundi:

---

18. "Sykes gave up and stalked back to his wagon, more depressed than ever" (Bhebe 38). Sykes, who worked with Robert Moffat and Thomas Morgan Thomas at the Matabele mission at Inyati, made this report to the Foreign Secretary in 1862.

19. Hebrews 4:12; Ephesians 6:17; Revelation 1:16, 2:16; Proverbs 12:18; Psalms 51:21. In John 9:28 "reviled" (eloidorhsan / *eloidorhsan*) is derived from *loidoria, logov*, "a word," and *doru*, "a spear," thus combining the ancient Hellenic morphemes to describe the cutting, piercing resistance of the old dispensation to the new order.

> I saw that one of them carried an assegai with a blade like a small claymore, and, seeing, coveted and resolved to have it if possible . . . Then taking up the assegai I began to examine it, suggesting that we should make an exchange, and throwing out all sorts of inducements. Not a bit of it; the jovial warrior would about as soon think of parting with his head-ring—or his head. He had fought with that very weapon 'kwa Jim' (Rorke's Drift) &c. &c; no, he couldn't give it away on any account. It was a splendid specimen of a spear, but on no terms could I obtain it. (*Zulu Country* 266-67)[20]

One might imagine that in life as in the novel the Mitford-narrator would be intensely mortified before the Zulus and such evidence of the British destruction of their capital (destruction more as retribution than strategic necessity); but later in his narrative Untúswa recounts the burning of the Basuto (now Basotho [pl.], Mosotho [sing.]) kraal as war at its best–when might makes all acts right. Like the romantic ruins of Kor in H. Rider Haggard's *She and Allan* (1921) or Robert Browning's "Love Among the Ruins" (1855), the setting for Mitford's narrative is symbolic, the hills overlooking overlooking the hub of the old Zulu kingdom, Cetywayo's kraal, scene of the last battle of the Zulu War. There at Ulundi the British lever-action Martini-Henry humbled the assegai. The destruction of this Zulu political center has prepared the way for the subsequent terrain of the story in which the Zulu-Ndebele narrator's memory will re-create the *ancien régime*, replacing its disquieting loss with a historical and clarifying *apologia* for tribal traditions.

Thus the king's spear in the hands of Untúswa as he looks out across the long-silent Ulundi emblematizes the memory of ancestral spirits once expressed through the royal word-as-sword and, with their passing, the final destruction of Zulu national pride. Yet the refusal of this prototypic old warrior to barter or sell his royal assegai to a mere collector of trophies is evidence of a refusal to betray Ndebele-Zulu cultural traditions to the emissaries of the European

---

20. Mitford's first literary publication was a poem, "The Defence of Rorke's Drift" in *The South African Magazine and Review*, Port Elizabeth, SA (1880).

world; that is, to acquiesce in their self-proclaimed religious, governmental or economic hegemony. Chief Gatsha Buthelezi recently commented that "another of my hopes for my people is the return of Zulu pride–pride in what they were, are and can be. Somehow, without the intention to do so, a feeling has been inculcated that we should be ashamed of everything that constitutes our past. To many people the old Zulu kingdom means just bloodshed, but it had other positive aspects in the sense that our political and social system was based on it. With the overthrow of the Zulu kingdom came the shattering of much of the Zulu national consciousness. We can get back this national consciousness, step by step, in the best possible way, if our people have the right once more to make decisions about their own future" (Gojwana, 4 October 2002).

Although a generalized patriarchal ideal of personal loyalty cast the Ndebele ruler as a father figure, with his people calling themselves the king's children, one may speculate that for Untúswa, whose real father was both remote and jealous, Mzilikazi fills the particular role of an authoritarian father and that he is the king's rebellious son. If one had more biographical information about Mitford, one might discover that this paternal semblance is the screen onto which the novelist projects his own psychological sense of a father-son relationship, especially since at about this time Mitford's father, Edward Ledwich Osbaldeston-Mitford, descended from nobility as far back as William the Conqueror, inherited the title "Lord of Mitford." If so, the tale of the emblematic assegai is more than Untúswa's first-person historical romance but is also a covert portrait of the artist as a young Zulu. Besides highlighting Untúswa's rash and rebellious nature, at its outset this romance performs one important task usually credited to later African writers. What set Chiuna Achebe's teeth on edge was a moment in Joseph Conrad's "Heart of Darkness" (1899) when Marlow watches Africans dancing:

> "Well, you know, that was the worst of it–this suspicion of their not being inhuman. It would come slowly to one. They howled, and leaped, and spun, and made horrid faces; but what thrilled you was just the thought of their humanity–like yours–the

> thought of your remote kinship with this wild and passionate uproar. Ugly." (*Youth* 109)

In implicit reaction, Achebe wrote what is perhaps the best-known African novel in English, *Things Fall Apart* (1958). His purpose was to go behind the slur of wildness and passion to the social and reasonable order of tribal life; and most of Achebe's story is about things "holding together" within a traditional Ibo culture. The initial scenes of *The King's Assegai* perform just this task also for Ndebele society.

Like Achebe, Mitford melds English with words, phrases, and songs of indigenous Africa, and supplies details not only of military discipline and the excitement of warfare but, especially in his opening chapters, of Ndebele courtship conventions, parental and sibling kinship patterns, social organization and customs, division of labor, religion (the *isanusi* and Masuka the Mosutu), and veldcraft. Furthermore Mitford's rather point-blank (for him) recognition of premarital sex without guilt anticipates that climatic moment in Ngugi wa Thiong'o's story, "Minutes of Glory," contrasting simple pastoral kraal-life to detribalized urban prostitution:

> Fallen from grace, fallen from grace. She was part of a generation which would never again be one with the soil, the crops, the wind and the moon. Not for them that whispering in dark hedges, not for her that dance and love-making under the glare of the moon, with the hills of TumuTumu rising to touch the sky. (86)

Perhaps Mitford permitted himself to half-believe in the special powers of those in tune with these occult forces of nature; and possibly this is why he allows Untúswa to experience the magic of the wizard's incantation bowl. The Mosutu witch-doctor is an alien to Nebele society and he brings a wisdom from the outside that the local *izanusi* find uncanny. If Masuka uses gunpowder hidden in his head bandage for his Fire Spirit display, the incantation bowl images can only be explained by spiritual powers that civilized man and even some Africans have lost by a fall from ancestral grace.

The Baputi-Gqunaqua cannibals whom Untúswa fights represent a contrasting nightmare to the social order of the Ndebele. Of course, Untúswa presumes an implicit class distinction between the military-caste Ndebele of Zulu blood and other inferior or mixed-ancestry tribes–an echo of Mitford's own intense consciousness of his upper-class birth. Mitford dedicated *The King's Assegai* to his second cousin, J. H. Bowker, commandant of the famed Frontier Armed and Mounted Police, a force similar to that in which Mitford himself may have served. Mitford's knowledge of the Ndebele may have come not only from the frontiersman Colenbrander but also Bowker, who was a military professional as well as an amateur naturalist of the highest order. As to such *published* sources upon which Mitford drew here, Bowker wrote a sensational first-person description of physical and oral evidence for past and recent cannibalism in South Africa, with dual submissions identically entitled "The Cave Cannibals of South Africa"(76-80) to *The Journal of the Ethnological Society of London*, under the pseudonym of "Mr. Layland"–a military officer can be depended upon to know the "lay of the land"?–and to the *Anthropological Review* under his own name, there also with addenda from two other scholars (121-28). Bowker's essay is no mere reflection of racist fascination with cannibalism in late nineteenth-century thought–even Richard Burton quotes "Mr. Layland" as authoritative (1: 215-16)–especially since, in the light of post-colonial discourse about "speaking for" the other, Bowker's citation of indigenous informants goes far to situate cannibalism within local cultural formations. Yet as these issues go, I have little doubt but that one could find Eurocentric assumptions in the bloodbath and beyond of Bowker's and Mitford's cannibal caves. On the whole, however, I think we can forgive Bowker's amusing but politically incorrect description of one reformed old cannibal as "a man of about sixty years of age, and (not to speak from prejudice) one of the most God-lost looking ruffians that I have ever beheld in all my life" (Bowker 123).

Bowker's rather Gothic cannibal caves are located in a semi-desert of open plains and archipelagos of mountains north and west of the Orange River, an area that in Mitford's time included

Bloemfontein and the diamond town of Jagersfontein where the Excelsior diamond was found in 1893, which became the inspiration for his next novel, *Renshaw Fanning's Quest* (1894). What *The King's Assegai* owes to Bowker's essay (who undoubtedly supplemented it with informal reminiscences) is the "savage looking" cavern in which the attack upon the mountain dwellers plays out, the reference to numerous skulls and jaws flung away, and the cavern's adjacent "larder," a "gloomy-looking natural gallery" in which "were stowed away the unfortunate victims not required for immediate consumption" (122). Mitford's story also borrows from one of Henry Callaway's oral informants cited in the essay: the episode of the wandering cannibals who "beguiled" their unsuspecting victims before trying to seize them. Bowker says that after spending "an hour or two in the cavern and its vicinity," the visitor "will, I imagine, return a wiser and a sadder man" (121). This echo of S. T. Coleridge's "Rime of the Ancient Mariner" is as much of a "moral" as Bowker draws from his experience; but insofar as Coleridge's wedding guest attempts to ignore the shameful realities of the human condition, Bowker is suggesting that those darker deeds both exist and will disrupt civilized life whether one wishes or not. This, I imagine in my turn, is also Mitford's purpose; and reading Bowker's scenes against Mitford's makes interpretation more compelling.

During the attack on the cannibals, Untúswa encounters his powerful rival Gungana in a secluded place and engages him in close combat. When Gungana falls into a crevice, Untúswa drops a large stone on his head: "There was a crunching sound, and a deep, convulsive groan; then the noise of a heavy body rolling and sliding further and further" (168). Soon afterwards, when Untúswa falls into the larder of the eaters of men, whose victims are themselves reduced by starvation to cannibalism, he dodges a head that is thrown at him and then is hit with "a human leg freshly torn off" which "was that of Gungana himself. What an omen, that the man whom I had killed should even in death continue to fight against me!" (178). The larger point here is that Untúswa has sunken to not much above the level of the *Izímu,* having murdered Gungana largely out of ambition and jealous rage. The martial prowess of Untúswa, intrinsically, is only meaningful in the context of duty to regiment, community, and nation, as implied in the *amabutho* oath of allegiance to the king and his "word." (Mitford seems to anticipate here Peter Mahlangu's historic epic, *uMthwakazi* [29-43]). The killing of Gungana was outside the Ndebele code. And when Untúswa brazenly runs off with Umzilikazi's wife-in-waiting, his bravado in defiance of the king's authority is both ostracizing and debasing, as he comes to realize: "I saw clearly that the man who should throw away his career as a warrior, and such dazzling chances as mine were–for the sake of a girl–is such a fool that he deserves not to live at all" (217).

This girl, Nangeza, has been a bad influence: she easily seduces Untúswa, invents the plan that gets his brother put to death, and suggests this idea of running off. As actively heterosexual, however, Untúswa's rebellious virility wins Mitford's approval, despite its ambition and dishonor. Irrespective of the illusion that closeness to nature directs sexual desire to its natural role of biological reproduction, Mitford recognized that homosexual practice was not exogenous to African society, certainly not within the age-grade regiments of unmarried young men required to live and work together. As a means of controlling procreation and overall work output, warriors were forbidden physical relations with women on pain of death until they had distinguished themselves in battle–and often were not permitted to marry until after decades, some not until age forty. Around this skeleton in the Zulu closet, Mitford dances with consummate adeptness by creating the girl-hungry Untúswa as his hero, whether mere fantasy or semi-autobiographical portrait one does not know (Untúswa's eventual sixteen wives would be the former, perhaps).

Mitford borrowed the incident of Umzilikazi's judgment upon the wayward Untúswa from the missionary Robert Moffat's account of his visit to Umzilikazi and the king's judgment upon a "man of rank," an *induna*. Both the fictional and historical soldiers are brought disarmed before their chief to hear an inevitable pronouncement of death. Because of Moffat's presence, however, the historical Umzilikazi proclaims "I spare you for his sake." "But," continues the king, "you must be degraded for life; you must no more associate with the nobles of the land, nor enter the towns of the princes of the people; nor ever again mingle in the dance of the mighty. Go to the poor of the field, and let your companions be the inhabitants of the desert" (541). Similarly, when Untúswa is brought before the king, Umzilikazi who has a fatherly regard for him decrees "I grant thee thy life. But" he continues "thou mayest no more be among my *izinceku*; no more shalt thou take thy place in the ranks of the warriors, or go out with them to battle, nor shalt thou ever be suffered to *tunga*. Thy place henceforth shall be among the lowest of the captured slaves who herd the nation's cattle, bearing no arms but a stick only" (236-37). In both scenes, the warriors' responses are similar; both prefer to relinquish their lives rather than lose their station in service to state and king. In Moffat: "O king, afflict not my heart! I have merited thy displeasure; let me be slain like the warrior; I cannot live with the poor. . . . How can I live among the dogs of the king, and disgrace these badges of honour which I won among the spears and shields of the mighty? No, I cannot live! Let me die, O Pezoolu!" (541).[21] In Mitford: "'I would prefer death O Black Elephant!'"adding as he tells his story, "I, a warrior, who lived but for battle, never again to bear arms! I, an *inceku*, to descend to herd with the offscourings of all the miserable and degraded tribes we had swept from our path! Of course, I preferred death ten time over, . . . any death, however hideous, however lingering, to life upon the terms of such awful degradation" (237-38).

Moffat's final comment points to the reason why the Nguni peoples appealed to the contemporary Britisher's imagination: "We have often read of the patriotism of the Greeks and Romans, and heard that magnanimity of soul extolled which could sacrifice honour, property, and life itself, for the public good, rather than become the vassals of a foe, and live divested of the poor trappings of human glory; if this be virtue, there are, even among Afric's sons, men not

---

21. "Pezoolu" is currently spelled "Izulu." The prefix *ili-/i-* is a noun marker for a person and *zulu* derives from the Zulu word for "heaven," one of the titles of the king: "heavenly one." Moffat also spells *induna* a half-dozen phonetic ways, including *tuna*.

inferior to the most illustrious of the Romans" (542). When A. T. Bryant quoted this "impressive incident" from Moffat, thirty-five years after Mitford had used it as his novel's climactic scene, Bryant says it shows "something of the better side" of Mzilikazi's character (*Olden Times* 439-40); but Moffat's and Mitford's intention was, rather, to show the soldier's character. Moffat's officer who preferred "death to dishonour" provides a parallel to the heroism of Tennyson's horsemen in his immensely popular "Charge of the Light Brigade"– the call to a duty that does not pretend to explain itself but that nonetheless is answered without hesitation, without consideration for self, simply because true character and right conduct require it. This is the authentic Roman *Pietas*, duty as unqualified fidelity to regiment and king. The famous scene in Haggard's *King Solomon's Mines* in which the condemned soldier accepts execution with the metaphor, "I am the king's ox" (130) also points precisely to this subordination of the individual to the higher will of the monarch; the warrior is a possession of the king to be sacrificed at his pleasure. Afterwards, Gagool the witch-doctoress screeches: "the king's word is spoken, the king's doom is done." This doom had elicited another sort of word from Sir Henry, a "great oath" because his values of justice and mercy are affronted. But in the event, Sir Henry turns up as a Zulu general swinging his battle-axe with all the gusto of a berserker warrior–as it turns out, the British really were crypto-afficionados of a rather violent justice and lethal mercy.

Ironically, only at the last moment, through force of will or telepathy, does the Mosutu wizard cause Untúswa to realize that without intending it he has carried out the basic challenge of the king: "perform some act bolder than any I have ever heard tell of" (26). It is solely by invoking the king's earlier promise of assegai and *tunga* for such an unheard of deed that Untúswa is able to avoid a seemingly inevitable death. He lives to fight another day; Moffat's antetype is thrown to the crocodiles "yawning to devour him" (542). When the king announces to Untúswa "thou shalt have thy wish," then twirls "the great assegai in his hand till it flashed–a band of fire," Untúswa understandably interprets this wish as his requested death-with-honor. Instead, Umzilikazi hands over to Untúswa the coveted assegai that had "halted–motionless but for a slight quiver–within a hand's-breadth of my heart" (243). Significantly, the *novelty* of Untúswa's exploit is also what saved the witch-doctor's life: "show me something I have never seen before," the King commands the Mosutu, "something new" (73). In the context of "a new nation" created by Umzilikazi himself, one theme of Mitford's romance might derive from the phrase which Pliny the Elder stole from the Greeks: *ex Africa semper aliquid novi*–"always something new is coming out of Africa." In antiquity this "something new" implied tribes of man-eaters–Bowker's African anthropophagic practices–and strange animals, human monsters with dog-heads, and the like; but in the age of empire the phrase suggested mineral resources and new economic possibilities. Mitford probably would have agreed with the part of Mary Kingsley's statement after the dash of her pen: that Africans were the "greatest world race–a race not passing off the stage of human affairs, but one that has an immense amount of history before it" (Porter 46).

If the king is surprised at that to which his words bind him, then of how much or of exactly what is he in control? If Umzilikatzi's word-as-spear can slay Untúswa or ennoble him, upending the seemingly irreconcilable differences of life and death, the king may not be a ruler of the historical process itself but at least he proves to be a force for choice of direction–and thus a facilitator of the historical process. In Mitford's estimation Umzilikazi stands between the cannibals of Pliny and the new commercial representatives of empire: he desired firearms (just for elephants and defense, so he said) and he was fascinated with Moffat's telescope and the construction techniques of his "moving houses" (wagons), as described in *Missionary Labours* (532). Umzilikazi is the pivotal figure between Ndebele customs and European culture, such as exists between Masuka's incantation bowl and the chalice of the Jesuit priest (in the second of Mitford's quartet, *The White Shield*). Mitford's missionary in that novel is not intent on stigmatizing the Ndebele as darkly superstitious nor on transforming their traditional values through a post-enlightenment colonizing culture. On Umzilikazi's watch, neither the Jesuit's Christianity nor Masuka's traditional animism suppresses the other as irrelevant to human spiritual needs; rather, each illuminates the other in interesting ways no one could foresee. And just as the king stands between that traditional past of witch-doctors and a broad provisional inculturation of ancestral spirits within the missionary's new religion, so also he straddles the Ndebele's formative stage as a military state and its future prospects for peace–peace not, however, as the autonomous (and currently over-stressed) entity of Zimbabwe; rather, as a future jewel in the imperial crown. And, finally, since Untúswa won't sell that kingly word-as-sword, the ghost of Umzilikazi hovers between an imperially imposed language that contributes to maintaining social inequities and an orature presenting itself in new literate forms that resist or subvert the cultural hegemony of the British Empire.

CHAPTER 4
LOVE AND MAGIC: WIVES

The indigenous woman by her wise use of love and magic as modes of power, status, and authority, enlightened romance writers as to the limits of Western rationalism and the reach of spiritual vision. Although this present critique may appear to stand on a long tack to the windward of such predecessors as Anne McClintock's *Imperial Leather* (1995), it will offer literary and philosophical specifics needed to understand the functioning of global events within the empire romances. McClintock's was a study of racial politics within imperial ideology as reflected in various forms of Victorian iconography, highlighting the intimate connections between power and its racial, social, and sexual expressions. She examined nineteenth-century novels, diaries, advertisements and photographs to show how British imperialists reinvented domestic patriarchy in the colonies–with Europeans holding a paternalistic power and the colonized peoples hidden in a kind of feminine subjection. Later, Laura Chrisman in *Rereading the Imperial Romance* (2000) and *Postcolonial Contraventions* (2003) drew on a stockpile of feminist, Marxist, and post-colonial theories to describe the ideological contradictions within empire. Her approach to imperial narratives and counter-narratives addressed the material bases of colonialism and the development of post-colonial studies. The present chapter, "Love and Magic: Wives,"considers the African women and her political role from a somewhat different perspective, as the eternal feminine, the visible "envelope of God."

In late imperial fiction, the charismatic woman may be either a beneficent influence who draws her power from nature or a threatening force hostile to the empire's ideals of honor and justice. Haggard's Gagool, as a practitioner of necromantic magic in *King Solomon's Mines* (1885), and Mameena in Haggard's *Child of Storm* (1913) are tribal figures who will not be subordinated by empire. Disentangled from the restriction of both African and British femininity, Mameena is a *femme fatale* who leaves Allan Quatermain socially and ruinously conflicted because neither her love for him nor his for her could fit the bourgeois and proletarian paradigms of either tribal or colonial societies. But Haggard's most dangerous woman was Ayesha in *She: A History of Adventure* (1887) whose magic, independence, aggressive sexuality, and intention to overthrow Queen Victoria and rule the British empire make her a threat to British ideals of civic order and moral standards. Merely to visualize the outrageous possibility of an Arabic-African queen from beyond the imperial frontier replacing Victoria on the throne of "a great civilizing race such as ours" raised concerns of whether such a divinely ordained mandate was merely a proud illusion.

Haggard drolly observed about himself that "From a boy ancient Egypt had fascinated me, . . . I venerate Isis, and always feel inclined to bow to the moon!"(Haggard, *Days* 1: 254-55). Isis, a moon-goddess like Astarte, was narrowly the divinity of agriculture but in her broader aspect she represented Nature, as testified to by an inscription on her veiled statue: "I am all that has been, all that is, all that ever shall be, and no mortal has ever raised my garment. The fruit which I brought forth became the Sun" (Blavatsky [1]). Isis is also the goddess the ancient citizens of Kor worshiped under the broader appellation of Truth: "Her perfect and most gracious form was naked, save–and here came the extraordinary thing–the face, which was thinly veiled, so that we could only trace the marking of her features" (*She* 264). Ayesha interprets: "It is Truth standing on the World, and calling to its children to unveil her face" (265). This "Unveiled Truth" (Blavatsky 2: 635, 640) had been the keynote in Helena Blavatsky's manifesto of spiritualism, placing Ayesha firmly within an empirical nineteenth-century science of spirituality. Isis as the Earth Mother, the goddess of Oriental-Hellenistic mystery religions, fuses nature and mystery. Carl Jung defines the antithetic/complementary facets of this Mother: "The qualities associated with this archetype are maternal solicitude and sympathy; the magic authority of the female; the wisdom and spiritual exaltation that transcend reason; any helpful instinct or impulse; all that is benign, all that cherishes and sustains, that fosters growth and fertility. . . . On the negative side she may connote anything secret, hidden and dark; the abyss, the world of

'The Dead,' anything that devours, seduces, and poisons, that is terrifying and inescapable like fate" (Jung 82).

Holly speculates on Ayesha's identity behind the curtain: is she "some naked savage queen, a languishing Oriental beauty, or a nineteenth-century young lady, drinking afternoon tea?" (141). His amusingly clichéd images are knocked over by Ayesha's face "wrapped up in soft white, gauzy material in such a way as at first sight to remind me most forcibly of a corpse in its grave-clothes, . . . the feeling crept over me that I was in the presence of something that was not canny" (142). Earlier Holly had dreamed of Ayesha's ambiguous, twofold identity as suggested by the beauty/corpse pairing: "a veiled form . . . revealing now the perfect shape of a lovely blooming woman, and now again the white bones of a grinning skeleton, and which, as it veiled and unveiled, uttered : . . .'*That which is alive hath known death, and that which is dead yet can never die, for in the Circle of the Spirit life is naught and death is naught*'" (109; 149). In the rhetorical figuration of European missionary doctrine, life is split into only two kinds of spiritual reality: moral/immoral; two paths: straight/crooked; and two destinations: heaven/hell. But this binary theology of the missionaries contrasts with spiritualism's cyclical or "dialectical monism" in which unity appears as duality and duality is an expression of unity. In mythic terms, Leo and Holly become the divine consorts of Nature, the light and dark duality or inherent opposition basic to the seasonal cycles of the earth in its changes, such as the summer and winter phases of Dionysus or Persephone in Greek mythology. As in the Greek myths of the twofold gods of joyful summer and dark winter, Leo (when ill) and Kallikrates (when dead) languish in the sterile chthonian phase of the wintry underworld, reflected also in Ayesha's lonely, hellishly tortured soul and in Holly's lovelorn yearning for her–until that "uncanny"(238) doppelgänger, Leo-as-Kallikrates, is restored to health and life. Like the rebirth of nature in spring, the divine consort's mystical return looks forward to the goddess's own restoration.

Unlike the grim ties between the mother and darkness, the magic of the African women in *The White Shield* and *The Induna's*

Wife by Mitford and in Plaatje's *Mhudi* belongs to the gentler tradition of the woman of knowledge, the "wise woman," whose prophetic vision and intuition are used for a moral, beneficent purpose, as the Boer mother in Olive Schreiner's "Eighteen Ninety-Nine": "And as time passed she came also to be known through the country-side as a 'wise woman.' People came to her to ask advice about their illnesses, or to ask her to dress old wounds that would not heal; and when they questioned her whether she thought the rains would be early, or the game plentiful that year, she was nearly always right" (*Stories* 19). Haggard also had created such figures of "white" magic–Rachel Dove, Nanea, Nobela, Noie, Nombe, Nya, Nyleptha, Lady Ragnall, Sabeela, Sheba, Sihamba, not to mention the Zulu Queen of Heaven. But Mitford's Lalusini and Plaatje's Mhudi deserve their share of focused attention inasmuch as they represent African spirituality as a less fanciful and exotic answer to the Empire's preoccupation with spiritual alienation. Both women were an epiphenomenon of late-Victorian debates on the status and social role of wives.

Such works as Mill's *On the Subjection of Women* (1869) helped to frame public discussions of what was called the "New Woman." Perhaps the allegorical figures of Haggard's Maiwa and Nada also should be read in the light of new 1890s social tensions–gender roles, marriage, family. The illusion of the angel in the house was rapidly being replaced by the new reality of a woman with a job and a menstrual syndrome. In the light of Lalusini's and Mhudi's symbolic roles as queens, Mill's comparison of queens and kings is most fitting. In comparison to kings, among reigning queens "a far larger proportion have shown talents for rule; though many of them have occupied the throne in difficult periods. It is remarkable, too, that they have, in a great number of instances, been distinguished by merits the most opposite to the imaginary and conventional character of women: they have been as much remarked for the firmness and vigour of their rule, as for its intelligence" (58). Mill also praises women's "more rapid insight into character, which is one of the admitted points of superiority in women over men" (60).

§

Solomon Plaatje's *Mhudi* was written circa 1917-20–not long after his *Native Life in South Africa* (1915-16) protested dispossession by the Native Lands Act of 1913–but was not published by Lovedale, a local missionary press, until 1930. Plaatje was a mission-educated Barolong whose family had been Christianized since the time of Moffat and Livingstone. *Mhudi* builds on the mystical "voice of Nada" as a cardinal icon of African spiritual existence as well as Haggard's critique of Shaka's and Dingaan's imperialism. *Mhudi* also thematically foreshadows not just Peter Abrahams' *Wild Conquest* (1950), but Achebe's *Things Fall Apart* (1958) by describing historically based pre-colonial encounters with European missionaries and colonizers as a way of understanding more-contemporary social/political problems. As fiction of action with powerful images, *Mhudi* to some extent overlaps the empire romance genre; it is "just like the style of Rider Haggard," says Plaatje of his novel (Chrisman 162). But primarily it is an edifying contrast of the voice of the *colonized* writer with that of the *colonizing* author. Although it is a critique of Plaatje's own pre-1920s circumstances, it is set in the 1830s in the same period and region as that of Mitford's Ndebele-Zulu quartet. As historical fiction, *Mhudi* portrays a traditional African society at a crucial stage of transition, chronicling the encounter of peaceful pre-colonial Barolong society with two imperialistic nations: the Matabele and the Boers. Plaatje's Barolong are portrayed as a community victimized by Matabele power in the 1830s, struggling to regain a lost national / cultural identity, only to lose it again in the political, social, and material oppression of European contact that culminated nearly a century later in the Native Lands Act. Plaatje's answer to social chaos presents the figure of Mhudi as an iconic mother of the Bechuana nation–or even of all Africa. Like Lalusini in Mitford's novels, Mhudi is ultimately in the "wise woman" tradition, a good doctoress, an even more-benign center of vision than Haggard's Nada or Mitford's Lalusini–and very much *un*like Haggard's Gagool in *King Solomon's Mines* or his Zikali in *Child of Storm*, typical likenesses of Zulu wizards, but darkly sinister.

It may be asked, however, if the all-male African nationalistic agenda as it unfolded in Plaatje's time perhaps made Mhudi its hostage rather than its goddess. Owing to a historically masculine society reluctant to accept the power and personhood of women, Plaatje cannot envision any plot-line that might give Mhudi the pragmatic political future that would allow her to be a character of great agency in South Africa. As present-day feminists allege, the lack of social and political power by African women suggests they continue to be controlled and marginalized in post-colonial society. Considerable debate within the empirical study of political structures has centered on a putative conflict between a masculine rhetoric of cultural identity as characterized in literature and the fact of women's limited social and political roles. How can Plaatje's glorification of Mhudi as the Spirit of Africa address the daily grimness women encounter in a post-Natives Land Act society or did this Mother Africa trope perpetuate the status quo of colonial domination? Plaatje did not believe wifehood and motherhood rendered women powerless, yet neither was he blind to the lived hardships around him by which many such women were beset daily. Mhudi's name means "harvester," and within the narrative she is the granary of Barolong culture, preserving the threshed grain of wisdom for years of scarcity. Mhudi thereby is an African goddess in domestic shape, no less a potential protector of the clan than Haggard's Gagool who warned of the bloodshed of imperial incursion. Mhudi likewise is suspicious of her "husband's friends" (117)–the Boers. As Plaatje's iconic hybridization of Christian morality and African wisdom, the figure of Mhudi echoes missionary teaching and African taboos as she struggles with the meaning of evil; although the stars are beautiful, her "heathen" heritage said numbering them is forbidden knowledge (75). Milton depicts the same warning when Gabriel admonishes Adam about counting the stars. Plaatje seems to suggest that elements of local folklore equate with Christian theology, thus easing if not erasing cultural differences.

in *Child of Storm*, typical likenesses of Zulu wizards, but darkly intolerance for customs differing from their own culturally sanctioned beliefs, especially in terms of punishment meted out to Africans. Mhudi endorses a more flexible indigenous system of justice that recognizes the relativity of circumstances to which the Boer mind is blind. This principle underlies the superior Barolong justice that Plaatje describes as both humane and "just," as well as profitable to the "state." The old tribal solutions, with which the Boers would concur, do not function in modern times; therefore, new tribal solutions emerge. The tribal system is flexible and recognizes the relativity of circumstances, but the Boers lack this practical flexibleness because they lack a historical and cultural ability to appreciate the two sides of every issue (106; 116-17; 121-124). Plaatje borrowed his motif of "two sides" from Protagoras (Laertius 9: 47) and although Edith Sitwell may have mocked the axiom– "It's more than platitudinous to say that there are two sides to every question but there is something to be said on both sides" (Glendinning xxviii)–in *Mhudi* Plaatje is rejecting a value-laden and ethnocentric dominance of one side over the other. His vision of Africa's social, political, and artistic future does not involve oppositions of man/woman, civilized/savage, Western/African but proposes an African episteme of pragmatic solutions without an illusory order or artificial and legalistic validation.

Mhudi's story is told by an oral narrator, Half-a-Crown, the presumed son of Ra-Thaga and Mhudi, to a hearer whom the reader supposes to be Plaatje himself. Half-a-Crown's name may be derived from a standard paper size watermarked with a regal coronet, as are also the crown and the double crown sizes. Possibly this hints he had an early African newspaper publishing career? As "the hoary octogenarian," he is at the time of his telling between 80 and 90 years old (164, 186). Given that this novel was written circa 1920, his approximate age would place its events at 1835-1840, plus or minus, which fits the time of the advance parties of Boers in that area. The narrative opens, however, in the pre-colonial era, about 1720-1730 (25). Life is an almost utopian existence, an original communal state of society seemingly without witch-doctors, certainly without missionaries. The impact of Mzilikazi's nation-making and the penetration of the Boers will very much change all this by the end of the story. It is an idyllic past, seen through a haze of nostalgia. The women enjoy the same respect as European artists. Yet Plaatje also offers the humorous tale of a Barolong who cross-bred an eland and an ox with disastrous results. The point of the story is either that new combinations of political alignments are dangerous–such as that which the Barolong will make with the Boers–or that that which God has created man should not try to improve. This suggests that if Plaatje espoused equality of socio-political rights in South Africa, he did not favor total assimilation, implying the early Barolong were not fully cautious about cross-cultural implications. At the end of the novel Mzilikazi tells a similar story of a farmer who raised a lion's whelp like a domestic puppy–until the day he discovered it "had eaten his children, chewed up two of his wives, and in destroying it, he himself narrowly escaped being mauled" (175). Mzilikazi as an imperialist in his own right makes the connection later to the Boers's rapacious taking possession of the African's land (170-71).

When Mzilikazi massacres the Barolong, Ra-Thaga flees into the wilderness left by the Matabele on their march to nationhood. After two months, he encounters a girl of his own tribe who has been driven by a lion straight into his arms. They both had assumed their tribe had been wholly exterminated. The prose at the end of the second chapter rises to an African poetic lament: "Kunana, where maidens sang and danced in the moonlight and made life merry with their mirth; Kunana, our former home"–and then the lyricism swerves into prosaic fact–"but now, one of the Matabele outposts"(39). Self-married away from society, the two live an idyll in their forest home, an almost drolly monogamous African Adam and Eve: "There was no room for suspicion of faithlessness, no danger of desertion, no long absences from home, no nights out!" (60). Could one generalize from the idyllic life of Mhudi and Ra-Thaga to society as a whole, one might sense some better social pattern is represented by this idyll in their fallen Eden. An important philosophical discussion occurs in the sixth chapter. When Tauana orders the tax-collectors of Mzilikazi killed, his motive is never explained by Plaatje. The provocation remains a matter of "two sides" (58). Gubuza's hypotheses about violating females, which favors the Barolong, possibly goes beyond ascertained facts. Ra-Thaga, on the other hand, believes that it was Mzilikazi's land and he didn't over-tax; indeed, he already owned all the animals, so his expedition was perchance justified–he who can take has a moral right to get: "might is right" (67). Mhudi, however, points out Mzilikazi was an interloper, an intruder who fled poverty to fatten on the Barolong, and that Tauana's crime was to kill "two potential woman slayers" (68). She believes that Mzilikazi's murderous overreaction could never be justified as a proportionate punishment. This symposium on justice perhaps should begin with pragmatic outcomes, not with first principles.

In the meantime the Matabele celebrate their victory and its "enormous booty of horned cattle" (51). But the general, Gubuza, a normative voice among the Matabele, suggests they "have made a fresh enemy" (55) and adds "I am convinced that the owners of so many cattle will never rest until they recover them . . . and I shudder when I think of the day when the revengeful owners of those herds will come back for them" (57-58). To his great credit, Mzilikazi, in a speech of folk wisdom, admits "there are always two sides to every matter"(58), a sentiment anticipated in Ra-Thaga and Mhudi's ethical discussion and ironically repeated later by the Boer leader: "there are always two points of view. The point of view of the ruler is not always the viewpoint of the ruled" (84). The issue is how to resolve these conflicting perspectives on the land and its inhabitants: the Barolong's prior claim and revenge after the fashion of Makabe (103) or the Matabele's "might makes right"? Justice, as Plato says in *The Republic*, can be neither of these; rather, it is a personal excellence of character constituting peaceful relationships within an ideal society. In the light of Moshueshue's reputation for a Robert Moffat-inspired "magnanimity" towards his enemies, cited multiple times (84, 130, 141), the political philosophy of Plaatje's novel cannot be too far from the Sermon on the Mount, particularly Matthew 5:39. This advances a politics neither of force nor guile but an entirely new science of peace. Given that Moshueshue afterwards faced no political hostility, evidently his loftier motivation broke the cycle of violence and introduced a spirit of conciliation that was pragmatically effective.

Plaatje allows for significant autonomy in all his female characters who are drawn in appreciable detail. He escapes those oppositional binaries implicit in the current debate on women and nationality by distinguishing Mhudi from traditionally held misconceptions that a mother or wife is a victim. Mhudi grants men bravery, but as a woman she too embodies bravery in facing lions and demonstrating a leader's assertiveness. Even before Ra-Thaga discovers that she had earlier outfaced a lion and was known as "the heroine of Motlhokaditse" (69), she ranked as "the only female native of Kunana who had thrice faced the king of beasts, and had finally killed one with her own hand" (66). Since the Barolong chief's name also means "lion," one supposes her encounters represent a test of courage and worthiness, an ordeal that invests this heroine with no less spiritual status than that of the biblical Jacob who wrestled with the angel. Even David Livingstone's *Missionary Travels* had opened with a lion attack, a useful gambit to involve his readers' interest, certainly. Not only her cool and sober "judgment" (73-74) but even her seventeen suitors–towards whom she is no less fastidious than a Victorian London debutante–show her unusual self-determination and freedom of will, making her "special," like royalty, mythically untouchable.

Mhudi, together with Umnandi, the Matabele chief's favorite wife and the "mainstay of his throne," and a Boer maiden, Hannetjie, are normative figures (137, 179). Mhudi approves of these "sisters" (172) despite their being outlanders. In contrast to the unhappy cross-breeders, each of these women nurtures a cross-cultural harmony without sacrificing her group's historic identity. Unlike Ra-Thaga, and more like Umnandi and Hannetje, Mhudi's style is flexibly interactive and emotionally focused on consensus and power-sharing which an African future of diverse voices requires. Umnandi, the beautiful though childless Queen, is framed by the king's other jealous wives and must flee. As the "central pillar" of the nation (180), national misfortune came with her disappearance says Mzilikazi (172). Mhudi's innate nobility makes her a Queen also, and she likewise is separated from her husband, Ra-Thaga. Umnandi tells Mhudi:"thine is a royal husband, the king of the morrow"(165).These women point the way to a future political paradigm, an eclectic melding of cultural values based–in Plaatje's vision–on the scriptural text that in Christ there is neither black nor white. Mhudi's anger at the original slaughter eventually dissipates and she wants peace; the voice of Umnandi likewise deplores bloodshed (167). The problem is, where in Matabeleland and Mashonaland in1835 or in 1920 *is* this Christ?

Mhudi's return to the remnants of her family is "a real resurrection" (82) but its joy is eclipsed by the arrival of a scouting party of Boers "in search of some unoccupied territory to colonize and to worship God in peace" (83). Perhaps the pagan resurrection eclipsed by the epiphany of the Christian Boers is meant to be ironic. Umnandi's return to Mzilikazi somewhat later is also a "resurrection" (179) and there is more than a hint of Shakespeare's allegorical meanings in *The Winter's Tale*. The humane yet courageous "voices" of these iconographic women exercise an indirect agency as hidden powers of redemption and political renewal. Plaatje's answer to Christ in Mashonaland is not unlike Olive Schreiner's in *Trooper Peter*: it is the one who is able to love all victims of oppression–men and women, Anglo and African, even the scorched earth. Through such an individual's integrative view of the human community, the colonized and estranged in South Africa will recover a national character and consciousness. This, of course, is Mhudi's implicit but unfulfilled role.

The attacking swarm of bees becomes the ultimate indignity as Mzilikazi's power is comically deflated and his hollow imperial dreams are blown away (146). His prophecy (analogous to Shaka's when assassinated) foretells what will become of the Barolong alliance with the Boers–including the evils of racial mixing: "they shall take Bechuana women to wife and, with them, breed a race of half man and half goblin, and they will deny them their legitimate *lobola*. With their cries unheeded these Bechuana will waste away in helpless fury till the gnome offspring of such miscegenation rise up against their cruel sires" (175). (This Ndebele reluctance to mix racially was not European only, found among the Boers certainly, but also among Zulus and as far afield as in the Ugandan myth of the leopard and goatherd.) According to the imperial script, the Boers say they do not want to be ruled by anyone but God and simply desire freedom of religion. The Barolong concede there is "plenty of land for all" (84) but the Boers try to cheat them. Plaatje shows unequivocally that the Baolongs are not willing to cede all their land (141-42) and he explicitly notes that their counter-terms were accepted by the Boers, demonstrating a bad faith that came to fruition in 1913. David Livingstone in his *Missionary Travels* (1858) vividly described the Boers, who believed that like the chosen people of old, God has delivered the heathen into their hands to be the hewers of wood and drawers of water:

> It is difficult for a person in a civilized country to conceive that any body of men possessing the common attributes of humanity (and these Boers are by now means destitute of the better feelings of our nature) should with one accord set out, after loading their own wives and children with caresses, and proceed to shoot down in cold blood men and women, of a different color, it is true, but possessed of domestic feelings and affections equal to their own.... It was long before I could give credit to the tales of bloodshed told by native witnesses, and had I received no other testimony but theirs I should probably have continued skeptical to this day as to the truth of the accounts; but when I found the Boers themselves, some bewailing and denouncing, others glorying in the bloody scenes in which they had been themselves the actors, I was compelled to admit the validity of the testimony, and try to account for the cruel anomaly. They are all traditionally religious, tracing their descent from some of the best men (Huguenots and Dutch) the world ever saw. Hence they claim to themselves the title of "Christians", and all the colored race are "black property" or "creatures". They being the chosen people of God, the heathen are given to them for an inheritance, and they are the rod of divine vengeance on the heathen, as were the Jews of old. (35-37)

De Villiers's gift of the wagon to Ra-Thaga is protested by the Van Zyls; however, De Villiers uses a strategy to undermine imperial attitudes similar to that from Olive Schreiner's *The Story of an African Farm*, quoting from the Bible so as to turn the Boers' proclaimed Christianity back upon their racist posture: "'What did Paulus mean,' he asked, 'when he said to the Galatians, "There is neither Greek nor Jew, bond nor free, male nor female, White nor Black, but are all one in Christ Jesus"?'" (184). The wagon might represent a new cultural level for the Barolong, even a hopeful symbol of colonial prosperity for all. Of course, it was "an old waggon . . . in rather a poor state of repair" (221) which, in connection with de Villiers statement to Ra-Thaga that "I always told you that you had brown skin over a white heart (189), suggests a certain paternalism. Never mind that Virgil had used the whitenesses of the heart as an image of purity, in an old cart like an impoverished trekker, Ra-Thaga is not a black African who is deVilliers's equal but a subservient "white" black man. Nevertheless, this friendship and gift breaks social conventions, as did Moshueshue's act, and suggests that St. Paul's vision may be utopian but is not entirely self-deluding.

Perhaps the young couple is traveling in a direction that will be "hard" yet amenable to improvement: the sound of "the waggon wheels on the hard road made a fierce yet not very disagreeable assault upon their ears" (188). One is reminded of nothing so much as the final lines of Milton's *Paradise Lost* as Adam and Eve leave the idyllic Garden: "There hand in hand with wand'ring steps and slow, / Through Eden took their solitary way." Perhaps the tempting alliance with the Boers was the snake in the garden that will drive the Barolong forever from any return to a past idyllic life or from that which Ra-Thaga and Mhudi had found in their forest home. At the end Ra-Thaga tells Mhudi he has ears only for "the call of your voice" (188)–not the politics of imperial aggression and revenge but of practical cooperation. In place of dominance and subjugation, mutual prosperity and–as in the Poe/Noko divorce–pragmatic solutions rather than ideological, racial, or tribal one-sidedness. This is a very different political paradigm from an imperial utopia where husband and wife, masters and servants are autonomous but in unequal balance with each other and the land. Doubtless then the best

Western minds believed this political harmony of stronger and weaker might betoken a less-flawed society once its internal logic of interwoven relationships was fully worked out. In sad historic hindsight, such an "assimilationist" goal of progress–the empire cherishing the smaller cultural "others" in a dialogic way–did not arrive in Plaatje's lifetime, nor yet has arrived.

§

Bertram Mitford's *The White Shield* (1895) is a closely felt story of strange events with telling specifics of an African-animistic world of magic. Details of psychology and anthropology, supplied by the novel's inner narrator, Untúswa, afford solidity to a past rooted in a natural or mythic time, shaped before the conquests of European imperialism. This is the second episode in Mitford's historical novels on the Ndebele-Zulu peoples. The Ndebele-Zulu, at the time Mitford wrote the first two of these novels, had been overrun by the Europeans–the Zulus by British troops in the war of 1879 and the Ndebele by the British South African Company under Cecil Rhodes in 1893. Each of these narratives might strike a casual reader as merely nostalgia for a vanished culture and its traditional life-ways; yet *The White Shield* and *The Induna's Wife* show the past to be not a mere shadow but a still palpable and perilous presence. Indeed, before Mitford could write the third of his novels, the Ndebele had risen up in 1896-97 against their British overlords and attempted to wrest back control of their hereditary lands. And a few years after the fourth novel in this series, the Zulus did the same. Mitford described Ndebele-Zulu history so that, even though seemingly constrained by the politics of colonial fiction, his presentations of indigenous cultural practices avoided cursory European stereotypes. Not only had Mitford lived and worked in the Eastern Cape throughout the 1870s, but later "at the close of the Zulu War, he trekked alone through Zululand, exploring battlefields and interviewing the principal indunas. On his various visits to Africa he has travelled in Matabeleland, and visited Zanzibar, Mozambique and other East Coast ports" (*Anglo-African Who's Who* 117). Undoubtedly here in *The White Shield* he drew on earlier missionary accounts, such as those of Robert Moffat and David Livingstone, as well as on the more recent experiences of Johan Colenbrander, guide and explorer. In the history of the Ndebele kingdom, Mitford found a wider symbol of Africa's advance towards skills and prosperity.

In *The King's Assegai* Mitford had told the story of how in about 1821 Shaka's headman, Umzilikazi (nowadays, Mzilikazi), member of a clan conquered by Shaka, fled with a band of followers (much smaller than Mitford suggests) towards the Transvaal. Umzilikazi, expecting another punitive attack after escaping over the Drakensberg mountains, laid waste the highveld country behind him, absorbing those of the Sotho-Tswana tribes and their cattle that he did not kill. Mitford's contemporary, A. T. Bryant, remarked that "This method of destruction and wholesale pressure into his service became from now on his settled policy, so that when the Boer farmers trekked up in 1836, they found the greater part of Orangia and the Transvaal a miserable wilderness" (*Dictionary* 48). This wasteland image has been disputed, but Umzilikazi's kingdom did not become powerful without the capture of cattle and local populations. The Sotho youths and others absorbed into Umzilikazi's expanding army were trained in Zulu tactics and were expected to take on Nguni customs. Owing to a gift of leadership, to disciplined regiments and deadly stabbing spears, and to his shrewdness in tactical and strategic objectives, Umzilikazi's power began to assume near-mythic dimensions of invincibility. His name, it has been alleged, meant Path of Blood; however, this would suggest that his parents who named him–chief Mashobane and Nompetu, granddaughter of chief Zwide–were unusually prescient to foresee these later events! His multiplying nation became known as the Matabele or Ndebele peoples, possibly meaning "those who duck," i.e., under their shields. In late 1823 he built his first military kraal on the Olifants river, calling it ekuPumuleni, the "place of rest." There the Ndebele remained for several years engaged in incessant warfare with all the bordering clans. Not only was this an unusual form of "rest" but Bryant observed that the place also was "somewhat prematurely named" in the light of the subsequent drought. An exploring party having already previously reported a fine land "of much water and green grass even during the dry season" away north, Mzilikazi forthwith determined to remove to those parts" (*Dictionary 48*). *The White Shield* continues the serial narrative at the point when this decision was taken, historically about 1827, to move through the territory of the "Bakoni" and their chief, Tauane. ("Bakoni" is the Sotho term for the Nguni peoples of southern Africa which include the Zulu, Xhosa and Swazi; however, in Mitford's novel used in a Zulu-Ndebele sense to mean everyone not originally Zulu.) The kraal of ekuPumuleni, the "place of rest," is historical; but the new kraal of Kwa'zingwenya which Umzilikazi establishes in *The White Shield* is a fictitious name that conflates, for the sake of fictional streamlining, multiple military kraals occupied at various times in this stage of the migrating Ndebele community. (*Kwa* means "place of" and *Zingwenya* is the Zulu word for "crocodile"–one of the rivers in the new Ndebele territory and an alternate name for its Bakwena people.) Historically, this would have been near the present sites of Pretoria-Johannesburg in the Transvaal.

As with the *The King's Assegai*, so also the title of *The White Shield* highlights the essence of Zulu military power–shield and assegai, a power that at the time these novels were written ostensibly had been conquered and superceded by the British rifles. Many historical and ethnographic specifics underlie Untúswa's tale, given Mitford's venturesome placement of himself in a tribal mind. But owing to the historical baggage that words impose upon users, Mitford's linguistic "equivalents" are inherently incommensurable. Even ethnographic documentation is subject to distortion by a transformation from the spoken local word to the printed English text with its colonized preoccupations. As in Haggard's Zulu epic, *Nada the Lily*, the relationship of the story-teller (in this instance Untúswa) to the hypothetical listener (Mitford-in-the-story) is unlike ethnographic reportage since both are the author's invention. But the touchstone here is not primarily the socio-political party to which the author belongs; rather, it is the explicit or implied values projected through his *dramatis personae*. Can those voices be relied upon–not for some merely literal historical accuracy, but for a humanistic and elucidating shaping of the past landscape, for insights that outflank the mindless botanizing of "facts" and their stereotypical interpretations? Mitford's chief accomplishment is not the twists and turns of "what next" in the narratives, though surprise and suspense are there, but his contextualizing details, those multiple levels of thematic connections wrought by the power of his personal and creative imagination.

One example of Mitford's subtly comparative assessments must suffice here. Since all his readers knew how central to the nineteenth-century's self-image the ideal of ancient Greek civilization was, the implicit parallels drawn by the authorial consciousness between Greece and pre-colonial South Africa may be understood as validating tribal life and lamenting the loss of the heroic and mythical in England's drawing-room culture of mass consumerism and accumulated possessions. Thus the astonishing Zulu/Ndebele concept that the warrior's life belonged to the king could not be explained by modern values of free choice and autonomy. The Western sense of individualistic selfhood–that one's life is own's own and that one has a right to resist sacrificing it at the whim of another–remained foreign to African concepts of social identity. Self-determination was a product of Christian values; but life, liberty and the pursuit of happiness were not inalienable rights for Zulus. For the Zulu his deepest definition of identity was collective and expressed through the king's "word"; therefore, the warrior had no independent life to lose. In this Mitford saw a parallel to the classic Spartan ethos. Those three hundred Spartans who died to the last man at Thermopylæ set the Western standard of moral as well as physical courage by their sacrifice. Like the contemporary Zulu, the ancient warrior's body did not belong to himself, but to his *polis*, ancestors, and kin; and he was trained to cultivate an unqualified contempt for a personal identification with his body or its pain or fear of death. His courageousness on the battlefield and unity with his battle-group was a product of *esoterike* and *exoterike harmonia*, self-composure or harmony within himself and externally with the larger fortunes of war. Mitford seems to have nurtured a frank sympathy for the

Lacedaemonian-like Matabeles, although recognizing the countervailing gospel of Christian peace.

At the opening of the novel, the author who appears in all but *propriâ persona* as a battlefield antiquarian or archeologist, is seated with the storyteller Untúswa "high up on the ill-omened Hlobane Mountain" (3) where in the Anglo-Zulu War the British had been grievously bested–briefly. Untúswa's story is set prior to that year of 1879, in the pre-colonial era of the Transvaal. The national events and figures of power are played off against local and marginal lives, both given equal priority. The outer narrator's portentous locale contrasts the pre-colonial with his own colonial era. Situated between a powerful past and the present, Untúswa's narrative thus dramatizes the act of calling up historic deeds from the shifting terrain of memory to show how modern society can be infused with–or threatened by–the values of the old; and, one might add, the twenty-first century reader's angle of vision adds yet another coordinate to the retrospective vector of Untúswa's account. The symbolism of the narrative setting here points to the end of the heroic, mythical period of tribal independence, the *ancien régime*. As in *The King's Assegai*, here also the story opens with a spear in the hands of a warrior that the author offers to buy. The possessor's declination again emblematizes his refusal to betray Ndebele-Zulu cultural traditions to the emissaries of the European world: "it took some time to explain that the weapon was wanted, not for use, but for show–in short, as a curio" (1-2). No slow evolution over time–no turning a somersault by gradual stages–is symbolized by this proffer of trade; rather, a sudden, irrevocable and unbridgeable change between an old world of native weapons employed in war amongst independent tribes on broadly equal terms and the new world of global British rule in which assegais are now merely "curios." Whatever their faults, the Zulus lived by a code of honor of which Jo'burg and its pursuit of gold knew nothing. This new world is industrial, commercial, and its love of money is the only love there is.

About 1829 Umzilikazi encountered in the far interior European trader-hunters and missionaries. Quite possibly Bertram

Mitford's Jesuit missionary among Umzilikazi's people in *The White Shield* may have been an evocative parallel to Robert Moffat who from his station at Kuruman visited the king on several occasions. Their personal friendship lasted many years, despite the fact that Moffat felt duty-bound to expostulate on what he perceived to be the chief's harsh and pagan practices:

> His government, so far as I could discover, was the very essence of despotism. The persons of the people, as well as their possessions, were the property of their monarch. His word was law, and he had only to lift his finger or give a frown, and his greatest nobles trembled in his presence. . . . Though but a follower in the footsteps of Chaka, the career of Moselekatse [Sutú rendering of his name], from the period of his revolt till the time I saw him, and long after, formed an interminable catalogue of crimes. Scarcely a mountain, over extensive regions, but bore the marks of his deadly ire. His experience and native cunning enabled him to triumph over the minds of his men, and made his trembling captives soon adore him as an invincible sovereign. Those who resisted, and would not stoop to be his dogs, he butchered. (542-45)

Such he acknowledged about the chief who bestowed his very own family patronymic upon Moffat and out of respect named a son after the mission station at Kuruman! Clearly the issue of whose traditional values must yield to the historical process and what others might be retained in a post-enlightenment colonizing culture here remains unresolved and papered over.

Although Moffat and his associates were Protestant, Mitford uses literary license to alter the novel's Christian missionary to his own personal persuasion of Catholicism. The British cultural paradigm in the eighteenth and nineteenth centuries did not always encourage missionaries to look upon those among those to whom they ministered as equals. Indeed, for maintenance and other services, missionary churches in the eighteenth century bought and sold slaves for their own use. And, unlike the Catholic missionary-priests who lived among their parishioners, the British missionaries withdrew into their own domestic enclaves. But translations of the Bible and Prayer Book into local languages represented a creeping recognition for African culture. Also the Good News was accommodated to local social and economic conditions; thus body painting and the problem of nudity was solved by transferring this graphic art to cloth to be worn, thereby also creating a market for indigenous goods. Before Mitford's "white isanusi" (156) dies at his post of a fever, he offers himself in substitution for several of Umzilikazi's subjects who were condemned to be fed to crocodiles, a form of Ndebele execution Moffat also had described. The heroic ministry of Mitford's Jesuit may have been a literary precursor to H. Rider Haggard's Mr. Owen in *The Wizard* (1896), since in both novels the new gospel of Christian peace is pitted against the tribal culture of war.

Catholic missionaries had been the first to go to the interior of southern Africa; however, when Jesuits later reappeared in Matabeleland in the time of Umzilikazi's successor, Lobengúla, the Ndebele had no interest in their religious teachings although their practical skills in the repair of ox wagons were welcomed. Such unresponsiveness was not entirely owing to Ndebele disapproval of priestly celibacy since, it has been asserted, the Protestant missionary William Sykes, a colleague of Moffat's son-in-law David Livingstone, preached and taught among them for almost thirty years and could not point to a single convert. Partly the Africans struggled not only with theological concepts such as the Trinity or bodily resurrection (hyenas and crocodiles ate many bodies and the rest putrefied–so what's left for resurrection?) but also with the Christian rejection of polygamy, of initiatory and marriage customs, of witch doctors and their "dark superstitions," and of internecine warfare. Miford more than half suggests (also noticed by John Moffat, Robert's son) that Umzilikazi was convinced opening his country to white settlers in the wake of the missionaries would erode or overwhelm indigenous social and religious practices. Only after the nineteenth century did a greater respect for African religions in contrast to the old-style conversion efforts emerge and emphasis on a social ministry to the poor, sick, and uneducated was increased.

The White Shield is organized around three main military engagements of increasing intensity and ferocity in the 1827-1837 period, grisly fighting, startling for Mitford's readers. In each battle, Mitford conflates multiple hostilites into a single encounter–one that always tips in favor of Ndebele success. The first fighting in *The White Shield* must have in fact occurred about June or July of 1836 with the earliest Trekkers who crossed the Vaal River with horses and wagons and shot game. At the time he wrote, Mitford had little documentation for the dates and details of these conflicts–thus, in historical fact Umzilikazi's move from Ekupumuleni predated the earliest wave of Afrikaner Voortrekkers ("pioneers") to his territory. But Mitford's character Kalipe (or MKalipe/Kaliphi as many modern accounts spell the name of this renowned Matabele warrior) was indeed the *induna* in command of several attacks when the Boers first appeared. Umzilikazi astutely realized the threat the coming swarms of Trekkers posed, and accounts do say Umzilikai sent an *impi* under Kalipe to kill the men and bring back their women and girls. Not long after, the tension between Umzilikazi and the Trekkers climaxed in a pitched battle against the Boers in laager at Vegkop (or Vecht-kop)– also fictionalized later in Peter Abrahams' *Wild Conquest* (1950) as the climactic encounter before Umzilikazi's flight north to Matabeleland. Though the Ndebele captured many cattle, hundreds of the attackers were killed. Mitford's incident of a girl-child captured from the Boers and sent to Umzilikazi was true enough though this occurred in previous skirmishes, not at the climactic encounter–and some later accounts say two girls and a boy. If the Boer women are amusingly described by Mitford as plug-ugly, this blue-eyed girl-child is British and "has the look of a child of a race of kings!" Indeed, her "eyes were blue as the heavens" (65); and since the Amazulu are "the People of the Heavens," she is a sort of nordic Zulu, much superior to the peasant Boers of whom Mitford thought much less, brave and good shooters though they were.

The second Ndebele battle described by Mitford–a foray against a tribe of the Bechuana clan of whom Tauane (or Tauana, "lion's whelp") was chief–actually had occurred about 1830 prior to the fights with the Trekkers. This battle may very well have been the attack on the Barolong later described in the opening chapters of Sol Plaatje's *Mhudi* (1930) since the episodes in both Mitford and Plaatje are initiated by a chief Tauane who "dared offer violence to the King's ambassadors" (*White Shield* 103). Plaatje, a journalist and politician, recounts from Barolong oral traditions the attack of "Mzilikazi" on his tribe from the viewpoint of the victims, Ra-Thaga and Mhudi; and, despite the inevitable discrepancies of oral history, Mitford's and Plaatje's accounts contain nearly a dozen smaller or larger similarities. Although British reformers and missionaries felt that such manifestations of "monarchical 'super-power'" (Michel Foucault 80) were unevenly distributed and thus capricious, within tribal social formations such punishments were not felt to be irrational or excessive atrocities.Seen as an attack against the person of the omnipotent sovereign himself, Ndebele punishment must "rewrite" the crime on the bodies of the offenders–a blood-for-blood logic that revolved around spectacle. Interestingly, both in Plaatje's and Abrahams' novels a Kalipe-figure named Gubuza warns Umzilikazi of the political and/or moral consequences of his vengeful massacre. Although Plaatje attempted to present Umzilikazi more favorably than in Boer accounts or in Barolong oral history, Mitford's 1895 novel had anticipated an even more sympathetic stance. Mitford's stance is not to see the king as a moral monster but to adopt the perspective of the chief's second-in-command, seeing him as did his loyal (and disloyal) followers–presenting a more impartial ethnographical approach or, perhaps considering the emotions displayed, a diversity of dissonant and subversive voices for the time and place in which the novel was produced.

When "Moselekatse" sent two *indunas* to visit the missionary Robert Moffat at Kuruman, Moffat agreed to conduct the emissaries upon their return to the border of their country because local tribes were hostile to the Matabele. They then persuaded him to continue on to see the king. In his *Missionary Labours and Scenes* (1842) Moffat recounts his visit with a local informant to the site of the battle:

> Seeing before me a large extent of level ground covered with ruins, I inquired what had become of the inhabitants. He had just sat down, but rose, evidently with some feeling, and, stretching

forth his arm in the direction of the ruins, said, "I, even I, beheld it!" and paused, as if in deep thought. "There lived the great chief of multitudes. He reigned among them like a king. He was the chief of the blue-coloured cattle. They were numerous as the dense mist on the mountain brow; his flocks covered the plain. He thought the number of his warriors would awe his enemies. His people boasted in their spears, and laughed at the cowardice of such as had fled from their towns. 'I shall slay them, and hang up their shields on my hill. . . . The vultures shall devour the slain of our enemies.'

Thus they sang, and thus they danced, till they beheld on yonder heights the approaching foe. . . . The men seized their arms, and rushed out, as if to chase the antelope. The onset was as the voice of lightning, and their spears as the shaking of a forest in the autumn storm. The Matabele lions raised the shout of death, and flew upon their victims. It was the shout of victory. Their hissing and hollow groans told their progress among the dead.

A few moments laid hundreds on the ground. The clash of shields was the signal of triumph. Our people fled with their cattle to the top of yonder mount. The Matabele entered the town with the roar of the lion; they pillaged and fired the houses, speared the mothers, and cast their infants to the flames. The sun went down. The victors emerged from the smoking plain, and pursued their course, surrounding the base of yonder hill. They slaughtered cattle; they danced and sang till the dawn of day; they ascended and killed till their hands were weary of the spear." Stooping to the ground on which we stood, he took up a little dust in his hand; blowing it off, and holding out his naked palm, he added, "That is all that remains of the great chief of the blue-coloured cattle!" (526-28)

Although Umzilikazi may have ruthlessly attacked Bakoni tribes, he was not the blood-thirsty despot described by the Boers. He welcomed small groups of strangers if they entered his country from Kuruman (where the missionary Robert Moffat screened visitors) and if they acknowledged his rule by asking his permission to shoot game.

The third battle of the novel is a large-scale retaliatory attack on Umzilikazi by Dingane's Zulus, probably the one in 1837. Although in the actual battle the Ndebele did in fact rally at the point of total collapse and thus stave off national destruction, their fictional success was nowhere nearly as unqualified as Mitford suggests. Dingane himself actually rated this same encounter a significant Zulu victory. The novel concludes as Umtúswa wins Lalusini for wife after this final battle. Historically, under continued pressure from Boers, Barolongs and Zulus, Umzilikazi not long afterwards was pushed north out of the Transvaal to settle for the final time in Matabeleland between the Limpopo and Zambezi rivers. As understood by Mitford, Umzilikazi stood between the Ndebele's military stage and future peace as a British colony. What this meant for Mitford is best encapsulated by John Buchan's statement "that we were laying the basis of a federation of the world," an echo of Alfred Tennyson's description of a utopian future in "Locksley Hall"–*i.e.*, what European colonization might have done for South Africa's future. The secret agenda of Lalusini, protégée of Shaka's best magicians and Queen of the Bakoni *múti* (magic), is deeply enmeshed in the Ndebele-Zulu struggle for supremacy. Like the mountain cave in *Nada*, the secret chamber in the mountain of death in which Untúswa found Lalusini, defines her roles as preserver and destroyer. In pursuit of her private objective, her warnings and legerdemain save Umzilikazi's life and the existence of the Ndebele nation. Although she will not abandon her revenge, Untúswa's "beautiful sorceress who had bewitched me with her love" (201) awaits a new turn of events in which Untúswa will act as her cat's paw or male shield. Should Lalusini achieve her aim, African history would be changed.

§

The Induna's Wife (1898) is the third episode Mitford's Ndebele-Zulu saga that began with *The King's Assegai* (1894) and continued in *The White Shield* (1895). These first two novels were written after the 1893 conquest of the Ndebele but before their 1896 Rising against the British, a period of complacency based on imperial hopes for peaceful but unequal coexistence. Mitford implies that the British are the new Ndebele, inasmuch as the Ndebele yield to the British as in the past lesser tribes had capitulated to Umzilikazi's *impi*s. The blue-eyed English girl ("of a far greater race" than the

Boers) who survived the attack on the laager in *The White Shield* is acknowledged instinctively as superior by the other tribal children; they *konza* to her as if she were born to rule them. But complacency in British invincibility had been undermined by the Rising in which a tenth of the settlers were killed in less than a week, and dread of another insurrection was strong among the settlers who feared they would have no chance against suitably armed warriors. Yet Mitford continued to admire the upper class Ndebele of Zulu origin who met the adversary on the field–unlike, so he apparently believed, those of lesser clans in the Rising who had murdered the women and children.

The warrior *induna* Untúswa, here initially fights for the Ndebele chief Umzilikazi, then joins Dingane and the Zulus. Untúswa says his tale is about "the fate of mighty nations and peoples, ... even that of the downfall and death of Dingane, and the dividing of the great Zulu nation" (126, 297-98). But it is equally about his own personal destiny and that of his sorceress-wife, Lalusini, the unacknowledged daughter of the Zulu king Shaka. In the previous novel, Lalusini urged a return of herself and Untúswa to Zululand; accordingly, Untúswa goes back to his roots and to the great ongoing struggle of Dingane and the encroaching Boers. (Later, after 1879, the Zulus would be swallowed by the British–never, Mitford believed, to rebel against the British as did the Ndebeles; but what history produced in the wake of the Zulu War–the Africans divided into "petty septs" and no longer a threat to settlers–was less desirable, he felt, than to see them reunited as a nation under a strong tribal leader, albeit one answerable to the rule of law as defined by the Empire.) In *The White Shield* Untúswa described "the witchery of the spell which this sorceress of Zulu blood had woven around me" (174). Here for Untúswa and Lalusini the temptation is power, to be the king and queen of the Zulus. Yet Lalusini ultimately is caught in the grip of her human love. She thus lives up to her own higher self–not Queen of the Zulus but rather beauty enthroned by the hearth.

Whether or not Mitford believed marriage sacramental, Lalusini's magical protection of Untúswa derives from their close spiritual union, soulmates beyond romantic love. With this wife Untúswa discovers a union wholly unlike traditional African polygamy. A sorceress of great power, passion, beauty, and ambition, Lalusini enhances the novel's uncanny atmosphere. Her personal beauty is a reflection of nature; she is more sorceress than wife and more goddess than sorceress, the spiritual form of all natural beauty and power–lion and fawn alike are responsive to her will. According to Untúswa, Lalusini and the Mosutu wizard, introduced earlier in *The King's Assegai*, are the only genuine sorcerers, the others are imposters. Haggard's Nada and Sol Plaatje's titular heroine doubtless double Lalusini as quasi-goddesses of nature's plenitude, uncolonized females, fallen but fearless Eves, whose courage defines their innate nobility and mythic status. Further, Lalusini and Untúswa love in the same personal manner as Nada and Umslopogaas or Muhdi and Ra-Thaga. Their loves echo a lost Eden, potentially modeling a wider redemption and renewal. Something of this also enters into Peter Abrahams's later novel, *Wild Conquest*, by way of Plaatje's influence in contrast to conventional Ndebele polygamy. In Abrahams's novel the figure of Gabuza, and to a lesser degree the figures of Dabula and Mzilikazi, display monogamous or near-monogamous devotion to a particular wife. One can only speculate that this is the influence of Christian values–and most likely a gesture towards late-Victorian debates on the status of husbands and wives, women's property and legal rights, and the social role of powerful women. Lalusini, however, contrasts with Untúswa's first wife, Nangeza, who was "proud and ambitious" (8) or with Haggard's queen, Ayesha, whose "proud, ambitious spirit" could "blast her way to any end she set before her" (256).

In *The Induna's Wife* Mitford's scenes strongly invoke a general indebtedness to literary Gothicism–Untústwa's ghost-bull, the horrors of devouring crocodiles and the magical powers of Gasitye or Lalusini. The literary Gothic crosses classes of readers, not to mention mixing in one sentence both classical and popular styles of writing. Gothicism often enshrines unresolved issues and fears about the author's cultural situation: marriage, wealth and power, race, and religion. In connection with this last, Mitford's amusing description of prelates at Westminster Abby, cited earlier, comes to mind: is Anglican ceremony truly superior to ornamented African animism?

This tale begins with Untúswa sent by the king to kill a ghost-bull known as the Red (*i.e.*, bloody) Death. Thought to be supernatural, this animal is bigger than life, perhaps as big as an elephant. As a creature of unchecked power and deadly territoriality, the demonic ghost-bull is a reflection of the lust for land. Untúswa goes, almost like Hercules to subdue the Cretan bull terrorizing the people or a Theseus to slay the dreadful Minotaur, a flesh-eating chimera reported to have the figure of a man but featuring a bull's head that could breathe fire. As an echo of "the valley of the shadow of death," the valley of the Red Death stands figuratively for the perils of life's looming and still growing risks; and the single way into or out of it suggests not some open-ended and brightly lit banquet hall but the malign trap of a "grey and ghostly" underworld where the voice of the ancient wizard Gasitye calls Untúswa into a cave that opened as magically to him as the cave of the thieves opened for Ali Baba; or is this like the enigmatical labyrinth of Minos? In Gasitye's cave Untúswa encounters, in a flash of green flame, visions of the dead returning to trouble the living, materializing like the ghosts in a London séance. He is imprisoned in the primitive and magical spirit world, the nether regions which are not governed by a living sense of temporality. These spirits bear hate and they desire vengeance, setting up the context of Untúswa's life as surrounded by threats, not the least of which is the wild strength of the animal that he must soon face. Despite the *múti* of Lalusini in the bag around his neck, Untúswa has every reason to fear this evil.

Walter Pater, in his eagerness to pioneer the psychological novel, had asserted such warfare of romance to be "flat and uninteresting":

> The chief factor in the thoughts of the modern mind concerning itself is the intricacy, the universality of natural law, even in the moral order. For us, necessity is not, as of old, a sort of mythological personage without us, with whom we can do warfare. It is rather a magic web woven through and through us; . . . this entanglement, this network of law, becomes the tragic situation. (*Renaissance*, 231-32)

But Pater threw the baby out with the bath water: the "mythological" threat of the ghost-bull initiates for Untúswa an increasingly complex series of moral and psychological challenges that he will have to negotiate, rising by levels of intensity and complexity. In the valley of the Red Death he crosses the threshold of adventure but is not yet confronted by his supreme ordeal–the cut-throat political struggle between duplicitous Boers and cunning Zulus. In legends, many victories entail a psychological transformation, a lifting of a curse upon the land, or personal triumph and honor. Here, Gasitye mocks as hollow the expectation that the slaying of the bull will produce any such happy ending. On the one hand, there is a mythological creature, antagonistic and deadly, whom the hero kills in order to restore social order; this is in contrast to the modern world in which–unlike that of the mythic bull–competing nationalities remain dependent for the essentials of life found on the same land. Contestation of the land by the assegai and flintlock brings chaos, fosters animosities, destroys liberties, and stimulates an unquenchable resentment–neither the tranquillity of détente nor joy. Though this ghost-bull episode may easily have stood as an independent short story the territorial scourge or threat links this episode with the later political struggle between Boer and Zulu.

Quite possibly there is a suggestion of British global domination in the ghost-bull, insofar as the personification of England in political cartoons (as in *Punch*) was John Bull. Olive Schriener's *Thoughts on South Africa* (c.1890-1901, posthumously published) describes how a progressive South African white would apply the "Bull" symbol:

> Our dream of the future of our race is of no John Bull seated astride of the earth, his huge belly distended with the people he has devoured and his teeth growing out yet more than ever with all the meat he has bitten and looking around on a depeopled earth and laughing till all his teeth show and the peoples' bones rattle in his belly: "Ha! I reign alone now. I have killed them all out!". . . The best thing the peoples of earth could do would be to combine and kill the ogre while there was yet time. But no such consummation of his fate is conceivable. . . . Our dream of the future empire of our race is not of an empire over graves but in

> and through living nations. The future of our race is never prefigured in our minds by the upas [poison tree] but as a huge tree, among whose shelving roots and under whose protecting shadow, endless forms of life may spring up and flourish that might otherwise be destroyed, and in whose wide umbrageous branches every form of bird and creature shall find resting place and nourishment, a tree of life and not of death. (354-55)

The archaic solution to the problem of the bull–"do warfare" (Pater) or "kill the ogre" (Schreiner)–can be applied to the perplexed currents of modern political strife only as parable. Like Schreiner or Buchan, Mitford's was a hope for an empire such as the Jesuit in *The White Shield* described to Umzilikazi: "The time will come–has come in some parts of the earth–when the strong no longer drive out the weak, but both shall sit down side by side in peace" (161)–a premature hope, as history has shown, but one in which Mitford himself would have wanted to believe.

The basic analogue in Mitford's *Induna's Wife* is that between the land-hungry Boers in the 1830s and the grasping hand of Cecil Rhodes in the 1890s, when the novel actually was written. Mitford had published the first volume of this quartet in 1894, one year after Rhodes conquered the then-king of the Ndebele, Lobengúla. Concurrently with this first volume Mitford published "Side-Lights on the Amandebili (Matabili) Question" in which he compared Lobengúla and the British in 1893 to Dingane and the Boers in 1838 (96-97). Mitford there criticizes contemporary British imperialism and its policies of land settlement. By the time he composed this third novel, the Ndebele, as noted, had recently risen up against their British overlords and attempted to wrest back control of their hereditary lands. The problem with both Boers and British, from Mitford's point of view, is that they violate their "word." This underlying struggle–who will possess the land–is possibly the single most contested issue in African history and fiction.

Perhaps influenced by Haggard's episode in *Nada* of Dingane's perfidious massacre of Piet Retief's Boer delegation, Mitford makes this bloody event the thematic (if not the dramatic) climax of his novel, offering a startlingly new Zulu justification.

Haggard's campfire buddy Fynney, for example, had applied such phrases as "treachery and foul murder" (1:15) to characterize Dingane's actions, casting the Boers (noble or at least honorable) as eager settlers victimized by deception and atrocity. But Mitford's interpretation of Zulu motivations is intensely pro-native: who really has broken faith? Even before beginning this novel, Mitford had defended Lobengúla, the Ndebele successor to Umzilikazi, by re-explaining motivation in the massacre of the concession-hunting Retief: "all grants of land to outsiders "must be absolutely rotten or fraudulent, or both; and this for the simple reason that no South African potentate dare–except under the direst pressure of circumstances, *i.e.*, Force–grant away the lands of his forefathers and of the nation or tribe at present beneath his rule" ("Side-Lights" 96). Mitford throws the charge of treachery back upon the Boers as more applicable to them than to the Zulus. Untúswa summarizes the Zulu viewpoint:

> "These people must in truth be mad, and worse than mad, to think that the King would give them a vast tract of country in exchange for their friendship and a few cattle–would welcome this swarm of buzzing devouring locusts beating down upon our lands. *Hau!* Mad, indeed, were they. They opened their mouth wide–very wide–and we thought we knew how we would fill it, but not with the country that lay between the Tugela and the Umzimvubu....For two whole days the Amabuna remained in their camp outside, and most of the time was spent in talking over the question of the large piece of our country they expected to swallow up." (161)

The image of the Boers with their land-hungry "mouths wide open" seems almost an anticipation of Joseph Conrad's ivory trader, Kurtz, when Marlow says: "I saw him open his mouth wide–it gave him a weirdly voracious aspect, as though he had wanted to swallow all the air, all the earth, all the men before him" (*Youth* 152). Fynney and most other commentators record that Dingane's signal for the massacre was his crying out "*Bulalani abatagati*"–kill the evil-doers; Mitford also quotes these words in his "Side-Lights" essay. But in *The Induna's Wife* Dingane instead speaks sentences of *double entendre* about the "new land, when ye come to dwell in it," concluding with "*Hambani-gahle*" (169)–go in peace; that is, to your deaths. To recognize Dingane's words as ironic is to appreciate that Mitford is implying the chief's intentions were invisible only to the dishonorable Boers who were so arrogant as to suppose the Zulus were childish and gullible–thus Retief deserved what he got.

Certainly, were one convinced from the outset that the Boers were untrustworthy and inimical to native rights–and historical hindsight does nothing to discourage that interpretation–Dingane's ruse was not pragmatically unwarranted. If the Zulus used opportunistic tactics to survive, the Boers on the other hand violate principles they loudly endorse, both here and later when they shoot the peace messenger, Tambusa. In "Side-Lights" Mitford describes with irony an analogous British abuse of good faith: "Men of rank who come openly and voluntarily into a hostile camp are sure to be spies. They ought to have been shot on sight, these voluntary ambassadors who trusted in British good faith–but they were only put under arrest. And instead of thinking themselves lucky in being so leniently dealt with they tried to escape! Of course they were shot!"(99).

After Untúswa's defense of Dingane, Mitford repeats the vindication in *propre persona* at the novel's conclusion, pointing out

> the senselessness of deciding offhand the morality of this or that deed which helpeth to make history from one hard-and-fast point of view, and that point of view the British; or of stigmatising even a savage potentate as a treacherous and cruel monster, because he is not particular as to his methods when it becomes a question of preserving his nation's rights and his nation's greatness, what time such are threatened and invaded by Christians, whom subsequent events show to be the reverse of models of uprightness or fair dealing themselves. (299)

Thus after the battle with Nongalaza, Untúswa commends clever trickery even when employed against themselves: "a good general will despise no method of snatching a victory, and Nongalaza was right" (266).

For Untúswa, the unsatisfactory father-figure of Umzilikazi is replaced by Dingane, also a reluctant and difficult mentor but ultimately convinced by Untúswa's new-found fidelity to become his patron. It may be that the opposite of fear in a world of betrayal and battle is not the warrior's courage, but that sort of honor which Miford in *The King's Assegai* had modeled on Moffat's heroically condemned *induna*. In the earlier novels, Untúswa's biological father, Ntelani, was jealous of his son's success and bravery. Then, in disgrace, "all wondered he did not take his own life rather than live on thus–he an *induna* of high degree, now forced to herd with Amaholi and the lowest of the people" (*White Shield* 75). In the final analysis the moral landscape of *The Induna's Wife* is determined less by tactics and strategy (the Boers and Panda enter into a political alliance against Dingane that is opportune but finally destructive of the Zulus) than by an overriding sense of honor or its lack. The story's leitmotif is epitomized by the question Untúswa asks of himself about Jambúla: "On whose faith could one set entire belief?" (114). Umzilikazi is noted repeatedly for having broken faith with Untúswa: "the faith of a king" often is treachery, "the faith of a slave" may be noble. Dingane's calculated promises of friendship and the paranoid suspicions of both Umzilikazi and Dingane towards him, not to mention Untúswa's own countervening aspirations to overthrow *them*, contrast markedly with the trust and fidelity between himself and Lalusini. As Untúswa moves through metastasizing complications to win approval from a father-figure, disposing of dangers skillfully and with Lalusini's magic protection (given that he lives to tell his tale), he grows in moral awareness of the sacrifices that loyalty demands, even to the very necessity of letting Lalusini go when she insists that he kill Dingane. Lalusini's intended revenge for Dingane's seizing the throne from her father is that through Untúswa's slaying she will rule in Dingane's stead as Queen of the Zulus. But the morality of "Gegesa's tale"–"Yet it is better to lose an *inkosikazi*, if by that loss you sit in the seat of a King!" (97)–is here inverted. Untúswa elects to lose his *inkosikazi* rather than to *usurp* the seat of a king.

But Untúswa's tale does not end with the tragic loss of Lalusini; rather, it concludes with her return–a poetic justice, perhaps, but more mundane than mysteriously ordained. From principles of honor Untúswa withstands Lalusini's temptation to power and renounces his life-long dream of kingship, even after she shows him his chance: "Thou art too faithful" (296), she tells him. Although Lalusini aspires to be a queen in a male society, in the end she is willing to submit to Untúswa's will, trading her ambitions for love: "'Thou wilt never be greater than an induna thyself, and I—well, I think I shall never be greater than an induna's wife.' And with these words she began to spread the mats in the hut, and heaped more wood upon the fire, and saw that things were in their places. Then she came and sat beside me" (297). Lalusini's magic depends no less on clever techniques than that of the male wizards. But although within her moral framework blood-revenge for the murder of her father is not only justified but expected, she emerges in the last scenes with her ambitions for power chastened.

As in *The Tempest* she is able to accept that "the rarer action is / In virtue than in vengeance" (5.1.27-28). She is reconciled to Untúswa's moral imperative. He will remain merely a subaltern, to be a witness for history by telling his people's story through a warrior's eyes. Haggard's Ayesha, too, may appear to have subjugated herself to Leo's will when she swears she "will be ever guided by thy voice in the straightest path of Duty," but only her death in the fire seems to have kept her, "at the cost of a terrible sacrifice of life," from having "revolutionised society" (284, 250, 295). Closer to the ideal of a beneficent and benign love would be Ra-Thaga's last words in *Mhudi*: "I shall have no ears for the call of war or the chase; my ears shall be open to one call only besides the call of the Chief, namely the call of your voice–Mhudi"(225). But neither Mitford, Haggard, nor Plaatje can persuade themselves that these women and the men who love them are predestined to become the immediate political agents of Africa's salvation. These couples may be the hidden "voices of Africa" personified; but only when Africa is ready will such woman and men be heard.

PART III

COLONIAL SETTLEMENT

CHAPTER 5
THE FARM AND THE COLONY

The connection among the works discussed in Part III, Colonial Settlement, is the contrast within imperial space of a landscape defined by exploitation and control for purely economic, political, and agricultural production or, by contrast, a land of utopian domesticity that harks back to the original Edenic "Garden," a "belonging place" linked by some spiritual affinity with other creative spaces inhabited in diverse cultural ways. This contrast underlies colonial narratives of love and hate, innocence and guilt, those shaping forces of personal identity. If the *romance* of empire required a focus on exploration and conquest of the wilderness–of harsh terrain, racial uprisings, uncanny beasts or demons–its more realistic counterpart would focus on *settler* domestication of the land. However, elements of conquest and settlement are interwoven themes in all empire narratives. Some version of a contested "wasteland" over against a harmonious pastoral utopia often appears. In many Anglo-African novels, the colonial characters, having failed in England to attain happiness or a career, arrive in Africa with large but flawed ambitions–hunting treasure, colonial administration, escaping a marriage or the law, fighting a war–that seem to promise freedom or wealth. In such narrations of the struggle in the pursuit of new lives, one thinks of Graham Wilmot in Douglas Blackburn's *Richard Hartley, Prospector* (1905), a would-be mining foreman who is depicted in the opening scene sitting forlornly above slag heaps as "the long-lurking anticipation of failure" arrives: "With the self-consciousness of an inexperienced and too-softly nurtured youth, he looked compassionately upon himself as the chosen child of misfortune, and his heart overflowed with bitterness against all things" (3). Of course, there were many colonists, even without the initial frustration of extravagant ambitions, who had looked to the agrarian life, perhaps to a stock farm like the Bowker's "Olive Burn," with a special sense of place.

§

Although Olive Schreiner is known primarily for *The Story of an African Farm* (1883), a novel of religious doubt and women's aspirations, among the very best of her shorter fiction is her long story "The Child's Day" (1888). Written in a flash of autobiographical inspiration and perhaps the summit of her achievement, it was intended to be a prelude to *From Man to Man* (1926), an unfinished novel that she had worked on at intervals since 1873 when she was eighteen. At the time of her story's composition, Schreiner apparently had been winding up an anthropological disquisition on "primitive and semi-barbarous womanhood" and beginning her analysis of current "sociological questions" (Schreiner, *Woman and Labor* 8-9). In "The Child's Day" her passionately felt social concerns were channeled into a more personal, yet artistic, self-expression, an integral part of her subconscious with a powerfully symbolic coherence. The story combines the regional color of an African settler farm with the profounder themes generated by five-year-old Rebekah's experiences of reproach, affection, and the ultimate incompatibility between her illusions and life itself.

This is a deeply felt account of a day in which Rebekah's mother delivers twins, one living and one stillborn. Rebekah must fend for herself, owing less to a psychologically unhealthy parental neglect than inattention because of the family's distress and distraction. Much to Rebekah's irritation, old Ayah, the comically despotic Khoi servant, constantly scolds her as "a wicked, naughty child" (41)–a gruff but protectively-meant expression of Cape settler values. In pursuit of affectionate reassurance she seeks some place that can accommodate her as she is. Schreiner is writing here a modern, autobiographical account of a fall from innocence and the reacquisition of paradise within, mingling fabrication and intimate experience. "I was sitting at my dear old desk writing an article on the Bushmen and giving a description of their skulls; when suddenly, in an instant, the whole of this little Prelude *flashed* on me" (*From Man to Man* xxvii). In a letter to a friend she inquires about the narrative's personal verisimilitude: "Did you think it a *made-up thing*, like an allegory, or did you think it was real *about myself?*" (*From Man to Man* xxviii) .

The temporality of the child Rebekah's "day" is outlined by clock time, an emblem of human mortality, which contrasts with the boundless knowledge that will last her a lifetime. Rebekah's twelve-hour day is tracked throughout by temporal references: 9:45; 10:00+; 11:30; 1:30; 3:00; afternoon past; evening cool; almost sunset; getting dark; twilight; pitch dark; 8:30; 9:30; 9:45. But the "day" of the five-year-old child is not merely this twelve-hour period in which she must fend for herself owing to her parents' inattention: it is the recognition of her mortality, the duration between birth and death. Rebekah's literal day is here allied to the fallen world in an almost biblical way since the mother is described in the first sentence as lying "in the agony of childbirth" (3). Inasmuch as the serpent beguiled the woman, her curse was to bear children in pain: "in sorrow thou shalt bring forth children; and thy desire shall be to thy husband, and he shall rule over thee" says Genesis 3:16. Particularly effective is the manner in which the mother's anguish in bringing forth a child contextualizes Rebekah's foretaste of her fallen condition as she comes to experience the human meaning of life and death. In this realistic parable, the nurturiant aspects of the child's farm are balanced with, but not overwhelmed by, a darker knowledge of guilt and death. She will have to sort out this original curse. The farm is an Eden, complete with a snake; and its orchard and tree support fantasies in which Rebekah, on an imaginary island of her own, is both a parallel to Queen Victoria and an ideal mother for an imaginary child.

There are two primary voices in this story: that of Old Ayah and Rebekah. The mother speaks only toward the end and her father, fleetingly, asks Rebekah to kiss her new-born sister. Old Ayah (Hindi *aya* or Portuguese *aia* from Latin *avia*, "grandmother," a common noun for any Khoikhoi maidservant in the former British Empire) ironically is the voice *in loco parentis* of genteel settler colonialism. Ayah is inflexible, structured, a mechanical and oppressive source of censure, like Waldo's ticking watch at the opening of *An African Farm*. She is always calling Rebekah a "strange child" on account of her unladylike and wild behavior. Rebekah's soap box was filled with things a proper little girl shouldn't have–true, its blue beads are feminine, as Lyndall had recognized in *An African Farm*, but certainly not its bugs. Ayah becomes the comic voice of a patriarchal God asking if Rebekah has, as it were, "eaten of the tree"; and Ayah's also is the primly Victorian forecast of Rebekah's dawning awareness of her "nakedness," her openness to sin: "And get your face washed and your hair done, and tell Mietje to put you on a clean dress and white pinafore" (42). Ayah's inability to control Rebekah is meant to be partly comic, much as Bonaparte Blenkins in *An African Farm* ludicrously impersonates all the authority roles of settler colonialism: father, school-master, preacher, judge, hunter, even storyteller and (outrageously) God calling to the wayward Adam. That Ayah, like Blenkins, should represent a power without sympathy that berates the child ironizes the ubiquitous tyrannies of colonial sexism, racism, and ignorance, whatever the gender, race, or class of the speaker may be. Such control is not a function of status but is simply a shared colonialism, its socially constructed façade. The important qualification here is that although Rebekah consistently expresses resentment toward her nursemaid, at the end of the story Ayah shows herself capable of a sympathetic response toward the sleeping sisters.

The other chief voice is that of Rebekah herself whose speech reflects the unformed materials of a self that seeks coherence– searching for a creative, adaptable, and organic identity, the inverse of the mechanical social role awaiting her. Among the farm inhabitants, Rebekah is laconic in the extreme; but as an author-to- be, Rebekah tells her imaginary baby stories in voices borrowed or created from across the human historical spectrum and the animal world alike. In contrast to Ayah's univocal and all but scripted exhortations to proper conduct, Rebekah invokes the various stories of her culture, her land, even that of "a Kaffir boy" (34). In her actual and imaginary discourses, she occupies a liminal space, a borderline position created by Schreiner's descriptions of her standing in or moving across thresholds–doorways, windows, or along paths between locations. Many feminists from Mary Wollstonecraft to Charlotte Brontë to Virginia Woolf have depicted strong-minded women liberated from a meekly self-sacrificing persona, or self-image as chattel goods, or a submissive domesticity. Although in *An African Farm*, Schreiner's Lyndall rages against the truly unnatural codes of behavior that subvert the growing child (172-73), the effort to rise above an obdurate patriarchal ideology in Africa may have been somewhat improved by the opportunity for woman on the frontiers, as for Issac Dinesen in the early twentieth century, to substitute her inherited European status for a more self-reliant and strong-minded identity. But those opportunities, however, did not present themselves within the tighter cocoon of the Cape Colony; instead, Rebekah is trapped in a colonial playscript, expected to follow customary social or cultural norms for the behavior of young females in the imperial system. She balks at those restrictions and her rebellion produces a liminality in which her position, in contrast to the conventional status and role of a colonial girl, is without guidelines, unclear, and contradictory–much to Ayah's consternation.

According to cultural anthropologists, such liminars as Rebekah, when renouncing position and prerogatives, would initiate a revision or "recention" of their (colonial) script. By virtue of her existence on the social threshold or margin where behavioral codes are provisionally abrogated, Rebekah can see more clearly and challenge those social norms expected of her, educing possibilities of alternate roles for herself. The archetype of such a normative challenge is prefigured in Adam and Eve's decision to eat the forbidden fruit so that by their lost innocence and expulsion from Eden (both a spatially geographic and a figurative transition) their status is irrevocably changed–but changed so that they re-emerge, even in the biblical parable, with enhanced dignity, inasmuch as Miton's Archangel Michael promises Adam "a paradise within thee, happier far" (*Paradise Lost* 12: 587). Rebekah too must undergo a similar *felix culpa* in her personal development that carries a new knowledge of life and death, sorrow and happiness.

The mood of longing and emptiness is set by a captivating (and autobiographical) description of Rebekah's visit to a "mouse house" that she has built of stones. She moves liminally from "kitchen doorstep" to the threshold of her mouse house under construction:

> Once a Kaffir boy told her he had built a house of stones, and as he passed the next day a mouse ran out at the front door. . . . . She sat down flat on the stone before it and peered in. Half, she expected the mice to come; and half, she knew they never would!. . . After a while she stretched out her right hand and drew its sides together and made the fingers look as if it were a little mouse and moved it softly along the stone, creeping, creeping up to the door; she let it go in. Then after a minute she drew it slowly back and sat up. (34-35)

The mouse house is empty, save for the hand of the child that perforce replaces the absent inhabitants. Thus imagination can replace the absent by escaping from the givenness of facticity into pure invention and wish-fulfillment. The emptiness is an ironic rephrasing of Rebekah's own baffled and balked condition, a house without those relationships that speak to the soul. The child's touchingly vain hope of inmates for her house, an epiphany of domestic fulfillment of mouse-like proportions, foreshadows the most dramatic event in "The Child's Day," her appropriation as her very own child of the stillborn twin to her mother's living baby.

After Rebekah re-enters the deserted kitchen, she continues on and knocks at "her mother's door" and is invited to kiss her new sister–which she says she "won't" because "I don't like it" (36), undoubtedly sensing the baby as not merely a competitor for her mother's love but as separate from herself, a purely objective "other." This recalls Lyndall's refusal to kiss her baby in *An African Farm* owing to her conflicted impulses between subservient maternity and independence. Lyndall cannot be a true mother to her baby even at its death because she never completed giving birth to herself. She says: "I am asleep, swathed, shut up in self; till I have been delivered I will deliver no one" (180). When Rebekah leaves the birth-room, the door must be opened and closed by an adult because "the handle was too high." Standing outside the closed door, "She saw her father and old Ayah come out of the spare room. Old Ayah locked the door and put the key into her pocket" (37). Rebekah has closed herself off from the living sister behind the door and is also locked out of the spare room, an unspoken prohibition to entrance. Her liminal status is, in Matthew Arnold's lines from "Stanzas from the Grand Chartruse," part of a psychological "wandering between two worlds, one dead and"–given her impending confusion of sisters–"the other powerless to be born." In what is clearly the story's major instance of liminal activity, Rebekah climbs through the ground-floor window of the darkened spare room, discovers her stillborn sibling laid out, and adopts it as her playmate.

Apart from any autobiographical memories, Schriener's motif may have been enhanced by George MacDonald's story, "The Gifts of the Child Christ"(1882), which doubtless was part of her permissible Sunday afternoon reading as a missionary's daughter, along with David Livingstone's *Missionary Travels*. MacDonald describes little Sophy, whose hair is too rebellious for the brush, as a neglected, unloved child. In a shadowy spare room, Sophy discovers her stillborn sibling, believing him to be the sleeping Christ child. She drags her chair to the cold doll-like figure and possessively wraps it in a coverlet before she realizes he has died. Sophy is discovered, her hair now an aureole, cradling the infant as if a Pietà. Here faith and love gain her the affection of her parents, who, in turn, recover "not the dead Jesus, but Him who liveth for evermore" (MacDonald 77). But Schreiner envisions a more astringent fictional resolution. In her reshaping of this episode, the happy ending and pious didacticism of MacDonald's story is replaced by a less doctrinal and more austere, though still mythopoeic, contextualizing of the event. Rebekah had imagined children painlessly found, not brought forth in agony–a misconception of innocence that permits her to suppose the stillborn twin responds to love.

This is an innocence that does not prepare Rebekah to live in the real world–Lyndall in *An African Farm* regards the euphemism that God sends babies as the worst "of all the dastardly revolting lies men tell to suit themselves" (209) and pious old Otto, naively and indiscriminately loving, is ruined by his childlike credulousness. Rebekah's dead baby had a "a curious resemblance" (38) to her own features but like some shadow, mirror image, or picture, it lacks the living baby's responsive personality. Rebekah offers gifts from her workbox to this inanimate object: an alphabet book, emblematic of access to language and knowledge; a silver thimble and needles, evoking the woman's domestic role; a "bushman stone," exemplary of the socially dispossessed; and so forth. Unlike her living sister, she kisses this baby. The adoption of the infant is, as far as Rebekah is concerned, a *fait accompli*. Rebekah says of the neonate: "It's mine; *I* found it! . . . Mietje found hers in the hut, and Katje found hers behind the kraal. My mother found hers that cries so, in the bedroom. *This one* is mine!" (41-42). Old Ayah bluntly tells Rebekah: "This one is dead: it'll never open its eyes again" (42). In contrast to the stillborn baby with never-to-be-opened eyes, the living Rebekah must inevitably have her eyes opened in Adam and Eve's manner at the fall (Genesis 3:7). Like her stillborn sister, who died in innocence before "Sin could blight or Sorrow fade" (Coleridge, "Epitaph on an Infant" 68), Rebekah's world of innocence is a deathlike, unreal, shadowy illusion.

As part of the dynamics of her personality transformation, Rebekah learns what she does not wish to know. Sigmund Freud's famous essay on "The Uncanny"(1919) illuminates Schreiner's story in terms of its relevance to period psychology. Freud devoted a full paragraph to a patient's childhood fantasy of "a doll that appears to be alive," noting that "it is in the highest degree uncanny when inanimate objects–a picture or a doll–come to life" (*Parapsychology* 37, 48). The uncanny, Freud says, is the perception of that which is "beyond" or "dæmonic" erupting into quotidian experience. Freud quotes Schelling: "everything is uncanny that ought to have remained hidden and secret, and yet comes to light" (28). Rebekah's doll baby is her hidden double materialized, imperiously reanimated by sovereign illusion, unlike the living sister who cannot become a creature of Rebekah's exclusive possession (any more than capitalists who formally possess title to the land, as Schreiner pointed out, truly *own* it). Schreiner achieves an uncanny convergence of reality and dream, the natural and the mythic. Freud contrasts "the world of common reality" to that of "poetic reality" (57); in romance-fiction, where "the world of reality is left behind from the very start, . . . many things are not uncanny which would be so if they happened in real life." But when "all the conditions operating to produce uncanny feelings in real life" are also found in fiction, the uncanny retains its power "in fiction as in experience, so long as the setting is one of physical reality" (57-58). Fictional believability produces the same uncanny feelings as does real life. For Freud, this experience of the *unheimlich* derives solely from the atavistic power of the mind over material reality and is implicit in animistic conceptions of the natural world–children and "primitive man" in an earlier evolutionary stage created a double, a second self initially beneficent but afterwards antithetical and hostile (46). The uncanny stillborn baby to which Rebekah clings embodies the overwhelming secret of her future identity. What Ayah's unmasking of it reveals is the awareness of knowledge just beyond reach that Rebekah would prefer remained repressed–a recognition that will oblige her to grant to others freedom from a controlled and prefigured destiny.

Although until now Rebekah has been living imaginatively within her farm world, fantasy intervenes to take her to an imaginary island with a little house "as high in proportion to her as grown-up people's houses are in proportion to them" (46). Rebekah's isle has a utopian exemption from pain, guilt, unloveliness, and isolation. She arrives, carrying "a large worn picture-book," following "a little winding foot-path among the grass to the middle of the orchard, where a large pear tree stood, with a gnarled and knotted stem"(43-44). She escapes her quotidian circumstances through her imagination: "Presently she made a story" (15). The child's mind segues into a stream-of-consciousness, a five-year-old colonial girl's interior monologue or, to borrow a less anachronistic phrase from Thomas DeQuincey, a dream fugue that seems both an inchoate arabesque of reading fragments yet with a controlled number of themes that later will define her writings: female identity in a colonial and imperial context. In this foreshadowing of modernism's psychological novel, Schreiner distinguishes Rebekah's inner and outer worlds of dream and reality by parenthtical insertions.

Queen Victoria's prominence is seen at the farm on everything from her rather ironic apotheosis "cut out of the tinsel label of a sardine tin" to the hanging pictures: "On the wall inside the large front room hung two great framed pictures of Queen Victoria and the Prince Consort, in regal dress" (62)–although Rebekah confuses the Prince Consort's name with that of her cousin and playmate, Charles. As the unifying force in a worldwide empire, Queen Victoria is a figure whose authority the colonists respect and admire. Rebekah in imagination meets a fantastical, magical version of the real Queen who tells her that "I have many islands that belong to me: but this island belongs to no one; why don't you come and live here? No one will ever scold you here, and you can do just what you like" (45). Since it "belongs to no one," Rebekah's island has much in common with the "fruitful waste ground" that John Ruskin had called upon the youths of England to colonize, a potentially troubling and dark invitation to the extension of empire that Queen Victoria emblematized. When Rebekah accepts the island, she unwittingly but wholeheartedly and uncritically accepts the notion of colonialism and white imperial domination. Although her claim to ownership of the dead baby is contested, in her land of dreams, at any rate, territorial possession and proprietary rights are unchallenged. This is because Rebekah and Victoria–"Queen of the United Kingdom of Great Britain and Ireland and Empress of India," to provide her full title–are sisters in power and rank. Much like Lyndall's admiration for Napoleon Bonaparte, Rebekah's passionate imaginative nature allows her to admire Victoria who is more powerful than any man–and *no one* would dare call that Queen "strange" or a "tomboy" or scold her for what she was.

Ayah's pestering may actually reveal her own feelings about being regarded as inferior: who truly is the monkey tied to the yard pole? Whereas Ayah's position is subordinate to the child in terms of colonial status, she has an authority Rebekah resents. Queen Victoria reflects Rebekah's aspiration to obtain supremacy over Old Ayah, the Khoisan maid, inasmuch as Rebekah's desire for power parallels imperialism. When old Ayah's iron-fisted control proves burdensome, Rebekah escapes into an imaginative landscape better than the one with its "dried" trees, "dull," "shriveled" leaves and grasses that she shares with snakes and farm workers. Her queenly alter ego empowers the child to inhabit the imaginary landscape without fear either of Ayah's disapproval or of her own shamed awareness of hoydenish behavior: "She knew she ought not to be there in the hot sun; she knew it was wicked; but she liked the heat to burn her that morning" (37). Story and dream become more satisfying lands to rule than the real ones governed from London or the Cape Colony. In her fantasy world, everything is harmonious–animals talk, nothing is dangerous–and her imagination seems to heal the harsh reality of her life's outer frame. Victoria allows her to escape from what she cannot comprehend as yet–her dead sibling. So she creates a reality where she can rectify her mistakenly directed maternity, acquiring an imaginary child that she can nurture, born asexually from a peapod.

As Rebekah's story-making modulates into a continuous reverie half-veiled by sleep, Schreiner provides an etymological play on the root meaning of sleep that goes back to the Latin *labi* and the Greek *lobos*, meaning pod, lobe: "she saw a snow-white pod nearly as long as her arm. It was like a pea pod, but it was covered all over with a white, frosted silver.... And there, lying inside it, like the seeds lie inside the pod of a mimosa tree–was a little baby" (47). This is a re-presentation, in terms of a child's sleep-induced fantasy, of the baby's emergence at birth from the mother's labia. The pod-child, a replacement for the sibling that Rebekah wished to posses and that Ayah denied to her because it was dead, is the product of Rebekah's idealizing imagination–found, not born in agony. Rebekah's dream-fantasy segues into a utopian story for her baby of the peaceable kingdom with the freedom and innocence of the original garden in which the child of the pod dwells. Central to this long intermediate section is Rebekah's unfallen childlike consciousness–though in her dream of the peaceable kingdom the animals, were this real life, do get deadlier. Like the baby Rebekah has imagined, the snake she here fantasizes is prelapsarian, of a gentle disposition and neither an overt nor disguised danger. Indeed, she invites her child to put its hand into the puff-adder's lair. This recalls the utopian vision of Eden in Isaiah 11:8: "And the sucking child shall play on the hole of the asp, and the weaned child shall put his hand on the cockatrice's den." As an author-to-be, Rebekah also tells her imaginary baby stories from the Bible, poetry, history, and morally edifying missionary texts. In them she tries to reconcile the conflicting fragments of maternal nurture and imperial power–the heroic Hester Durham of the Indian Mutiny (at the time "What Hester Durham Lived For" was published, Schreiner would have been about eight years old), or Boadicea's defiance of the Roman invasion of Britain, as in William Cowper's lines which she quotes: "Rome, for Empire far renown" ("Boadicia"). Because art is incubated within cultural interstices or on its margins, Rebekah's early storytelling both critiques the current norms of the colony and will later usher in new social paradigms. Although some critics have supposed that the conflicted ideals of the child will persist to cause the adult Rebekah's failure as an artist, what this story implies is that art grows not in the utopian illusions of childhood but is realized in the artist's ability to bring those visions into connection with the complex practical relationships of real life, such as gender and labor, domesticity and wealth, race and servitude–precisely the vision of Plaatje's Mhudi.

With the pear tree of knowledge above her, Rebekah "half opened her eyes" as she hovers on the threshold of Eve's knowledge. Her dream ends with a visionary scene: "A spasm of delight thrilled up the spine of the child under the pear tree. When a full-grown woman, long years afterwards she could always recall that island, the little house, the bricks, the wonderful light over earth and sky, and the swans swimming on the still water" (58). Though this is a utopian vision about to be shattered by the snake in the grass, in later years Rebekah is able to attain an independent *modus vivendi*, finding both a physical means of support and a psychological equilibrium between sorrow and joy–a life immersed in a dystopian world with an aesthetic turn or twist toward a utopian future, such as a commonwealth of men and women in "an Eden nobler than any the Chaldean dreams of" (*Woman and Labour* 282) as visualized in Olive Scheiner's own turn-of-the-century allegories. Rebekah's transition to reality is greeted also by "A herd of little pigs a short way off, feeding under the peach trees" (59). Schreiner's story has another pig that appears in Rebekah's alphabet book echoing these pigs in the outer frame of her factual experience (within the literary convention that fiction presents authentic reality). The dramatic doubling between these animals and the incident of Augustine's pear tree in the second volume of his *Confessions* introduces the theme of the Fall in the Garden of Eden. Augustine recounts how he and his friends stole "an enormous quantity of pears" from a neighbor, "not to eat them ourselves but simply to throw them to the pigs" (2: 80). Augustine chose this incident to illustrate that such an act committed simply for the sake of doing evil testifies that human nature is out of kilter.

Already an observant naturalist, Rebekah's encounter with a trail of ants recalls H. D. Thoreau's "battle of the ants" in *Walden* and Darwin's observations of ants in *Voyage of Beagle* and *Origin of Species*. Though Rebekah's description is partly behavioral, its covert anthropomorphism makes this a philosophical, if not satirical, parable of human competition and rapacity. Rebekah's mediation between the fighting ants can be paralleled to the empire's role of protector and its interventionist policies, an echo of rescripting of the lives of others. And at this juncture an all-too-real threat shows that her actual world beneath the pear tree is red in tooth and claw. She is conscious that "some one was looking at her." As the apocalyptic manifestation of the knowledge of good and evil, a yellow cobra seems to accuse Rebekah much as in *An African Farm* Waldo's prickly-pear had accused him:

> Had it been there all afternoon? . . . . She was not afraid of snakes. When she was three years old she had carried one home in her pinafore, as a great treasure, and been punished for doing so. Since she understood what they were, she was not afraid of them, but they had become a nightmare to her. They spoiled her world. . . . Her heart was beating so she could hear it; she had a sense of an abandoned wickedness somewhere: it was almost as if she herself were a snake, and had gone krinkle! krinkle! krinkle! over the grass. She had sense of all the world being abandonedly wicked. (61-62)

Apart from the local specter of punishment because the child must learn to shun tall grasses to avoid a poisonous bite, the snake is associated with the original blood-curse upon mankind. Rebekah feels guilty, the result of lessons, prayers, and missionary teachings about original sin. As with Charles Dicken's Pip in the graveyard or Esther Summerson or Oliver Twist, Victorians often seemed to link reproach to lack of power–the weakness of the marginalized in contrast to the wealthy–thus Brontë's orphaned Jane Eyre is censured for her rebellion and Bertram Mitford's wealthy Jo'burg businessmen are considered respectable.

Returning to the house as the daylight wanes, Rebekah ignores portraits of Victoria and her Consort. Victoria may be more exotic than her multiplication tables, but her mind is now drifting liminally. When envisioning a more ideal order of existence, Rebekah said to her imaginary child: "If you should wake in the night, my baby . . . and hear anything, don't be afraid: just call to me. I'll be close by. And if you hear the clock ticking, *don't* think it means any of those dreadful things–it doesn't. I'll stop it if it makes you sad"(47). In *An African Farm* a watch that incessantly ticked out men's death and damnation drove little Waldo to despair. Although Rebekah's imaginary child is no more real than her stillborn twin, both await replacement by a better infant–but it will be in the "dreadful" world of the ticking watch. With the picture of Queen and Consort hanging on the wall above, there comes to Rebekah in a moment of clarity the realization that the world, "abandonedly wicked" (62), cannot be how she imagined it was. The fantasy snake and the real snake bring the biblical symbol of sin to where dream and reality intersect. The real snake establishes the terms on which the child will be admitted to an understanding of the human condition–birth, sexuality, and death.

Shortly thereafter, in the large front room as she repeats the multiplication mantra, "looking out dreamily" over her book and

> through the open door, her mind almost a complete blank . . . something had flashed on her! She knew now what those figures had meant which she had seen walking down in the flat in the afternoon when she stood on the sod wall. She knew now what it was Long Jan was carrying; she knew why her father walked behind him, and the two Kaffir boys had spades over their shoulders. . . . She knew, also, something else; she knew at the moment–vaguely, but quite certainly–something of what birth and death mean, which she had not known before. She would

> never again look for a new little baby, or expect to find it anywhere; vaguely but quite certainly something of its genesis had flashed on her. (63-64)

Rebekah suddenly understands the meaning of the funeral procession for her stillborn sibling and also, significantly, the connection of human sexuality with the new baby: "something of its genesis had flashed on her." This vision is what comes instead of the mouse to its house or the dead child awakening to life. Schreiner's identical word *"flashed,"* to describe her own "unconscious cerebration" leading to a sudden grasping of this narrative, suggests that Rebekah's insights and the author's imagination are identical revelations of a knowledge that reshapes life. Perhaps Schreiner selected the noun "genesis" with attention to its usage in the biblical account of Adam and Eve who also had their "eyes opened" to a sense of human sexuality that brings shame.

Just as Rebekah's surroundings constituted the fabric of her idle fantasies born of naivete, now the world around becomes the subject of understanding; she watches the wick of a tallow candle and studies the "long dark shadow" of her hand cast on the wall:

> Why was the shadow so much longer than the hand, and why did it fall just where it did. . . . If only one were grown up, one would know all about these things! She dropped her hand on her side. Perhaps, even grown-up people didn't know all. Perhaps only God knew what lights and shadows were! (67)

Her optical curiosity suggests her acceptance of the real physical world as opposed to the imaginary one. Though the desire for knowledge is a function of her fall and the "long dark shadow on the wall" its emblem, her tentative "perhaps only God" recalls both the subtitle of the volume in which this story appears and the Preface to *An African Farm* where Schreiner observed that human life is a play without a name and that "If there sits a spectator who knows, he sits so high that the players in the gaslight cannot hear his breathing" (viii). Less significant for Rebekah than justifying the ways of God to man is, in the light of his fallenness, charity from man to man.

(Schriener had taken her novel title from John Morley's sentence: "From man to man nothing matters but a boundless charity.")

Though originally she had refused to kiss the infant in her mother's arms, Rebekah now realizes the surviving baby needs her. She receives the live child in the place of the stillborn one, not as a possession but as a being with whom she shares an identity, keeping her fantasy of nurturing but letting go of her innocence. At the price of lost dreams, nurturant strength now becomes an essential constituent of her personality. The "oppressive" quiet anguish at the opening of the story is here balanced by the peaceful room with all "quiet and asleep"at the ending. In this final scene when Ayah comes to take the baby Bertie, Rebekah is found asleep, protectively intertwined with her living sister: "But when she turned down the cover she found the hands of the sisters so interlocked, and the arm of the elder sister so closely round the younger, that she could not remove it without awakening both" (43). The landscape of Rebekah's island was an imperial fantasy that must be replaced by a reshaped space open to all the diverse qualities, modes, and ways of existing. By giving up her utopian island, by sharing the surviving sibling with her mother, and by opening herself to the uncertainties of an emotional investment in her sister, Rebekah brings her dreams constructively into reality. Her new relationship with Bertie unifies the sisters within "the valley of the shadow of death," bonded by their common mortality.

Ayah's figure casts–as did Rebekah's hand earlier that evening–"a long dark shadow on the wall" (73). If the nursemaid's and the child's shadows allude to Plato's parable of the cave, perhaps Schreiner's intent is to describe a society immured by its imperfect conceptions of truth, unaware of its imprisonment in a self-deluding and morally blind system of values, of the racist and patriarchal ideology behind the roles children, women, and Africans are assigned. Yet even in the grip of the Original curse, Rebekah finds that those "deep shadows" of birth, activity, death, and rebirth are the human context in which the bonds of sisterhood and love are forged. She gains those qualities of strength, intensity, or purpose that humanly suffering women, like Hester Durham, possess. Her imaginary baby, with its unreal exemption from life's dangers and griefs, enjoys everything that Bertie and Rebekah will lack; but the implication here is that, for Rebekah, perhaps Bertie may offer more. Surely in this last scene Schreiner's readers are meant to see that the entire woman–the already nurturing personality and its artistic analogue–is sleeping "well."

As liminar, Rebekah moves through interwoven levels of invented narratives and reality to come to terms with the real world. The thimble, thread, and cotton in her workbox perhaps additionally represent the possibility of covering the spiritual nakedness of the material empire, first as a child clothing and shielding herself from reality in fantasy, then as an adult turning the imperfections of reality back upon themselves in the artistry of the text: "should one sit down to paint the scenes among which he has grown, he will find that the facts creep in upon him. Those brilliant phases and shapes which the imagination sees in far-off lands are not for him to portray. Sadly he must squeeze the colour from his brush, and dip it into the grey pigments round him. He must paint what lies before him" (*An African Farm* viii-ix). Rebekah awakes to her mortality and discovers how to bring her fantasies into productive contact with real, though painfully imperfect, life. As she finally moves into the outer frame of reality, her magical empire granted by Queen Victoria fades away. But parent or mother is another role filled by Victoria, who was the "Grandmother of Europe." Thus as an "Ayah" or "Grandmother," Rebekah's alter ego is herself figuratively at the site of intercultural dialogue with the Khoisan maid. By creating out of life's imperfections the vision in "The Child's Day," Schreiner both acknowledges the fallennesss of self and society and recognizes that against the background of shadowy existence, human sacrifice, loyalty, and love are immeasurably deepened.

§

The Weird of Deadly Hollow (1891) is set in the frontier area of the Eastern Cape not much more than three years after the Gaika rebellion of 1877-1878 (aka the Ninth Frontier War). This area inland from East London is that to which the "1820 Settlers" came, among them relatives of Mitford. When Mitford lived in the Karoo village of Tarkastad, near Fort Beaufort, the settlers and the Xhosas were then fighting in the region. The contract that Mitford's agent Watt negotiated for an initial edition of 2,000 copies of *The Weird of Deadly Hollow*–this was his second novel–paid him "one shilling per each and every thirteen copies sold for each shilling of the published price." Such self-referential precision makes the dark psychology of Mitford's protagonist appear straightforward by comparison. The plot of *The Weird of Deadly Hollow*, apart from its settler background, includes elements of folk superstition and quasi-supernatural agency: "But all are agreed–overtly or tacitly–that the Weird of the awful blood-curse brooding over Moordenaar's Hoek will never be removed" (315)–so reads the final sentence of this romance. The use of "Weird" here and in the title means ill-fortune or fate; but capitalized as it is, it also signifies Fate's three sisters who weave the fabric of human life: Clotho spins the thread of life in the beginning; Lachesis weaves the thread into the thick weft of daily existence; and Atropos cuts the thread hereafter when life is at an end. Ominously, "Moordenaar's Hoek" is, in the regional Dutch speech of Afrikaans, a "deadly" or "murderer's hollow."

The longer of the novel's two epigraphs, from Thomas Hood's "The Haunted House," belongs to the popular literary tradition of Gothicism so evident in, say, E. A. Poe's work, which is also found elsewhere in Mitford's fiction–premonitory dreams, repressed sexuality, the taboo, rage, violence, and, at times, imagery demonizing the African "other" as monster or ghost. But this said, Mitford's tales are by preference only marginally supernatural–ghost stories without a ghost, although premonition and second sight do hover around the fringes of his narratives. Mitford's penchant for rational, empirical data does not run counter to curiosity and open-mindedness, but it does contrast with H. Rider Haggard's deeply felt disposition to believe in spiritualism, intuition, apparitions, and clairvoyance. Mitford toys with mystic powers, but we're not quite sure if they actuate the plot. He often introduces an aura of preternatural weirdness only to walk away from its implications by the narrative's end. It is as if that which possibly goes beyond the empirical remains both inexplicable *and* unbelievable, thus what seems supernatural may be only coincidence. Can Mitford be accused of decoying the reader, tricking him into supposing situations are more supernatural than they really are? Or are we supposed to be left wondering whether humans or the Weird controls fate?

Mitford's *Weird of Deadly Hollow* avoids the more cliched elements of Gothicism; and insofar as he uses the genre's motifs of passion or pathos, wild landscapes, horror or inherited curses to probe cultural, social, or psychological tensions, his novel stands alongside many mainstream works of literature. Indeed, the first and shorter of the novel's epigraphs (*not* from Shakespeare) is taken from William Wordsworth's "Hart-Leap Well," which blends Gothic imagery in the first part with a didactic lesson from its second part about an innocent stag cruelly killed for the pleasure and pride of the hunter. Possibly the novel's extended scenes of "the chase" are meant to be construed in terms of Wordsworth's censure. Whether or not the hunted stag in "Hart-leap Well" is an image of the poet or of Christ, the unnecessary trophy-killing by the callous knight is strongly condemned: his pleasure-house turns to "dust" while contrastingly Nature perennially renews "her beauty and her bloom." Just as the noble hart suffered cruel pain and death, so Wordsworth's reader becomes aware that the ruins of the hunter's pleasure-house represent everyman's own slender hold on life.

Thomas Hood's "The Haunted House," quoted in the second epigraph, rated highly with E. A. Poe, who found it "thoroughly artistic," "powerfully ideal" and "imaginative" (100)–certainly an appreciative comment but analytically useless. Although Hood's poem alludes to domestic murder, it steadfastly refuses to supply specifics. Its aim is to use imagery and suggestive phrases–"a cloud of fear," "a secret curse"–to create an atmosphere of horror finally beyond any rational explanation. As the narrator-dreamer enters the courtyard of the haunted house in Part I, crosses the threshold in Part II, and mounts the stairs to the bedroom in Part III, the reader is plunged progressively deeper into its abnormal psychological violence and supernatural malediction. Perhaps in such generic

Gothic imagery and subject matter Mitford saw a way to critique–whether as a reactionary or reformist, it is hard to say–nineteenth-century cultural dislocations.

Behind all the voices of these fictional speakers–behind this realistic rendering of African and colonial personalities–Mitford's distinctive authorial voice reveals itself, not only in the more expository or editorial interludes of his discourse but also in the suggestive patterns, structures, and ironies of the narrative's historical situations. Often in his introductory chapters or in genteel settings or interludes, his style is less natural and more artificial, displaying a Victorian elaborateness, complete with authorial voice-over as when the narrative consciousness leaps ahead of the chronology (prolepsis) to hint darkly about the future. In *Weird* the chapter entitled "Barabastadt *en Fête*" caricatures the lower-class citizens of the town with the bold strokes of broad satire. Mitford begins with caustic contempt for their vain and provincial notion that they are the center of the earth, when in fact any visitor to Barabastadt would have concluded "that he had, for his sins, dropped into the ugliest, most commonplace, and most utterly God-forsaken hole on this sad earth . . . .'Where the very deuce *is* Barabastadt?' had been the helpless and hopeless cry of more than one Civil Service official, as, with the utmost consternation depicted on his countenance, he perused the Government communication appointing him to office and banishment thither" (215-17). (This jab, we may be sure, was an autobiographical reminiscence from Mitford's own days in the Cape Civil Service.) Next, halfway through this chapter, Mitford's style puffs up to mock-epic phraseology in imitation of the citizens' absurdly pompous notions of themselves, echoing such biblical phraseology as Jeremiah's diatribe against the sins of Judah: "graven upon," "unto this day."

Significantly Mitford took up the most pressing intellectual challenge of his or our generation: in a culture increasingly without ultimate passion, how does one regain a sense of life as meaningful? His religious sympathies emerge most explicitly when Ida describes Catholic belief as "a grand old creed" and, in a passage using Custance as an authorial mouthpiece, Mitford has him describe his grounds of belief, concluding by identifying Catholic doctrine as "one that has stood the test of time and hard knocks" (144-45). Owing to his own Catholicism, Mitford's most important narrative patterns are often powerfully religious–guilt, despair, damnation; or love and salvation. If the *Inferno*, *Purgatorio*, and *Paradiso* are mystical realities in Dante's *Divine Comedy*, they are no less real in Mitford's vision, though emphatically less mystical. Unlike the events in *La Commedia*, Mitford's literal storyline is every bit as essential and consequential as the allegorical lesson within it. Heaven and Hell, not to mention the intermediate world of penance and hope, are all for Mitford as much in the here and now as in the hereafter. The year after *Weird of Deadly Hollow*, Walter Pater, a Victorian "skeptical probabalist" who commented on the signs of the times, characterized the religious mood of his and Mitford's generation thus:

> An age of faith, if such there ever were, our age certainly is not: an age of love, all its pity and self-pity notwithstanding, who shall say?–in its religious scepticism, however, especially as compared with the last century in its religious scepticism, an age of hope, we may safely call it, of a development of religious hope or hopefulness, similar in tendency to the development of the doctrine of Purgatory in the church of the Middle Age:–*quel secondo regno / Ove l'umano spirito si purga*:–a world of merciful second thoughts on one side, of fresh opportunities on the other, useful, serviceable, endurable, in contrast alike with that *mar si crudele* of the *Inferno*, and the blinding radiancy of Paradise. (*Purgatory* xx)

In a modernizing culture of superficial business pursuits, in which stark evil and awful suffering are torn from their ontological moorings in the supernatural, redemptive grace cannot be assumed as inevitably countervailing; nevertheless, as an alternative to the failures of conviction, Mitford portrayed a world of "merciful second thoughts" and "fresh opportunities" forged in the symbolic arena of hope.

T. S. Eliot once described Charles Baudelaire as a soul who welcomed "the reality of Sin. . . . The possibility of damnation is so immense a relief in a world of electoral reform, plebiscites, sex reform and dress reform, that damnation itself is an immediate form of salvation–of salvation from the *ennui* of modern life, because it at least gives some significance to living." Eliot added that to be human "what we do must be either evil or good; so far as we do evil or good, we are human; and it is better, in a paradoxical way, to do evil than to do nothing; at least we exist" (*Selected Essays* 380). This is the logic of Bertram Mitford's novels also; however immediate or distant the supernatural may be, evil and love are capable of being direct realities on earth. This is not to contradict the fact of Mitford's religious allegiances; rather, if one is not to be condemned to living in a world without redemption, a profounder innocence is needed to strip bitterness from one's heart. Some characters find this force, while others–good lovers but better haters–lose all hope, such as Custance or the protagonist of *The Gun-Runner* who instigates tribal attacks upon his countrymen to revenge the death of his beloved.

Ida plays the typical Mitford role of the heroine, softening the misogynistic male who "had not a grain of faith left in the genuineness, let alone the durability, of any human affection" (132). If Haggard and Mitford support an idea of manliness embodying physical vigor, courage, moral restraint, and a firm will, the role of their women is not to maintain this trope with its associated male privilege and power but to complete it on equal terms. In most of Anglo-African fiction the element of romantic love plays a central part. If this popular subject catered to a mass readership, the fiction nonetheless probed how the realities of race, class, and ethnicity unsettled nineteenth-century gender beliefs, as in the presentation of colonial women who resist both a marginalizing of their experience and a subordination to male dominance. Mitford, for example, named his first child and daughter Yseult, perhaps because of that moment in the legend when Tristram and Iseult drink the love potion which may have epitomized for him an intensely personal phantasy. Certainly Mitford and Haggard undercut the nineteenth-century's stereotypically beautiful and submissively conformist heroine of good breeding, dependent yet coyly manipulative, by recasting her in terms similar to the traditional heroines of Shakespeare–Portia, Rosalind, Viola–by stressing her interior qualities of passion, intelligence, character, and especially an unwavering courage in the face of grave danger. In these women, the seemingly discordant forms of maidenly chastity and nubile sensuousness are not mutually exclusive but are held together within the daily dynamic of life and death. Indeed, the heroines' purity may have greatly added to these novels' popularity as it did to Shakespeare's, it being as great a stimulus to the heterosexual masculinity of his readers as it is to the male characters within his fiction.

Ida, together with other Mitford heroines, becomes an emblem of Dante's Beatrice–but an earthly Beatrice. Dante's beatific icon was the mystic bride in Solomon's "Song of Songs," a symbol of spiritual love (or of the soul or of *Sapientia*, Wisdom). But Mitford's "Junoesque" (20) Ida also embodies sexual desire as well as an inconceivable tenderness. Christianity portrayed woman as either radiant (Beatrice, the Madonna, muse) or dark (she-devil, temptress, witch, destroyer). Victorian man, traumatized by the idea that sexuality was sinful, unable to create an authentic connection to that half-scary, half-fascinating creature, found himself lost and confused between her extremes. Ida creates a middle ground of love; she resolves guilt and fear and charms Custance by the power of her voice "into dreamily wondering whether he might not be called upon to take up the threads of his life where he had dropped them–to live over again–to open up once more the possibilities of the future" (166-67). The fates, of course, cut these threads of life, foreshadowing a possibility less fortunate. Yet a nurturing, protective role–almost like a pagan virgin mother–is denoted by Ida's name. Ida was the nymph of Crete who in her mountain cave nursed Zeus when the newborn god had to be concealed and protected from his father Cronus. This Titan devoured his offspring out of fear of being dethroned, as had been foretold. Certainly the haunted "hollow" has its antecedent in the mythical cave of Ida, ambiguously a haven of peace or, under the aegis of the Weird, a devouring maw. While a golden dog guarded the cave of Ida–reappearing in Mitford's story as the comically-named Kruger and Joubert, Afrikaner heroes–youths beat shields and spears to mask cries of the infant, to which the noises in the hollow seem analogous. For a time the reader interprets those noises as inexplicit superstitious fantasy; but by the end, in what is called retrospective meaning attribution, Mitford's reader begins to credit them as evil omens.

In particular, the biblical motif of a "blood-curse," as punishment for deeply flawed behavior, underlies the metaphoric structure of this tale. As the kings of Judah degenerated, God finally pronounced a curse upon the royal line of descent from David: "Thus saith the Lord, Write ye this man childless, a man that shall not prosper in his days: for no man of his seed shall prosper, sitting upon the throne of David, and ruling any more in Judah" (Jeremiah 22:30). Accused of the death of his own child at the narrative's opening by his embittered wife, Custance flees London because he believes his push has killed her. At first, in search merely of escape, homeless and wandering, Custance finds refuge in the isolated, haunted hollow where before crops never grew. When Maud Rendlesham and her sister call Custance a hermit crab, they merely take a jab at his isolation; but for the reader the symbolism of the crab appropriating an empty shell *to protect its soft underbelly* is also apparent (whether indeed Mitford knew that hermit-crabs love the society of their species, one cannot speculate upon).

Custance eventually falls in love with Ida and suddenly glimpses an impossible redemption in her love, an astonishing and dimly providential deliverance from beyond the flaming ramparts of the world. But the guilt and hate from his ruined marriage in England seemingly follow him like the lineal curse of Judah. He allows his anger to get out of hand; provoked, but without compassion he beats and humiliates Wildschut, a snake in the grass, triggering his venomous revenge. Ominously, while lovingly feeding an ostrich chick, Ida accidentally kills it: "With words of consternation and sorrow she dropped the knife and snatched up the wounded bird, staining her fingers and dress in its blood. But the little thing was dead in a minute, stiffened out in her hand" (239). This figuratively echoes what we assume is Custance's tragic loss of his child. On a number of previous occasions Custance had rescued Ida, but now with the innocent blood of chick-as-child on her hand, Ida's own blood must be shed. Yet for whom will Ida's blood-stained death be redemptive?

Mitford's fascination with the emotional intensity of retribution and with the incongruous "way of the world–our blessings, when they come to us, invariably do so a day too late" (342), is spoken in summation by the eponymous hero of *Fordham's Feud*, whose villainy only a Corsican view of vendetta can explain. Mitford's novels suggest an underlying anguish with the nature of earthly justice and the silence of God, with what Miguel de Unamuno–Mitford's more-philosophical, younger contemporary– called the tragic sense of life, man's quixotic desire for the perfection that makes his life a senseless irony. Christ forgave his tormentors as well as the thief crucified with him, but Custance fiendishly enjoys watching Wildschut's body slowly turn chalk-white in the fire. Custance destroys himself–psychically, spiritually–as surely as his "devilish" vengeance kills the African. Custance's twisted vengeance is ironically analogous to, but whole octaves more deadly than, Barabastadt's distorted sense of itself. Mitford had joked that the name of the town, given its "seat of magistracy" and ceaselessly quarreling citizens, might be a significant characternym: "there were wags who protested that the place was well named" (216). When Pilate, anxious to release Jesus, offered the mob the option of the unoffending Jesus or the murderer Barabbas, they chose the murderer with the blood curse on their heads (Matthew 27: 16-25).

Barabastadt is the colonial equivalent to the mob before Pilate that prefered the guilty Barabbas to the innocent Christ.[22] One never quite knows how far to push interpretation, but the weathercock on the new church steeple of which they were so proud "pointed east when it should be pointing west" (222). Reformed church steeples were capped by weathercocks instead of crosses as a reminder of Peter's betrayal of Christ at which Jesus said, "I tell thee, Peter, the cock shall not crow this day, before that thou shalt thrice deny that

---

22. The *Advertiser* for 3 January1888 (Leader article) entitled "Barabbas at Fault" echoes Mitford's struggle with those (obtuse publishers) who prefer the worse to the better.

thou knowest me" (Luke 22:34). The rooster that crowed the morning of Jesus's trial served to remind the faithful not to deny Christ as Peter had done; and, because cocks crow early in the morning as the sun/Son is rising, to admonish the faithful to remain vigilant against Satan. A wrong-way rooster (and the literal physical preposterousness of this only goes to reinforce its symbolism) faults the Christianity in that Dutch Reformed community. Might not also, then, the casual epithet for the village, "God-forsaken," have a deeper significance? In contrast with Psalm 22:1 and the uttering of these words from the Cross, Mitford intended to contrast a genuine faith with this colonial culture that has lost its spiritual direction.

Mitford has nothing but contempt for Barabastadt's indifference to sin or grace, for its lack of sympathetic involvement, for its simplistic, literal-minded and materialistic life. Andrew Baird's requital for his smug rationalism upon meeting the bewitched leopard is no less humorous in its way than the citizen's childish pride in their malfunctioning weathercock. Those such as the Scotsman Baird or the second Mrs. Rendlesham and her daughters are, as Dante might allege, among the *per se* (entirely for oneself)–they like the other citizens of Barabastadt are neither among the rebellious damned nor the faithful saved, nor even among those undergoing the cleansing fire of purgation. Dante remanded these souls of the selfish to the entryway of Hell, without redemption: "Abandon hope, all ye who enter here" (*Inferno* 3). Thus Barabastadt's citizens were solely concerned to put Custance on trial for his unintentional bigamy. They had no intention of punishing him for his merciless torture-murder, even though he personified Barabbas in choice and deed. Who really, then, is on trial here for uttering vows not underwritten by the Logos? For Mitford, the crowd's sense of guilt and innocence is as like as two peas in a pod; unlike that world of moral difference behind the superficial similarity in the names of Jesus Barabbas and Jesus of Nazareth.[23] As with Barabbas, Wildschut is the dark doppelgänger of

---

23. Origen of Alexandria, one of the early theologians of the church, was uneasy with the full name Jesus Barabbas (*bar* son + *abba* father "son of the father") in the early manuscripts because Jesus, son of God the Father, should not share both name and imprisonment with Jesus, son of the father–indeed, capitalized *Abba* is a holy

Custance, his repressed side of anger and violence. Wildschut is thus like Mr. Hyde who overwhelms Dr. Jekyll; or perhaps he is like the old dramatic "vice figure" who carries his victim to damnation.

But does Wildschut drag Custance to hell? The fire-torture scene of Wildschut the rapist-murderer may avenge the innocent Ida, but her love and suffering do not rescue Custance from his overwhelming hatred. When Custance calls Ida "an angel of light"(196), he ominously echoes 2 Corinthians 11:14 in which Satan (Lucifer the light bearer) becomes an angel of light for the sake of temptation and deceit. Mitford seems to ask: Where is the victim left in the light of forgiveness? Does forgiveness diminish or discount the offence, pretending it did not occur? What will inhibit the making of future victims? The offence has happened and *someone* has to be responsible. For Custance, Ida's death becomes what he makes of it–not a divine ransom from hatred but a Satanic invitation to fall anew. What is clear is that Custance who exacts punishment is assuredly not innocent; and, further, he who is the malefactor (Wildschut) may not be eternally condemned; indeed, Wildschut's torture could be a salutary foretaste of the purifying fire of Purgatory.

At the end of the novel we are left wondering what will become of Custance. His destiny seems to raise the difficult issue of whether innocence and guilt, love and hate, are contingent upon human choices that allow a rebirth of spirit or whether they are foreordained by the unseen hand of the Weird that no soul or thing can escape? I tend to imagine Custance in the words of one of the greatest and, in Mitford's generation, least known of poets, a Jesuit priest:

> I am gall, I am heartburn. God's most deep decree
> Bitter would have me taste: my taste was me;
> Bones built in me, flesh filled, blood brimmed the curse.

In the last scenes of the novel Custance has not escaped from the blood-brimmed curse. Unlike the poet Gerard Manley Hopkins, he will relive his bitterness in the ruins of his suffering until death. And,

---

name of God.

judged by the failure of his earthly remorse, at the time of his death he merits damnation:

> ... I see
> The lost are like this, and their scourge to be
> As I am mine, their sweating selves; but worse.
> (Hopkins 110)

There in the *Inferno*, everlastingly "selfwrung, selfstrung, sheathe- and shelterless, thóughts agaínst thoughts ín groans grínd" (Hopkins 105). But yet . . . maybe . . . if the love of Beatrice is an outcome of the sinfulness that marks Dante as fallen, perchance good and evil each have a role as dialectical elements in the redemptive scheme of God. Haggard once observed that in his novel *She* the chastening power of Ayesha's love redeems her, "gives her strength to cast away the evil" and, as "her hardened nature melts in the heats of passion," her love becomes "a saving grace and a gate of redemption" (*Pall Mall Gazette* 13-14). If so, perhaps despite the fact that Custance welcomed damnation for the sake of a supreme love, a love that, like the maw of Cronus, consumed and devoured his soul and everything else in this world of any importance–perhaps somehow his stupendous passion for Ida may win for him, like the thief on the cross, Paradise.

Whether Mitford converted from Anglicanism to Catholicism as a form of rebellion is purely conjecture, yet his novels express a perplexingly provocative play between an indistinct providential framework and the diabolic ironies and frustrations that baffle love and hope. But more frequently, with the same combinations of tragic circumstances, Mitford provides a happier, nearly miraculous, unknotting of events. This does not expunge injustice or death; rather, terror and loss invest these moments with the joy of an astonishing and dimly providential deliverance from beyond the flaming ramparts of the world–though in at least the one instance of *Haviland's Chum* (1903) the sudden rescue is so implausible as to unwittingly anticipate the ironic farragos of Evelyn Waugh's *Black Mischief* (1932) or *Scoop* (1938). Indeed, Mitford's mingling of the ironic and the spiritual puts one in mind of the famously misguided attack on

Evelyn Waugh's *Black Mischief* by the editor of the Catholic journal *The Tablet*–"a disgrace to anybody professing the Catholic name" (Oldmeadow 10). Insofar as Mitford strikes a moral chord, it is the motif of forgiveness. If one is not to be condemned to living in a world without redemption, forgiveness is needed to pluck bitterness out of one's heart.

CHAPTER 6
THE LAND AND ITS RICHES

The issues of land and culture, both in narratives of heroic exploration-conquest and in the realistic fiction of settler life, originate in and react upon debates on colonial affairs such those as at the Anglo-African club. These social and political tensions of imperialism in southern Africa were by no means limited to Europeans with the Zulu/Xhosa/Ndebele tribes. Cross-cultural interactions and the problems of land tenure are even more starkly presented by the relation of settlers to the Khoi peoples, where the Stone Age met the nineteenth century. In the land of the Khoi-Khoi and Khoisan societies (in colonial terms, "Hottentots" and "Bushmen") sun, drought, and rare seasonal storms spread over some of the most dramatic landscapes in South Africa. The struggle with such a harsh land plays out in different ways according to societal levels of technical skill and applied cultural wisdom. Here the British and the Boers are both recent occupiers of the land, with its thin resources and troubled intergroup relationships. Among the Khoisan, their physical landscape provided the cultural framework for the voices of their disappearing culture. Viewed symbolically as an expression of the inherited wisdom of these hunter-gatherers, physical space had no formal separation from cultural space–their ancestral spirit world, their stories and songs together with the sky, plants, and animals constituted a single cultural and natural fabric.

Although missionary or travel accounts of the Khoi peoples would belong to non-fictional ethnography, they also sometimes blur the line with fiction when using dramatic techniques. In these accounts, their social, geographical and historical perspectives are forms of personal observation, reflection, and social critique. Such elements become paramount in William Charles Scully's *Between Sun and Sand: a Tale of an African Desert* (1898) and *A Vendetta of the Desert* (1898) as well as in Henry Anderson Bryden's "A Bushwoman's Romance" from his *Tales of South Africa* (1896). Scully and Bryden had opportunity to observe the Khoi peoples directly in their original habitats, and their narratives have depth, complexity, and startle or catch out the reader. By contrast, Mitford probably had little opportunity to observe these groups at first hand. On its surface, Mitford's *Renshaw Fanning's Quest* (1894) seems to present the Khoisan with the single role of guarding their evil-eyed diamond. Dramatically the Khoisan play only this single role of primitive obstacle; they say or do no more than give hair-raising chase. But rather than embodying atavistic traits exactly the opposite of the heroes', the Khoisan display the same sense of exclusive possession. Renshaw and Maurice feel they have a right to the diamond because they were able to identify and take it; the Khoisan feel they have a right to the stone because it has traditionally been part of their lives and religion. The struggle defines ownership, physical possession, not of a particular gem but of the land and its exploitable resources. Beneath the formal dissimilarity of romance to realism, Mitford finds in the stolen stone a less heroic and more perplexing vision of the social tensions of empire: Khoisan and settlers are both driven by a similar desire for what is perceived as the essentials of life found in the same land. Just here, by illuminating the problematics of possession, the contribution of high romance to imperial debates is situated.

§

After various stints that included prospecting in 1871 for diamonds with Cecil Rhodes, Scully served as a magistrate variously in the Orange Free State, the eastern Cape, and Namaqualand. If he was, by virtue of his vocation, an imperial presence, yet he sympathized with the displacement of the indigenous inhabitants in the face of inexorably advancing encroachments, and he lamented the imperialists' excesses, their selfish exploitation cloaked by a paternalistic rhetoric that did little for the aboriginal peoples. The missionary Robert Moffat, often much loved by his parishioners and influential in opening up the continent to European enterprise, had been twenty-three years among the Khoisan and related tribes when wrote his ethnographic masterpiece on his life's calling, *Missionary Labours and Scenes in Southern Africa* (1842):

> They have neither house nor shed, neither flocks nor herds. Their most delightful home is "afar in the desert," the unfrequented mountain pass, or the secluded recesses of a cave or ravine. They remove from place to place, as convenience or necessity requires. The man takes his spear, and suspends his bow and quiver on his shoulder; while the woman, in addition to the burden of a helpless infant, frequently carries a mat, an earthen pot, a number of ostrich egg-shells, and a few ragged skins, bundled on her head or shoulder.

Moffat is able to describe their diet and hunting with first-hand ethnographic observation:

> Though their poisoned arrows cannot take in one third of the length of a musket shot, they aim with great precision. I have known men shot dead on the spot with poisoned arrows; and others, who did not at first appear to be mortally wounded, I have seen die in convulsive agony in a few hours.

Moffat tempers his rather substantial reservations about their daily routines with a recognition of their better qualities:

> When they have abundance of meat, they do nothing but gorge and sleep, dance and sing, till their stock is exhausted. But hunger, that imperious master, soon drives them to the chase. It is astonishing to what a distance they will run in pursuit of the animal which has received the fatal arrow. . . . He knows no God, knows nothing of eternity, yet dreads death; and has no shrine at which he leaves his cares or sorrows. . . . But, degraded as the Bushmen really are, they can be kind, and hospitable too; faithful to their charge, grateful for favours, and susceptible of kindness. (53-59)

Nearly forty years later in *A Hunter's Wanderings in Africa* (1881), Frederick Courtenay Selous records a Khoisan life-style only slightly less aboriginal than that of Moffat.

The desert of Namaqualand (or Bushmanland as it was then called) is part of southern Africa's Karoo-Namib region encompassing the middle and lower Orange River valley. It remained practically unexplored until the nineteenth century when European hunters, subsistence farmers ("trekboers"), and missionaries entered and encountered the Khoi Khoi and the related but more ancient Khoisan peoples, living there as hunter-gatherers since the early Stone Age: "The term 'Bushman,' strictly speaking, only applies to the diminutive former inhabitants of the Desert, who are now practically dispersed to the south of the Orange River. The Trek-Boer, however, usually calls every Hottentot of low stature a Bushman" (Scully, *Sun and Sand* vi). Because as hunter-gathers the Khoisan pillaged the animals and crops of other African tribes and of the early European settlers (Barrow 1: 272-75), these Stone Age people, living conjointly with the animals and the seasons, were driven away. Particularly after the arrival of Europeans at the Cape they were exploited or hunted, so that by the 1870s they were facing cultural extinction: the "glottophagy" or "eating up" of their language and dispossession from a landscape stocked with their stories, music, dreams, and rituals. During the nineteenth century and into the twentieth, the semi-nomadic trekboers, pioneers of Dutch-German-French extraction, pastured their goats and sheep in Bushmanland areas of summer rainfall, moving in the winter to the coastal regions.

In his two volumes of autobiographical reflections, *Reminiscences of a South African Pioneer* (1913), Scully's Namaqualand experiences do not figure prominently, yet in his novels, short stories, and poetry he added greatly to an understanding of the 1890s inhabitants of this area. Among his best fiction is *Between Sun and Sand* (1898), drawing on memories of northern Bushmanland from "1892, when the author held the appointments of Civil Commissioner for Namaqualand and Special Magistrate for the northern Border of the Cape Colony" (vi). Namaqualand is rich in Afrikaans "*kontreistories*" or tales of the land, but the first novel descriptive of the region was by the science fiction writer Jules Verne: *Meridiana or Adventures in South Africa* (1872/1873) in which Verne's characters begin their survey of longitudes and latitudes in Central Africa by taking a steamboat up the Orange River–apparently using a local name, Morgheda, for the loud cataract of the Augrabies waterfall (from the Khoi *aukoerebis*, the place of the

Great Noise). In his poem, "Namaqualand," Scully suggests something of the existential ambiguity of his spiritual connection to this deadly region where only the adaptive survive its rigors. It is, he says:

> A land of deathful sleep, where fitful dreams
> Of hurrying spring scarce wake swift fading flowers;
> A land of fleckless sky, and sheer-shed beams
> Of sun and stars through day's and dark's slow hours,
> A land where sand has choked once fluent stream–
> Where grassless plains lie girt by granite towers
> That fright the swift and heaven-nurtured teams
> Of winds that bear afar the sea-gleaned showers.
> The wild Atlantic, fretted by the breath
> Of fiery gales o'er leagues of desert sped, . . .
> The waves for ever roar a song of death,
> The shore they roar to is for ever dead.
> (Helps 286-87)

In "The Bushman's Cave" Scully fills this space with the vanished race of Khoi, though "withdrew" is surely a colonial euphemism:

> The shades of long-dead forms arisen . . .
> That from this land of ours withdrew
> To silence, leaving scarce a trace. (Helps 289)

Between Sun and Sand depicts the fortunes of a lonely young Jewish shopkeeper or *smous* who falls in love with a trekboer girl. Its subplot features Gert Gemsbok, a Hottentot-Bushman (here only colonial labels evoke the fictional meanings) who is ostracized by the trekboers for telling the truth in court about one of their own. Gert finds six diamonds in the shoe-soles of a red-bearded man tied to a raft about to go over the Augrabies Fall. Gemsbok's name is tied to the cruciform red-bearded man on the raft with his hidden gems and the odd "V" cut into his forehead. Plot is linked to subplot through Max the shopkeeper, who is the only one willing to hire the starving Gemsbok–a name enshrining both the most elegant of desert antelope, the gemsbok or oryx, and an echo of his diamonds. H. A. Bryden says of the "noble gemsbok" that it is the "prototype of the fabled unicorn"

("Bushwoman" 44), a detail he may have found in the description of its beautiful horns by a hunter of the 1830s, Cornwallis Harris; originally, this pagan symbol of the unicorn had been used by ancient Christian writers as a symbol of Christ. Thematically, Gert and this antelope species are both victims of man's "unreasoning cruelty" (76)–Gert, as a ramkee instrumentalist of exceptional sensitivity, is kicked to death in revenge for his "crime of truth-telling" (54); the graceful antelopes are slaughtered for sport. When Scully describes the murdered Gert as "an innocent fellow-creature" (213) the two G(g)emsboks of the cultural and natural landscapes are elided.

Max's older brother Nathan, owner of the trading station and dealer in illegal ostrich feathers, deliberately encourages the attack on Gert. The killers of Gert destroy themselves, by greed and guilt, in the sand dunes, the fingers of which Scully describes as legs of a spider (128); elsewhere they are the limbs of a dune-monster. This sand-creature is the primordial earth in its changes, not beautiful and procreative but demonic and deadly. Over against this force of change and death is the sturdy, slow-growing koekerboom (or kokerboom, *Aloe dichotoma*) also called the "quiver tree"–because Khoisan cored out sections and attached animal skins over the ends to make quivers for their poisoned arrows. It is often found singly or in small clusters in its extremely arid habitats and flowers in July: "the yellow buds which a few of its less mature twigs had put forth tentatively, as though half ashamed of such frivolity, burst open and sent forth a faint show of pollen, which fell like a spangling of gold-dust upon Susannah's hair" (39). Ethnobotanists call this tree a "cultural keystone species" owing to its unaltered persistence through time and its connection with the daily life of the indigenous peoples. Merely by naming such things and particular places tribal elders renewed social values and traditions; every such tree may be a cultural space with its own tribal life-stories or information about the land. More specifically here, the unfolding buds are linked with the young girl's emergent sexuality–perhaps not unlike the golden shower of Danae. Scully's similes fulfill Ezra Pound's ideal of a "one image poem," the figurative *hokku*-like verse he acclaimed in "Vorticism." Like the koekerboom, the migratory antelope are also a keystone species; later to be described in Scully's *Lodges in the Wilderness* (1915) and also in S. C. Cronwright-Schreiner's *The Migratory Springbucks of South Africa* (1925). Scully almost seems to anticipate that an increased population and hunting, if not the future fencing of livestock and rinderpest/drought, will put an end to their treks as part of the overall disintegration of the karoo ecosystem owing to forces of economic consumption.

In a review of this novel, *The Athenaeum* wrote:

> The innumerable writers with whom salvation by local colour is an article of faith should strive to discover from this book the way it is done. We do not say that they will succeed, for the more carefully Mr. Scully's style is analyzed the less it seems to yield its secrets. After some considerable time and pains spent in seeking for an extract which might give some idea of the descriptive power here displayed, we have given up the unsuccessful search. And yet the book is full of descriptive writing, and the descriptions unmistakably attain their end. The reader passes at once into the very atmosphere of the African desert; the inexpressible space and stillness swallow him up, and until he turns the last page there is no world for him but that immeasurable waste of sun and sand. Truly the mystery of style is insoluble. Try as we may, the closest study of Mr. Scully's definite sentences reveals nothing which need seem out of place in the veriest guide-book. Yet these same sentences paint the very spirit of the veld as (with all deference to those who have thought otherwise) no writer has succeeded in painting it before. (531)

Because "such a story is so impossible outside South Africa, and so inextricably interwoven with what cannot without injustice be called its background" of the African land, the meanings created by Scully's stylistic "voice" in his scene paintings are the same meanings created in his story–they are interdependent. The reviewer throws down a gauntlet by suggesting that the narrative, even the romance between Max and Susannah, cannot be understood without defining the qualities of Scully's stylistic voice in his descriptions of the land.

One perhaps should begin by asking what is it that lies "between sun and sand"–oases? dust devils? oven-like heat? More likely, human life, its loves and hates. Scully's is the art of calling up the familiar within the unfamiliar, rendering them together as a visible, sensible presence: ignorant Dutch Calvinists, secularized Jewish immigrants, and despised aboriginal inhabitants, all in a mythically charged land. The story pleads, without oversimplification or misplaced dogmatism, for sympathy with the social and ethical issues between cultures and races. Scully's artistic selection, utilizing the least possible elaboration of material, produces a natural design and fluid movement reflected in the simple and straightforward plot of loves and hates artistically subordinated to his description of unusual regions and lives. His characters are drawn from direct personal observation and are historically authentic. For example, Max the *smous* might seem a false note; however, Namaqualand at this time was home to a small contingent of impoverished Jewish immigrants. Although relieved of traditional restrictions and integrated into the societies of Western Europe, Jews were prompted to relocate by state-sponsored pogroms in Russia and Eastern Europe at the end of the nineteenth century, a few of whom established trade in this remote and isolated region (Jowell and Folb *Kokerboom Country*).

The land itself is described with striking details rich in local color. Scully's is a simple style of clarity and purity; like his beloved desert, it is sharp, economical, and uncontaminated. His purpose is not merely to express ideas or political polemic, but to communicate a state of mind, a mental attitude, with imagistic immediacy. He eschews the rhetoric of abstractions and, like William Blake, thinks in images and energizes his prose with poetic tropes. Scully's narrative becomes an autobiographical counterpoint between his personal experiences and the reader's curiosity so as to produce an almost shared experience of discovery. Although minimally allusive to classical and biblical literature, this prose has a natural dignity and an instinct for the right word developed by Scully's reading. One recalls H. D. Thoreau's formula: "Sentences which suggest far more than they say, which have an atmosphere about them, which do not merely report an old, but make a new impression; sentences which suggest as many things and are as durable as Roman aqueducts; to frame these, that is the *art* of writing[–words] kinked and knotted up into something hard and significant, which you could swallow like a diamond, without digesting" (*Journal* 2: 418-19).

Scully's image of a "land of deathful sleep" recurs in a description that reminds one of T. S. Eliot's lines in "Whispers of Immortality," where the dramatist Webster is notably described as "much possessed by death / And saw the skull beneath the skin" (1:1):

> No more dreary prospect can be imagined than that afforded by Bushmanland in its normal condition of drought. After rain, however, it turns for a few short weeks into a smiling garden. This is especially the case around the northern and western margins where, among the rocky kopjes forming the fringe of the plain, gorgeous flowers cover the ground with vivid patches of colour, and climb and trail over the grey stones. This combination always suggests to the traveller a skull crowned with flowers. The stark rocks, blasted by æons of burning sunshine, are always in evidence, and the wanton luxuriance of the garlands seem to mock at and accentuate their death-like rigour. (7)

The paragraph turns around the almost violent paradox of "a skull crowned with flowers." This single image, however, is embedded throughout the one-hundred-seventeen word paragraph which opens with a contrast of drought to rain in which the blooming desert has been resacralized. For a few "short weeks" after the rain Bushmanland becomes "a smiling garden"–of Eden or, more likely, of an Eden about to fall. One recollects Lord Byron's lines: "In thy once smiling garden, the hemlock and thistle / Have choak'd up the rose, which late bloom'd in the way" ("On Leaving Newstead Abbey" 1: 3). The implicit fall of this "garden" leads quite naturally to thoughts of man's mortality and the "skull." Prior to this image the connotative tenor has been calm, direct, casual; but at the skull the restrained voice forsakes its neutrality of tone for strongly marked emotive words: "stark," "blasted," "wanton," "death." What emerges in the final phrase, "death-like rigour" is a corpse. The land is now felt to be a metaphor of life's passage: life mocks death but life is brief ("a few short weeks") and death is eternal ("æons").

Old Schalk, the patriarchal trekboer, hopelessly ignorant and darkly humorous, makes the Jews and Catholics together scapegoats for the Crucifixion of Christ, thus reenacting the original sin of Jesus's killers by creating scapegoats to rid the community of its social outsiders. Not only does Schalk decry Max for violating the community's religious-ethnic taboo of racial mixing by proposing to marry Susannah, but as Assistant Field Cornet, Schalk even plays the role of Pontius Pilate in the inquest on Gemsbok's death. What makes him like the Roman prefect who washed his hands of responsibility for Jesus's crucifixion is not his governmental role as representative of the magistrate (in point of historic fact that was Scully) but his complicity in the trekboers' desire to close ranks against the victim, to make the victim guilty of his own victimization, to discover only a clean conscience and no victim at all. Schalk's arrogance is emphasized by the poignancy of Gert's smashed ramkee beside his body: in this society, the arts are another spontaneous beauty scorned.

The identical point was made in Olive Schreiner's *An African Farm* when the child Waldo, who had been appreciating the cave art of the Khoisan observed: "'He used to kneel here naked, painting, painting, painting; and he wondered at the things he made himself,' said the boy, rising and moving his hand in deep excitement. 'Now the Boers have shot them all, so that we never see a yellow face peeping out among the stones'" (17-18). The boy's devastatingly matter of fact acknowledgment of this genocide is owing not to his lack of sympathy but to the all-too-familiar fact that the colonial mentality cares neither for the artist nor for those at the margins of its daily life–disparate ethnic factions, the marginal or weak, all those thought to be different–such as Gert Gemsbok. The mythical and sacrificial dimension of violence directed toward the unjustly accused and wrongly murdered is recognized explicitly by the reader in the killing of springboks and Bushmen. Neither springbok nor Bushman willingly seek death to assuage the evil powers, but the rains that annually bring life to nature suggest that despite man's blighting guilt "deep down things" are awakened by a hidden power.

Like Schreiner, Haggard, or Mitford, Scully also anticipates something of Roger Fry's response in "Art of the Bushman" (1910) and "Negro Sculpture" (1920) to African aesthetic and spiritual capacities. Scully is here contributing to a cross-cultural aesthetic, both anthropological and philosophical:

> This Hottentot was an artist, carrying in his heart a spark of that quality which we call genius, and which might be called the flower that bears the pollen which fertilises the human mind, and without which the soul of man would not exist, nor would his understanding have sought for aught beyond the satisfaction of his material senses. Gert Gemsbok was a musician. (51)

Gemsbok speaks extensively in San to his wife over the campfire (wholly unrecorded, untranslated in the narrative), but very little to outsiders–except for his ramkee music. His indigenous "voice" for the world is "his favourite air" that, startlingly, is given by Scully in full musical notation. "Upon it he would improvise and invent fantastic arabesques and ingenious variations" (53). Possibly there is a Western influence in its rhythmic structure from his time at the diamond mines–in its major-minor tonal system and eight-note range with skips–but on his native instrument and in all its variations, especially in his improvisational duets with Oom Schulpad (78-79), this musical "voice" represents a cultural harmony that otherwise is lacking in the Namaqualand desert. After his wife dies, Gert's music "was all in a minor key; no more reels and jigs that made one long to caper. The old, stock melody ran through all he played, making it like an endless, barbaric fugue–weird and melancholy. His nocturnal performances sometimes made the dog leap out of the scherm and howl despairingly at the stars" (118). Sadly comic, the dog's ululation nevertheless has joined in a duet with the ramkee no less than Oom Schulpad's fiddle. The death and burial of Gert is in a chapter entitled "The Broken Ramkee," an image that is both literal and, when applied to Gert himself, figurative.

Justice for Nathan and Koos does not await some never-to-materialize human intervention, as Scully's use of biblical imagery makes clear. The title of chapter thirteen, "Whoso Diggeth a Pit . . ." is from both Proverbs 26:27 and Ecclesiastes 10:8, concluding ". . . shall fall therein." And chapter fifteen "Whoso Breaketh a Fence..."

also from Ecclesiastes 10:8 ends ". . . a serpent shall bite him." (Although nominally both are from the King James version of the Bible, the choice of the word "fence" rather than "hedge" seems to derive from Rabbinic translations of the *Tractate Hullin* of the Babylonian Talmud.) Clearly the pit and the serpent that bites the intruder both represent justice whereby the plotters of death perish by their own stratagems. Nathan, who intends to use Koos's guilt as an opportunity to blackmail his wife for sex, is clearly an ironic characternym, inasmuch as it was the prophet Nathan who accused King David of his sin with Bathsheba (2 Samuel 12). The story Nathan tells is designed to get King David to pronounce judgment on his own crime before he realizes that he himself is the criminal. David does not make the connection to his stealing Uriah's wife until Nathan's dramatic accusal: "You are the man!" Nor does Scully's Nathan see what is coming for him among the dunes.

The dunes, centered around "the weird form of Bantom Berg," are a "vast death-trap" (189). Scully describes this Namaqualand feature later also later in his hunting memoir, *Lodges in the Wilderness* (1914):

> When day had fully dissipated the faint haze of morning we endeavoured to appraise the contours of this gross, amorphous entity, for the concept that it was one and indivisible had gradually but irresistibly formed. It grew more and more enormous; more gross and inimical. Irregular and convoluted ridges arose from it here and there; it appeared to be absolutely bare of vegetation. In the centre was piled a humped, bulging mass; out of this Bantom Berg lifted its clean-cut cone of granite, a soaring sphynx still waiting for the carver's chisel. Here and there columns of dust slender beneath but widely dilating above at an enormous height, stalked slowly over the body of the prone monster, marking each the path of a miniature whirlwind. As we drew near, the face of the dune tract once more became indefinite and complicated; for a time the eye could not follow nor appraise its details. But suddenly the thing explained itself; from the central mass, the prostrate carcase of the obscene creature, a number of league-long tentacles, consisting of sand dunes, extended. These were thick at the base, but they tapered away to nothingness. Like a crouching spider or a half-huddled cuttle-fish

> the monstrosity sprawled, its talon-tentacles seeming to gather in the plains to infest them like a malignant cancer. . . . It seemed to be endowed with some low-graded form of rudimentary life. . . The dune-monster was the slow-pacing steed of the Thirst King; it was his throne, his host and his strong city; it was the abhorrent body of which he was the resistless and implacable soul! (36-37)

This diabolic form is the primordial earth, not in its benevolent manifestation of rain and life but in its grim aspect of thirst and death.

Koos Bester abandons Nathan, suffering with thirst, to his death in this desert. Nathan dies almost as a failed scapegoat sacrifice to a demonic idol that will bring no peace. Nathan missing, a party of trekboers follows Koos and Nathan's spoor into the dunes. The jackals have cleaned Nathan to his bones, but his clothes and effects identify him. His remains are brought back in a sack:

> The sack containing the horror had not been opened, pending the arrival of the Special Magistrate; it was hung in the fork of a high koekerboom about fifty yards away. Towards this tree which bore such terrible fruit furtive and frightened glances were shot from time to time. . . . The children . . . took up positions in small groups around the koekerboom, but at a respectful distance. For hours they silently gazed, wide-eyed and fascinated, at the Thing which hung in its fork, lifted thereto by its own act when a sentient being, even as Haman of old was hung upon the high gallows which he had prepared for Mordecai. (214)

The "fruit of the tree" of which Adam and Eve partook proclaims its evil effects to the trekboer children who find no temptation here. Neither hanging upon Adam's tree as the tempting apple nor upon Christ's cross as redemption from sin, "the Thing" is an object that cannot be named specifically. The ironic justice of Nathan's reversal of intent and its result suggests a mysteriously appointed self-punishment for a man without conscience or god. Scully's reference to Haman hanged on a gallows of his own contriving (Esther 7:9-10) was a routine cross-reference in sermons expatiating on the blow-back of sin.

The same nemesis awaits Koos Bester, but it is Koos's conscience that accomplishes his death beneath "the accusing stars"

(218): "Like Abiram, God had doomed him for his crimes to go down alive into the pit" (222). Abiram and his cohorts had rebelled against the leadership of Moses and "the ground clave asunder that was under them: And the earth opened her mouth, and swallowed them up. . . . They, and all that appertained to them, went down alive into the pit, and the earth closed upon them: and they perished from among the congregation" (Numbers 16: 31-33). Koos himself, however, summons this divine punishment. He believes the early-morning fires of the herd-boys to be demonic: "To the demented brain of the fugitive it appeared as if the whole Desert were full of fiends seeking him with torches, far and near. Where the Milky Way dipped to the horizon the thronging stars seemed each a torch lit at the nether flame, and borne by a searching demon" (223). Thus the stars and diamonds that were enshrined in Gemsbok's name now return like the horribly familiar music of the dead man's ramkee, to pursue Koos as "the torch of a tracking fiend" (224). Symbols of serpent, spider, pit all conspire to define the damnation of Koos, who is returned from the dunes by his wife the day following his mental breakdown: "It was late at night when she arrived at the camp, with the corpse of her husband tied, stiff and stark, on the seat beside her" (226). This gothic image of wife and husband, living and dead, riding home as if in some early allegorical painting of personified death, points to Koos's sin of hatred and to Nathan's lust as corrupting forces delivering the sinners to hell.

Scully's *A Vendetta of the Desert*, published in the same year as *Between Sun and Sand*, is a cultural documentary with a strong oral flavor of Dutch history and life in which the young female protagonist's blindness creates a bond between the traditional adversaries of Boer and Bushman. The characters of a Khoisan boy, Kanu, and a Boer girl, Elsie, are explored in the context of a fraternal feud that, given a lifetime of space and suffering, finally works itself out. The epigraph for the nouvelle, from Romans 12:19, is "Vengeance is mine; I will repay, saith the Lord." The setting of this novel is not long after the establishment of British rule in the Cape Colony in 1806 and it takes place on the isolated Karoo near the Tanqua River in the Cape Colony, south of what is now Calvinia. The anonymous narrator presents his story as if it were partly a tale of incident once handed down by word of mouth to which the author's reconstructions of psychological and moral motivations are seemingly super-added. Scully's narrative opens with surely one of the most arresting Afrikander ghost stories in literature–bearing all the earmarks of a true folk tale–of a howling dog that over the centuries foretells the imminent death of the family patriarch. At the time this novel begins, the horrified paterfamilias demands his son shoot this incubus or suffer disinheritance: "There was an old and tattered family Bible on the loft, with a strong and heavy metal clasp. This clasp Tyardt broke into fragments about the size of ordinary slugs, and with them he loaded his gun, using portions of the leaves as wadding" (3-4). Those familiar with the Dutch *Statenbijbels* of elephant-folio size with their brass clasps and the *familie register* in the front, grasp immediately the symbolism. Religious but not reverent, as were many Boers in that era, son Tyardt in effect shoots the dog with the Bible: "He fired, and a horrible, half-human yell followed the report of the gun.... Beneath lay the huddled, bleeding figure of an old man of hideous aspect, clad in a garb unknown at the Cape but which, it was afterwards thought, suggested some woodcuts in an old book brought out . . . from Holland" (4). This diabolic figure then mystifyingly vanishes–but remains as a "baleful influence" (6) to afflict the family until the present-day "vendetta of the desert."

Two brothers, Stephanus and Gideon both fall in love with the same girl; years after she has married the former, the rivalry of the brothers has grown to embrace even the ownership of grazing rights. In a heated exchange Stephanus accidentally shoots his brother who, surviving only because of the skill of the herbalist, "Uncle Diederik," maliciously claims the shooting was deliberate. Stephanus is brought to trial for attempted murder; and although he is convicted and imprisoned by the false testimony of his brother, his blind child Elsie's love for him ultimately dissolves his anger. His reformation is unassailable. A certain neat symmetry underlying this vendetta reveals itself as Stephanus' prison-widowed wife lies dying. She confesses to the jealous bother Gideon her life-long love for him, revealing that she married the wrong man only because she had been told he himself was otherwise bespoken. She had assumed her husband shot Gideon because he'd discovered her secret. But the conscience-stricken Gideon's confession to her of his perjury kills her on the spot. Elsie, who afterwards overhears the guilty Gideon's prayer-confession of false witness, naively treks to Cape Town to rescue her father by telling the Governor what she has learned.

Elsie's blindness, because it creates a bond between her and Kanu, the Bushman, is really a spiritual benison. As the lovers in *Sun and Sand* were from culturally conflicting spheres, so here the traditional adversaries of Boer and Bushman become allies in Elsie and Kanu, indeed nearly inseparable companions. British punishment is a theme: Stephanus and Kanu are both unjustly punished, yet each finds in the penalty an opportunity for spiritual growth. Stephanus works out his salvation in humble acceptance and Kanu makes of it afterwards stories to entertain his clan. In contrast to the illusory pride that haunts the feuding brothers, Elsie's unqualified purity is only surpassed by Stephanus's forgiveness of his brother. He and Elsie pursue Gideon into the deserts of Thirstland to effect a reconciliation. Nearly dying of dryness, they are reunited with Kanu who rescues them from death in the drifting sand. With the help of the Khoisan, Stephanus reaches Gideon and the brothers are reconciled. Here the different voices of indigenes and settlers meet in cross-cultural recognition about their lives and relationships to the land. The larger context for this novella is expressed in its last scene, the rain coming to the parched earth: Elsie stood "her face turned to the mighty thunder-chariot from which a refreshing wind, laden with the ichor of the fallen rain, stirred the richness of her hair" (206). "Ichor" is the colorless liquid said to flow "from the wounds of the blessed immortals" and here it is certainly also a hint of the crucifixion, the blood and water from the soldier's spear. The renewed brotherly affection confirms the desert, for settler as well Khoisan, as the physical setting for the spirit's reconstruction.

Between Sun and Sand and *A Vendetta of the Desert* are novels about the destruction of beauty, the obstacles to love, and the fallen nature of man. Yet it is also about the desert, not merely as a wasteland presided over by the monstrous "Thirst King," but as the vehicle for hope. Scully avoids any artificial exaggeration or sentimental nostalgia for this harsh life; rather, he finds in the desert a paradigm both new and old–as with the "desert fathers" of antiquity, Scully finds in this arid landscape a place for the construction or reconstruction of the spirit, paradigms of wisdom.

§

Among the most powerful short stories about the Khoisan is Henry Anderson Bryden's "A Bushwoman's Romance," collected in *Tales of South Africa* (1896). Set in the area of the North Kalahari among the "Masarwa Bushmen" and centered on the figure of barely mature Nakeesa, married off by her father to a lazy husband, this story is about the moral choices within a Khoisan society, a "houseless race of wild hunters" (Bryden 41). As a nineteenth-century writer finding the moral basis of action undermined by rationalistic modes of thought and religious skepticism, Bryden seems to have curiosity about the motivations of a race believed to lack many of the traditions of the African tribes around them. How does love prosper in a world that either worships the demonic or "knows no God" (Moffat 59)? As a Stone Age hunting-gathering race, this ancient society might disclose something of the hidden origins of human morality, as well as the origins of art, magic, and storytelling in its cosmogonic tales of stars, moon, rain; animals and man. Wonderfully remote from Western thought and science, the world-view and spirituality of the Khoisan, whose imagination led them to become mankind's first hunters and fantasists, is polytheistic animism, primarily a belief in nameless spirits of the dead who bring sickness and death. Their most spiritual animal is the eland and a dance of occult healing is their most important ritual–by which evil spirits are warded off, the future is predicted, the weather ameliorated and favorable hunting made certain–all in a trance of mind-altering herbs.

In the story's last sentence, Bryden says Nakeesa's romance was meant to illustrate the complexity of her emotions in this seemingly brutish society. The task to which Bryden apparently had set himself was to reveal the enduring Khoisan humanity despite their predilection for a phlegmatic life and love rather than for a Victorian expressiveness. Cultural differences of material comfort, technological attainment, and economic development clearly exist between settler and African but often emotional complexity is not so different. Bryden undertakes to psychologize the consciousness and point of view of Nakeesa. He remarks: "She had shown two great extremes of evil and good in her nineteen years of existence. She had refused to save the life of Sinikwe (the man who treated her ill, and whom she loathed) from the puff-adder–an act as good as murder, most men will say. And for Kwaneet, who had treated her with some kindliness, and whom she loved with as much love as a Masarwa is capable of, she had given her whole being–life itself" (62). Bryden seems to ask whether what "most men" would praise or condemn as good or evil applies in her society; does she knowingly break a moral rule or, as Socrates would suggest, is her choice owing to ignorance, to having no moral code? Bryden says: "Conscience goes for little in the world, yet something like conscience told her that if the puff-adder reached Sinikwe and caused his death, hers was the blame" (57). Bryden suggests that she is morally capable of both heroism and treachery, as is "most" of mankind; and therein lies her complexity.

But her father and Sinikwe and Kwaneet, by contrast, have no social self-image where moral considerations apply, and their actions contain no moral distinctions or judgments. Her father's primitive self-interest decreed her sale to Sinikwe; and Sinikwe treated her with a loveless patriarchal indifference. Kwaneet shows himself even worse:

> having satisfied himself, without much emotion, at a later period of the day, of the death of his wife and child, and having taken as much zebra meat as the lion had left, he went his way. Nakeesa's elder child–now three years old–was, of course, a perfectly useless encumbrance to him. He therefore sold the boy to some Batauana people for a new assegai, and soon after returned to his desert life. (62)

Kwaneet's "kindliness" is not love. Nakeesa aspired to marry him because she confused with love his offer of titbits of meat from successful hunting. But he is unwilling to offer his one treasured brass snuff cartridge case for her *lobola* or bride price and he has no "spare ones to offer" (43). Later, he gives her a very small "pinch" of snuff (52), no larger than the "pinch" Sinikwe had extended (48); and although this prompts her to offer him water in return, it is because she misconstrued his sexual desire as love. Kwaneet then selfishly drinks half the water in her ostrich shell, exposing her to a potential beating from Sinikwe: "She herself had had but one sip since she started. She dared to take no more. But she knew her risk, and cheerfully accepted it–for Kwaneet's sake" (53). Thus *neither* husband proves loving; she only has an easier time of it with Kwaneet. She kills one mate and sacrifices herself for the other, all for a delusive romance.

Bryden's strength of narration lies, first, in the ethnographic and desert details that are rendered in fluid and authoritative prose. Thus, in the brilliant moonlight, Nakeesa suddenly awakes to the presence of a snake: "It was a great puff-adder; and the gentle vibration of the reptile's scales against the sand, as it slowly crawled, had aroused her" (56). The image is both eerie and informative, since such auditory powers are unprecedented in "superior" cultures. Second, his narrative foreshadowing and irony support the complexity of his vision. In addition to the subtle hints of Kwaneet's selfishness, the lion's sudden killing of Nakeesa ironically fulfills her prediction pertaining to Sinikwe: "Our life is short, and has many dangers" (53); and her abandonment of his body duplicates her own demise: "She left the body to the vultures and jackals and hyænas. A Bushman needs no burial" (58). Finally, Bryden's allusion to the treasured brass cartridge cases ties this Stone Age society into the modern empire– even if one ignores other travel book references to tea, wine, and a deer park in England. Sinikwe's making snuff with tobacco while his wife labors in the hot sun is a cross-cultural activity of sorts, but the spent cartridges of the modern rifle, symbol of imperial power, are the agents of the story's central selfishness.

Whether the snake, its temptation of freedom to remarry, Nakeesa's conscience suggesting "blame," and the her act of eating– gorging on–the meat of the giraffe add up to a parable of the Fall becomes a matter of creative convention. It is generally safe to say that when there is a garden and a snake, there's an allegory of the fall. However, the garden here is a desert nearly without food. Yet the giraffe is unfallen nobility: "you may search all Africa–ay, all the world–for a more wonderful, more beautiful picture of feral life in its most primæval form" (45). Perhaps the experience of nature is an experience at every moment in time of a fall. Yet equally, by the rule of opposites, to fall may be also to rise; and Nakeesa's giving of herself for the amiable but unloving Kwaneet, unable to appreciate her sacrifice, is an intimation of her redemption.

What seems especially to link the realism of this narrative and those by Scully to the narrative of Mitford that follows is the sweep of life upon the landscape, from its sand and sun to the ambiguities of good and evil in the human heart.

§

The debate of conquest and settlement–that is, the issue of who owns the land and on what moral footing–is equally alive in Bertram Mitford's *Renshaw Fanning's Quest: A Tale of the High Veldt* (1894). The historical discovery of diamonds and stories of pick and shovel prospectors heroically pitted against earth and rock–in those few years before individual diggers were supplanted by mining-consortium geologists–hovers in the background of this novel's narrative, underpinning its pursuit of fortune set variously in South Africa's eastern Cape, in the high grasslands of its semi-arid central Karoo (a name derived from the Khoi, *Karusa*, meaning a barren and thirsty land), and finally in Bushmanland where the Orange River pierces both desert and archipelagos of mountains. It is a treasure quest tale, complete with deathbed directions to a great diamond in a mythical Valley of the Eye, in which it may be more than a little redolent of A. C. Doyle's first published story, "The Mystery of the Sasassa Valley" (1879) or H. Rider Haggard's *King Solomon's Mines* (1885). Yet if even today Haggard's and Mitford's masterpieces have not lived down the stigma of their adventure formats, they both are classics of this genre and will in time be appreciated as works of wide and undoubtedly permanent interest. In 1893 a mine at Jagersfontein, South Africa, yielded the "Excelsior" diamond of 971 carats (old units; 995 metric carats), the world's heaviest-known uncut diamond up to that time. Of wide local interest to diggers, this exceptional stone may have been the immediate inspiration for Mitford's plot.[24] It had a flat cleavage face on one side and rose to a peak on the other, hence its name meaning "higher." Renshaw even puns on the name as he climbs to the Eye's location: "And now, excelsior!" (223).

But one may wonder why Mitford chose for his tale such a pedestrian title as he did, when the much more suspenseful "Valley of the Eye" begs for titular employment. Yet just as there are two kinds of "heart" in Joseph Conrad's "Heart of Darkness" (1899)–the literal geographic place of the Inner Station and the figurative psychological state of fallenness–so in Mitford's novel the title designates two "quests"–the literal quest for the diamond in the Valley of the Eye and the hero's unarticulated search for that Miltonic "paradise within, happier far," which is found in the "veritable garden of Eden" (29) at Sunningdale where Marian Selwood's love awaits. By taking his place ultimately in the local community and its network of social relationships, Renshaw's truer quest is fulfilled. Similar to the antithesis of civilization against primitivism in the contrast between the English Thames and Africa's Congo in "Heart of Darkness," so the antithesis between the Cape's domesticity and the Valley's call to rugged individualism in *Renshaw Fanning* reflects a distrust of the primitive "heart." So intensely ingrained in nineteenth-century psychology was suspicion of instinctual impulses that they required forceful repression, as in Stevenson's allegorical *Dr. Jekyll and Mr. Hyde* (1885). Hence early European settlers were militantly opposed

---

24. The *Cape Times* made no mention of the discovery for that July, but the *Cape Argus & Cape Mercantile Advertiser* carried the following in the edition of 3 July 1893: "A SIX OUNCE DIAMOND / Fauresmith July 1st (Special) / A diamond of good quality, pure white and weighing 974 carats was found at Jagersfontein last evening"–but no follow-up article appeared and no account of the find appeared in major British newspapers afterwards, possibly because its name, "Excelsior," was a cliché or because it did not come on the open market for more than a decade.

to the African animist religions, and they approached Africans like the Bushman with hatred and suspicion for reasons both territorial and theological. The settlers had landed in Africa brave and pious, with the flintlock in one hand and the Bible in the other, ready to defend the kingdom of God against the kingdom of Satan. Isaiah 8:19-22 had written of "familiar spirits" and "wizards that peep and that mutter" consulting the dead on behalf of the living and had said of such fetishists that "there is no light in them" and "they shall be driven to darkness"; therefore, the early evangelical literalists rejected any inculturation by Christianity of African beliefs. But the worship of Mammon at the Cape, Mitford suggests, may be more evil than the animism of the Valley.

Mitford's colonial philosophy is based on hard, practical considerations rather than on sentimental ethnocentrism or idealistic clichés. He believes every country gets the government it deserves (*Seaford* 221), that "fortune does not favor the brave" (*Averno* 10) and that inventions have been known to make fortunes, but practically never for the inventor. He doesn't believe in "poetic justice"; or that "honesty is the best policy" (*Seaford* 103); or that Zulus need missionaries (*Seaford* 117). Mitford's typical protagonist is upper class, in his later thirties, and is often some combination of a psychologically injured "renegade" (sometimes in disguise) with "a clouded and shipwrecked life" desiring revenge on society, like Lorraine in *Gun-Runner* (69), or a wanderer running from an unhappy marriage whose "life is behind him," cynical about love that for him is "a thing of the past," as in *Palliser* (6) or *Aletta* (137). At times a lack of money is coupled with the hardening process of despair and loss of conscience, as in Lawrence Stanninghame's pursuit of the "oof bird" of wealth in *Sign of the Spider* (98). Whatever specific form this estrangement takes, the Mitford figure exists to some degree lost outside the traditional domestic space. Occasionally, this protagonist manipulates native attacks upon his countrymen for his own purposes of revenge, as in *Gun-Runner, Ames,* or *Palliser*. At other times he is the "victim of circumstances" (*Official* 89) who dies at the end because of the "pitilessness of life" (*Palliser* 341). Within those extreme situations of suffering, struggle, guilt and death, Mitford's protagonist must make choices, take a stand, and define a place in the world. If the deeper and more-sensitive heroes and heroines die, they first undergo a creative suffering and self-discovery and find in love a value that surpasses justice, happiness, or life. But often this is accompanied by ironic coincidence; in *Palliser* the tormented hero is *not* married, though his mistaken belief that he indeed was married provided the whole impetus for his tragedy.

  The Mitford heroine is often a British relative sojourning with her distant colonial family, only erroneously regarded merely as a sop to his younger drawing-room readers in a pinafore. Sometimes of "Junoesque" (*Weird* 20) proportions, she has a "strong passion-fraught temperament" (*Palliser* 11), "a free and unaffected self-possession" and an "open, sunny nature" (*Waynflete* 59) with grace, beauty, pride and puts love before socially-constructed values. She won't scruple at courtroom perjury if the cause be love. Her romance is often set against the background of Zulu warfare, plot and subplot complicating and enriching Mitford's action. The union of the lovers, so desired by the reader, is always forestalled by new complications of social circumstance. Sometimes the woman (*vide* Lalusini in *The Induna's Wife*) is wiser or stronger-minded than her mate, and at other times she physically saves her man. Beryl in *Veldt Vendetta*, Aurelle in *Seaford's Snake*, and Verna in *Forging the Blades* all shoot blacks in confrontations: "Never still, Sapazani dodged the volley and laughed exultantly. But even as he did so he leaped in the air and fell flat. Those in her neighbourhood looked up at Verna Halse, who, pale as death, with a red spot on each cheek and dull eyes, after one quick glance began refilling her magazine" (*Blades* 320).

  Sometimes, as in *Harley Greenoak's Charge*, *John Ames*, or *Forging the Blades*, cynical Mitford actually seems to believe in a sentimental romanticism, though perhaps by the rule of contraries. He simply may be amusing and enriching himself by pandering to the expectations of the marketplace–perfect lovers who fall in love in minutes, sudden wealth, happy endings. Watt once wrote to the Northern Newspaper Syndicate about a proposed novel, *Raynier, Political Agent* (retitled *The Sadir's Oath* [1904]), that Mitford quite understood a bright love and adventure story was wanted and that although there was no objection to an African element, he was to avoid all mention whatever of the Anglo-Boer War. More likely, Mitford's sunny plots reflect his contrarianism. As with Olive Schreiner, more often than not it is the problematic whites who find a material answer to their quest. So in *Renshaw Fanning* "the way of the transgressor" (307) is rewarded, monetarily at least.

Renshaw, a prospector/stock-farmer situated several hundred miles to the north of Sunningdale, is bankrupt by the dry season in the "howling desert"(14) of the Upper Karoo, quaintly called Thirstland on some nineteenth-century maps. Mitford's wonderfully vivid, at times comic, description of this land under a curse includes all but the second and the last of the ten plagues of Egypt, at least if one counts as the first of the plagues such images as the "red and turgid water"(5-6) on a landscape parched to the "hue of blood" (13). Maurice Sellon stumbles upon Renshaw's dry farm and the two agree to seek their fortunes in the Valley of the Eye after Renshaw recovers at Sunningdale from his malarial bout. His friends, Chris and Edith Selwood and Chris's sister Marian and their stunningly beautiful twenty-two year old visitor, Violet Avory, with whom Renshaw has been in love for some time, live at Sunningdale.

Several coincidences could be said to impair the plot, such as the fact that quite accidentally at Sunningdale Maurice encounters Violet with whom he has been conducting an intense but secret affair or, again later, when the Koranna servant Dirk fortuitously discovers and rescues Renshaw. However, a nineteenth-century novel is very unlike a twenty-first century novel, and this problem of impossible coincidence was for Mitford's readers, implicitly and unconsciously of course, an accepted self-referential gesture to the fictiveness of the narrative. Because it was a story, they expected it to use coincidence, this being a convention of the genre. After all, they were not so naive as to take stories *literally*–as did old Otto Farber in Olive Schreiner's *An African Farm*, the butt of an enlightened readership's amusement. Thus as long as coincidence is kept this side of absurdity, it was as integral to the artifice of fiction as the willing suspension of disbelief has always been to poetic faith. A century and more later we may grumble (because of our *lack* of narrative sophistication?), but even the canonized Charles Dickens took advantage of this liberty. Another sort of improbability is the extensive and apparently verbatim dictation Renshaw takes from Amos Greenway concerning how to locate the Eye–so exhaustively detailed, the poor man dies before he supplies the final crucial fact of the location of the Valley. These details do lend credibility to his claim and also create the challenge to construe incomplete directions, generating suspenseful plot complications. A thematic justification for this bulky directive's fragmentary data lies in the quest idea itself. Just as Sellon's character is undetermined and Renshaw's emotional knowledge is unripened, so the frustrating process of deciphering and completing Greenway's directions is a make-or-break ordeal, a turning of a mere sequence of landmarks into a characterological challenge that summons at the darkest point hidden resources to do what seems impossible.

Although Mitford places his fictional locale of Sunningdale in the Umtirara range above Fort Lamport, it is a thinly disguised version of the actual Fort Beaufort in its bend on the Kat river and the nearby Katberg Mountain foothills. Mitford himself had resided not far from this frontier outpost as an official in the colonial civil service. The date of the novel's action could be contemporaneous with its publication but, given the uncharted terrain of the Valley of the Eye, it more likely is set during Mitford's own tenure in the Eastern Cape, fifteen years earlier. Neither Cecil Rhodes's war to occupy the more northerly Matabeleland a year before this novel's appearance nor the Ninth Frontier War with the Xhosas, that occurred during Mitford's residency in the later 1870s, is alluded to in the text. The attack on the homestead early in the plot was not indicative of any tribal frontier uprising, but simply a specific instance of banditry in which other ethnic locals were the preponderate victims.

Though the reader takes Mitford's scenes and characters to be a model of empirical reality, on a deeper level their exoticism and conceptual novelty are symbolic socio-cultural constructions of his personal vision. When Mitford was vacationing in October 1902 at the Hotel de Londres in Cava dei Tirreni on the Amalfi Coast, he wrote Watt that the first edition illustrations for this novel were "too vulgarly grotesque for words" and urged that with the exception of "the third in the book-showing the battle" (Monsman, *Haggard* 277) they be excluded from the new edition being planned. As much as a Mitford adventure seems at times to rely upon a low-mimetic formal realism, to which these illustrations contributed, it in fact pushes toward extended levels of meaning, particularly in situations where the individual escapes existential alienation and loneliness by attuning himself to his reflection in another's authentic selfhood: "The glad mirth danced in his eyes, reflected from hers" (*Gun-Runner* 23). Mitford suggests the Platonic theory that the lover's search for his own best self takes place through his idealization of the beloved.

A brief, perhaps elementary, example of Mitford's extended levels of meaning occurs as Renshaw Fanning lounges in his cane chair, contemplating Marian Selwood:

> The boom of bees floated upon the jessamine-laden air, varied by the shriller buzz of a long, rakish-looking hornet winging in and out of his absurd little clay nest, wedged, like that of a swallow, beneath the eaves of the veranda. Great butterflies flitted among the sunflowers, but warily and in terror of the lurking amantis--that arrant hypocrite, so devotional in his attitude, so treacherously voracious in his method of seizing and assimilating his prey--and a pair of tiny sugar-birds, in their delicate crimson and green vests, flashed fearlessly to and fro within a couple of yards of Renshaw's head, dipping their long needle-like bills into the waxen blossoms of the fragrant jessamine. (98)

This passage, opening and closing with the jasmine's fragrance, evokes all the five senses–taste and touch not least in the operations of the preying/praying mantis. Nature's fecundity is suggested by bees, butterflies and birds; and feminine grace, elegance and sensuality are foregrounded in the symbolism of the jasmine. But the Freudian imagery of "dipping . . . needle-like bills into . . . blossoms," in conjunction with the "terror" of the butterflies, intensifies the masculinity of Renshaw's gaze on the veranda, though his desire is still subconscious. At first glance this scene is merely a transcript from domestic reality–just what one would expect to see in that semi-tropical latitude; and in point of fact this sugar-bird has migrated to the farm veranda from the final pages of Mitford's non-fictional *Through the Zulu Country* (1883), feeding there without Freudian overtones and footnoted as "a species of humming bird" (320). Among Mitford's favorite plot episodes are attacks on such homesteads as this. Needless to say, the readers' *prima facie* sympathies, as controlled by the author, are all on the side of defending these colonial verandas.

The Valley of the Eye lay across the Orange river, several days' trek into the dry savannah of the nomadic Bushmen. The great diamond that Renshaw and Maurice seek is variously described as the "stare of a basilisk"(65) and as a "devil's eye that would scorch up whoever looked at it too long" (171). The basilisk, also known as a cockatrice, is mentioned in the older translations of Psalms, Isaiah, Jeremiah, and Proverbs (or less mythically as an "adder" in modern revisions). It was known in folklore as a serpent with the head of a rooster, supposed to have the power to strike dead any upon whom it looked–"From powerful eyes close venim doth convey / Into the lookers hart, and killeth farre away" (Spenser, *Faerie Queene* 4.7.37). To this traditionally African chimera, Heliodorus in *Aethiopica* had linked love at first sight with the basilisk's evil eye; and Lucan's *Pharsalia* had suggested its connection to Medusa's snaky *coup d'oeil* (Heliodorus 3.8; Lucan 9.696ff). The noun "spell" is applied by Mitford both to Violet Avory and to the diamond, and so the Eye emblematizes Violet Avory's enthralling *coup d'oeil* that Renshaw must surmount–"His heart was seared"–before he recognizes his real love, Marian, an ever-weaving Penelope. Moreover, a basilisk figuratively denotes a pernicious person intent on treachery: "They will kill one another by the look, like cockatrices" (*Twelfth Night* 3.4.193)–one of a dozen such allusions in Shakespeare. So the Eye also emblematizes Maurice Sellon, whose punning on his and Chris Selwood's names invokes the slang sense of "sell," a swindle or hoax and thus prefigures his treachery. In Marian's metaphor of intrinsic merit, taken from the ring or sound of genuine coin, neither Maurice nor Violet, because of their hidden love affair and exclusive self-seeking, "ring true."

All of this would be in danger of over-reading were it not that Mitford introduces a likeness of his basilisk into the narrative–a homologous embodiment, as it were. The crest that crowns the chimerical reptile's head is described as the "cock's-comb-looking peak"(214) of the mountain in which the crater with its sinister diamond is located. The adventurers in their quest arrive literally *on* the basilisk to plunder its Eye, causing Renshaw to stand "as one turned to stone" by the "diabolical" power "luring men to destruction" (231). The cobra Renshaw killed during the thunder and lightning of the storm in Thirstland foreshadowed in Maurice's nightmare a landscape under the curse of the basilisk at which they arrive. Lucan had described the powers of this king of serpents as "releasing hisses dismaying to all these pests, its breath lethal before its bite, the basilisk thrusts the entire brood aside and lords it over empty sand" (9.724-26ff). And slightly later Pliny's *Natural History* not only cites its hiss but comments that its breath "scorches up grass and bursts rocks" (13.8.33) to create the desert in which it is always found. The dead snake with which Chris teases Violet at Sunningdale (if it's a fallen paradise, nonetheless the snake of evil there is dead), the hissing that Maurice hears when Renshaw kills the cobra in his farmhouse, and the puff adder that kills their pack-horse in the mountains, to say nothing of the arrow point of the Bushman (guardians of the Eye, and therefore its doubles) that nearly kills Renshaw–all these dead or living venomous powers are aspects or echoes of the Eye. Either Renshaw is performing a kind of exorcism on this heathen object when the four white chalk marks on its exterior rock took "the relative formation of the stars composing the Southern Cross" (241) or Mitford is suggesting that the primary spatial dimensions of up-down are moral also and that by bringing the "eyes of the stars"(229) down to earth, this "'Eye' shining like a star" (231) is an idol or a fallen version of the heavenly *crux* of stars. Lightbearer the Eye may be, but it is the malign angel in eclipse, a Lucifer or some pagan Isis.

On the other hand, it could argued that in the estimation of the Bushmen, the prospectors commit a "sacrilege" (171) because the Eye is a sacred and venerated fetish / icon, fully as much as the silver cross in Renshaw's room presaged those four bright stars. This raises the issue of the novel's conflicted meanings, whether to read with or against its grain: at the moment the Eye is descried, Renshaw's thoughts of "riches lying waste" that must "yield to the grasping hand" (243) could be an echo of John Ruskin's vision of "seizing every piece of fruitful waste ground" and of Haggard's "strong aggressive hand of England" that "has grasped some fresh portion of the earth's surface" ("Zulu War-Dance" 94). But perhaps we are invited to question this imperial perspective on the land and its resources by reading in "a contrarious spirit" (*Weird* 145). Does the Latin cross comment on Europeans pillaging Africa in the name of Christ? For the Khoisan, such physical sites as the Valley of the Eye are spaces of access to an intangible ancestral knowledge where the land expresses and transmits the voices of oral culture. Perhaps also Mitford expects us to see that the ethnocentricity of the British is subtly ironized by Dirk's intervention? Admittedly, through Fanning's eyes Mitford invokes the imperialist's stereotype that the Bushmen are "like a troop of apes" (262) and, again, "human apes" (263); the only African unstintingly praised is Renshaw's Koranna servant, Dirk, "ready to defend him if necessary at the cost of his own life"(294). This is certainly a familiar sentimental imperial stereotype–the loyal servant. Yet Renshaw's recognition here is a corrective to his original disgust with "these wretched people" (158; a Khoi-Khoi subgroup) when Dirk had taken leave without permission to go hunting. Could Dirk's value no longer be merely the practical services he can render Renshaw? Perhaps having saved his master's life, the nearly-insurmountable colonial barrier between black and white has been breached, and the victim has begun to redeem his oppressor. Still, Mitford never wrote a novel in which the master was willing to die for his servant.

Put simply, because the Bushmen do not appreciate the *economic* value of their Eye, Renshaw does not grasp the immorality of appropriating it. However, the text certainly does imply that the evil in this "devil's eye" which turns Sellon into "Judas" (248) is the product of a European commodity fetishism that, in contrast to the diamond's setting in nature, imparts to it the diminished status of a mere salable object. Implicit here is a loss of the heroic and its replacement with the material comforts of mass consumerism in a spiritually emasculated society. Like the thirty pieces of silver paid to Judas, "the price of blood" (272), the economic wealth conferred by this Eye upon Sellon inhibits redemptive possibilities. Sellon's greed is the intangible basilisk that bars him from Eden's primal innocence and love. With Violet and the diamond Eye, he sails forth to enact the drama of great wealth in foreign parts, never to be seen again. When, earlier in the narrative, the band of local brigands attack the farmstead, the readers' sympathies were all with the Anglo-African settlers. They were the intended victims of criminal despoliation; the defeat of the vicious bandits is a victory for order and tranquility in the kingdom. The storyline reason for this episode is to demonstrate Marian's courage in defense of her family in contrast to Violet's conventional womanly hysteria. But there is also an unintended implication. How different from the intentions of the bandits are the actions of Renshaw and Maurice in plundering the native stone? As they pocket the diamond, Sellon jokes: "I wonder what the '*schelm*' Bushmen will think when they find that their 'devil's eye' has knocked off shining?" (244). Why are these Bushmen *schelm*, i.e. sneaky, devilish rogues? Because they defend their Eye from profanation, whether it be god or devil? Interestingly, the leader of the attack on the farm, who is given his quietus by Marian, is the villainous evil-eyed Muntiwa: "The empty eye-socket and the brutal pock-marked features seemed distorted in a fiend-like leer beneath the moonlight" (129-30). The moon links Muntiwa to Renshaw, but particularly Sellon, who has taken full possession of the moon-reflecting Eye. The act of carrying off the moon-lit Eye, recalling Milton's fallen angle Isis (*Paradise Lost* 1:478) or H. Rider Haggard's Isis-like Ayshea, is a profanation of the moon-goddess. Proclus reports this inscription on a statue of Isis: "I am that which is, has been, and shall be. My veil no one has lifted. The fruit I bore was the Sun" (Blavatsky 1).[25] Hence to lift the veil of Isis is to encounter one's subconscious self, in this case the dark manifestation of

---

25. See also Plutarch, "Osiris and Isis" (Ch. 9) in *Moralia*, Vol 5 (Loeb Classical Library). Trans. Frank Cole Babbett (Cambridge, MA: Harvard UP, 1936); see also Proclus's commentary on the *Timaeus* of Plato.

Renshaw's double, Sellon's greed. Nevertheless, Renshaw's apocalyptic double, who had seemed to interrupt and impede his quest for wealth and love, concludes, once he disappears with the devilish Eye, by imbuing our eponymous hero with the rays of the sun's life-force at *Sunning*dale.

Mitford does not believe that the "way of the transgressors" is always "hard" (307); in the last report of them, Maurice Sellon and Violet are "flourishing like the green bay tree" (307). This arboreal image is from Psalms 37:29, 35-36: "The righteous shall inherit the land, and dwell therein for ever.... I have seen the wicked in great power, and spreading himself like a green bay tree. Yet he passed away, and, lo, he was not: yea, I sought him, but he could not be found." Maurice and Violet's transgressions are less positive evils than mortal weaknesses of character: his being the same love of money for which Judas sold his Master; hers, selfishly to flaunt social and sacramental restraints–but she does warn Renshaw, whom she genuinely respects, that "there are reasons" (3) she cannot love him. The Latin title for the final chapter, "*Eheu!*" (Alas!), invokes Horace's poem, "Eheu fugaces," which targets Sellon's years ahead: what will come to pass, asks Horace, when the fleeting years and death take your land, your house, your lovely bride? Renshaw had read into Violet qualities better than those she actually possessed, confusing lively beauty with moral worth, and well-nigh paid for his fault with a disastrous misalliance. The "feline" (143) Violet had been described in the same terms as the leopard that almost kills Fanning at the end of the story (272); and the leopard has "scintillating eyes ... glittering like green stars" (27-72), similar to the diamond in its "incandescence" and "green scintillations" like a "flashing star" (230, 235).

Could it be symbolic that Renshaw spends a good deal of the novel sick, in need of healing? As he lies dying, he supposes, on a ledge after the Bushman attack with poisoned arrows, his thoughts turn to the irrelevance of the diamonds: "The treasure–the precious stones which he had thrown into the balance against his own life– what did they count now? . . . Mere dross" (270). This is a moral strikingly similar to that voiced by Allan Quatermain in Haggard's

King Solomon's Mines as the adventurers lies trapped in the "absolute silence" of King Solomon's treasure chambers: "Truly wealth, which men spend all their lives in acquiring, is a valueless thing at the last" (287). The material comforts of a spiritually arid society are themselves the real trap; Renshaw Fanning's ledge or Allan Quatermain's cave are merely the "objective correlatives" of the desire for wealth that appears to have destroyed them. In so much of Mitford's or Haggard's writing, the need for the hero is to break free of contemporary society's stifling obsession with artificial economic definitions of the self. They seek somehow to bring their lives into contact with the light and fertile landscapes or the dark and passionate myths of Africa's body.

When Mitford's readers responded uncritically to this tale of European conquest in Bushmanland, he may have felt his contempt for violent imperialism vindicated. Haggard often toyed with his readers in this fashion. Although the seeming-fantastic elements in *She* are ostensibly grounded in documentary evidence, a close reading finds such documentation ironic, i.e., itself a strategic part of the fantasy, ironizing the illuson of factuality through narrative inconsistencies. Likewise in Mitford's *Renshaw Fanning*, the religious imagery and locutions about the land's "riches lying waste for ages"strongly suggest an ironic attack on imperial racism–yet irony can be elusive, and one is never wholly certain when unmasking such byzantine strategies. At a bare minimum, one might observe that the twenty-first century's privileged perceptual sophistication predictably faults the imperial romance for not being *au courant* by today's standards, viewing this work from the catbird seat of post-colonial criticism. Yet a sympathetic leap of the historical imagination is necessary to understand the cultural environment of that time, to hark back to the world of late nineteenth- or early twentieth-century observers, to realize how they understood the romanticism of life on the frontiers. At the end Renshaw realizes what a fool he has been about women and wealth; indeed, Marian's "golden hair" (97) equates the two. Only the Eden of Sunningdale, to which Renshaw ultimately returns, offers spiritual tenure of the land and–by his allusion to "some day, when the quiver is full" (307,

Psalm 127:5)–of procreative love. Although it is an *imperial* utopia–husband and wife, masters and servants in unequal balance with each other and the land–yet this imperial harmony contains within it the seeds of a less-flawed society once its internal logic of interwoven relationships is complete. Perhaps this claims too much for Mitford's forward-leaning stance; but after a period of critical discussion and re-evaluation, he should re-emerge for a twenty-first century readership as an Anglo-African writer who, by narrating with irony and taut suspense the details of colonial interactions, broadens and enriches our sense of the nineteenth-century's all-too-human quest for survival and love in that portion of the globe.

Part IV

COLONIAL BLOODSHED

CHAPTER 7
RENEGADES AND REBELS

With Victorian social codes attaining to epidemic proportions, a disconnect between the overt stance and covert feelings of the empire writers must have become an inevitability. Part IV, Colonial Bloodshed, considers how in numerous ways the empire writers were in advance of popular opinion. Their cultural relativism and theological dubiety led them toward a broad sympathy with figures who resist the values enshrined in the dominant, socially constructed ideals and practices of imperial culture. Thus the character of the renegade allows his author to mount a counter-cultural challenge without the author himself being tainted by association with turncoat actions or views. Mitford will often put a criticism of British policy into the mouth of Boers or Zulus. In *The White Shield* (1895) or *Aletta* (1900) when the Zulu Untúswa or the Afrikaner character Botma declare that the British are rapacious, Mitford either reveals an unconscious distress and uncertainty counterbalanced by invoking the glories of imperial power or a very conscious sympathy for the underdog that would be unpatriotic if openly acknowledged–the latter most likely, given his handful of comments in *propre persona*.

One strong and direct anti-British statement occurs in Mitford's *Expiation of Wynne Palliser* (1896) in which a peaceful kraal at sunset with "contented and pastoral people" is depicted:

> Small wonder if even up to the present day the Zulu has not yet mastered the logic of the benevolence which moved that humane and Christian power, Great Britain, to invade his country and exile his hereditary rulers–to yield up half of that fair land to filibustering nomads [the Boers, who employed private military force in a country not their own], in their way certainly not less barbarous than himself–to force him to pay hut-tax for the support of English officials and missionaries, and practically to send his young men to be inoculated with drink and disease and ruffianism at Kimberly and Johannesburg and elsewhere. (209)

Wynne's disloyalty to his group, his incitement of the blacks to attack, echoes the revenge strategy of Lorraine in *The Gun-Runner* (1893) who is, perhaps, the most notorious of Mitford's renegades. Harriet Ward's *Jasper Lyle* (1851) is probably the eponymous prototype of Mitford's English figures of resistance. Like Lyle, Lorraine is wanted by British justice; both hide on the edge of the frontier under aliases; both run guns to the Africans–Xhosas or Zulus. Jasper Lyle, as a white agitator in Kaffirland, had a history in England of Chartist agitation, stirring up discontent (296; 342; 391) and does the same in Kaffirland. His complaint is that the law crushed him with its iron heel (295) and he dies in a kind of crucifixion (416). If Jasper were not a wife beater, he could well be an anti-hero of contemporary fiction. Lorraine is the furtive figure who is also cited in *The Curse of Clement Waynflete* (1894) and *The Expiation of Wynne Palliser* (1896) as well as the mysterious god-like puppeteer in *John Ames* (1900), and he evidently is also the *agent provocateur* of *In the Whirl of the Rising* (1904) and *Forging the Blades* (1908).These novels dealing with historical and political conflict are among the best Anglo-African romances of imperial conflict.

As Allan Quatermain was for H. Rider Haggard, so the patrician and perplexing Lorraine, first introduced in *The Gun-Runner* (1893),[26] is for Mitford, but a darker, a much, *much* darker figure than either Quatermain or even Mitford himself, who was, he joked, a "general reprobate."[27] Haggard's Quatermain, as a blunt, unpolished hunter and trader of ivory was intended to undercut or at least critique the imperial agenda of foreign rule and African dispossession. Haggard's alter ego, a "gentleman" not unlike Rider himself, subjects British assumptions, practices, and jingoistic persiflage to a practical

---

26. The *Dictionary of South African Biography* (1968-87) attributes *The Gun-Runner* to 1882. Although a frequently cited date of publication elsewhere also, neither Sidney Mendelssohn's *South African Bibliography* (1910) nor its updated edition (1925) list an 1882 edition; nor has one been found in any library. The 1882 publication is probably a ghost edition.

27. Inscribed on the front flyleaf of a presentation copy of the American edition of *Sign of the Spider*.

common sense and African experience largely free of politically self-serving myths. Bertram Mitford, whose elevated social pedigree included peers of the realm, created a similar alter ego across a range of his texts.

§

The Gun-Runner (1893), set during the outbreak of the Zulu War (1878-1879), depicts African resistance to a British invasion implementing the colonial policy of confederating the crown colonies, Boer republics, and African tribal states. In particular, Zululand, which refused to accept British dominion, was an untapped arena of potential workers for the mining industry. Lorraine, who has been the victim of an inflexible legal system, has fled England to become a trader and gunrunner to the Zulus. That this novel was written in the same year that Cecil Rhodes and the British South African Company were prosecuting war against King Lobengúla and the Ndebele people is no coincidence. In each invasion a national culture is annihilated by imperial expansion. Mitford's protagonist, Lorraine, operates a trading station with a partner on the Natal-Zulu border. Lorraine's sympathies lie with the Zulus and he considers the British ideal of race solidarity "sickly sentimentality" (21). Lynette Causand is a beautiful twenty-nine years old visitor from England staying nearby on the Natal border at the kraal of the Reverend Mr. Jeremiah Gibbs, a psalm-quoting imperialist. Although, as we learn belatedly, Lorraine has left a wife back in England, he loves Lynette wildly and she reciprocates with a virginal passion, cautious about their assignations.

Using a plot more complex than is usual with him, Mitford introduces Brooke Mounteney as a recently commissioned British officer looking for some "fun" "nigger-shooting" (42). Brooke has eyes for Lynette but fails to recognize his elder half-brother in the guise of Lorraine. From motives of jealousy and greed, Brooke in the past had framed Lorraine on a legal technicality. The citizens endorse this judgment of Lorraine because they fail to recognize the truth and discount his history, rights, and emotional responses; they empathize with and support the half-brother and the legal system. Thus, "injured past all forgiveness" (130), Lorraine jumped bail to begin a "clouded and shipwrecked life" (69) of wandering in Africa. The novel's basic analogy is that Lorraine's hatred of his half-brother Brooke is akin to the hatred between black and white–both reflect a history of injustice or struggle for dominance. If this pattern of outrage begetting outrage is not healed, the discord will become entrenched.

Lorraine's impediment of a previous marriage is a common one among Mitford protagonists: *The Weird of Deadly Hollow*, *Wynne Palliser*, *Sign of the Spider*, even Maurice Sellon in *Renshaw Fanning*, all have men trapped by a misalliance. If Charles Dickens rescued David Copperfield from his disastrous choice of Dora by contriving her death, Mitford's characters must carry this blighting incubus into their new African lives. The moral problem in a Mitford novel, for one who imperfectly knows himself and futilely tries to diagnose the poison in his soul, is how to set aside the pride or anger that blocks the deeper, truer power of love's redemption: "to melt the soured hardness of an atrophied life" (*Heath Hover* 246). And yet, can there be redemption without transgression?

When hostilities with the Zulus begin, Lorraine promises a bounty to his Zulu friends if they bring him Brooke's head. In a macabre twist, Lorraine is brought the wrong officer's blood-smeared head. But when Brooke turns up helpless and wounded after battle, love for Lynette tempers Lorraine's mortal hatred for his inveterately treacherous half-brother; he restrains his hatred and aids him. But slowly, Lorraine's past history and present gun-running begin to close in upon him, owing especially to Brooke's efforts, having discovered who he is. Lorraine flees into Zululand and Lynette, seeking her beloved, stumbles into the hands of the Zulus who have also captured Brooke. Owing to Lorraine's status with them, Lynette is reunited with him; and for a brief period, until she dies of a fever as the direct result of Brooke's villainous treachery, they are supremely happy. Brooke then is turned over to Lorraine for whatever punishment he intends:

> From the great bole of the tree, about three yards above the ground, there grew a ragged projection. By the gun-runner's order, the victim was hoisted up by thongs until his feet rested on this projection, and bound against the tree with his back to it is

> such wise that his arms, stretched out to their utmost tension, were made fast to the trunk overhead. He could move neither hand nor foot. He was, in fact, crucified. (344)

Lorraine, himself now contemplating suicide, would have allowed the crucified Brooke to suffer to death but for the merciful intercession of Lynette's disembodied voice–much as Stanninghame's life is saved by Lilith's phantom presence in *Sign of the Spider* (chapter eight).

Taken together as brothers (or half-brothers) the nominal guilt of Lorraine and the explicit jealousy, greed, and deceit in Brooke becomes a symbolic-allegorical representation open to several interpretations. The one brother is innocent or seemingly only legalistically guilty in Britain for perjury and in Natal for gunrunning; but the other, who had hid behind the ramparts of the law, appears guilty on a far deeper moral level. He becomes an ironic Christ, tortured and crucified, made to look out over the endless depths of an existential abyss:

> Is he in hell already? The broad, cold moon seems to float within a yard of his face, scorching it like a lamp. The tall tops of the trees are as spectral giant-hands, nodding down to clutch him. The mountain walls in front seem towering upward, only to fall upon him. Sky, earth, moonlit glade, seem to go round and round, and ever a crowd of grisly wild-beast shapes below is surging and leaping with ravening snarls and saliva-dropping jaws to rend out his vitals as he hangs there alive. (351)

This is the punishment of Christ or Prometheus; but the sufferer is not heroically innocent. He is at best like the "other" thief on the cross, the unbelieving one. Yet once again by the rule of relational opposites, Brooke's guilt intimates innocence, particularly since this is a fraternal relationship–one who is innocent and one guilty, but which one? Lorraine's vengeance, after all, is likely a disproportionate response. Vacillating between revenge and forgiveness, Lorraine is offered healing in Lynette's revitalizing love, a forgiveness that sets him free from hate and empowers him in turn to offer pardon and reconciliation to others. After Lorraine renounces his vengeance of the cross, Brooke retires to England emasculated, stunned, uncertain; for Lorraine in the ferocity of his lost love after Lynette's death, there remains only an abyss of hate and self-torture–much as Custance and Wildschut in *The Weird of Deadly Hollow* both seem ambiguously innocent and guilty.

Lorraine's is the tragedy of a man who *can't* forgive and embrace his lost love's merciful Christanity. When Lorraine is placed under sufficient pressure, by numerous people, for a considerable time, he switches positions and does the same to them as was done to him. His hatred begets more anger and revenge, putting others on the receiving end of his own experience. Lorraine wrecks his vengeance upon the British and their settler-supporters by inciting the tribes to throw off every trace of colonial rule. He becomes sociopathic, acting out what he was not allowed to talk out because when he challenges, questions, or threatens majority authority, the judicial process places him on the defensive, suggesting any moral lapse belongs entirely to the one who suggests the system is dysfunctional and challenges authority; thus the original victim can now be defined as a renegade since only he apprehends a truth or reality the others do not. But in Mitford's ensuing novels, Lorraine's murder and mayhem seem designed both to attack the myth of white power and privilege and also to celebrate the courage and steadfastness of the common settlers. This seemingly paradoxical set of goals is not irreconcilable. Mitford supports the ordinary settler as well as the Ndebele codes of culture. Insofar as Lorraine is an *agent provocateur*, his effectiveness among the Ndebele flows from imperial abuses originating in the deep-seated iniquities of the laws of "Grandmama" (as Rhodes termed the London home administration)–its policies, its legalities, its lies, its sinister self-interest.

§

After Lorraine fades from the scene of the Zulu War, he reappears again twice: seventeen years later in 1896-97 in Matebeleland in the wake of Cecil Rhodes's occupation of that territory and then once again in Zululand during the Bambatha rising of 1904-06 and thus serves to explain–albeit fictionally–the shocking historical tribal uprisings. Lorraine's monomania is not without justification, inasmuch as the humanitarian language of empire-building conflicted most egregiously with the greed of Rhodes's occupation of Matebeleland. Although Mitford in no way condoned the full range of Ndebele objectives in that 1896-97 Rising, inasmuch as he would not reverse the British presence in southern Africa, he nevertheless would accord the tribes a measure of autonomy–restoring their hereditary king under a capable and progressive British Resident; prohibiting any "crowd of missionaries" from trammeling their animistic religious beliefs; and giving them an opportunity to flourish economically:

> When Civilisation first comes into contact with the savage, it is nearly always in one of two capacities–that of invader or that of beggar–more commonly the latter. And the object of such mendicancy is the cession of land.
>
> Whatever may hold good elsewhere, it is my firm conviction that, as regards South Africa, all such "cessions" existing or asserted to exist, must be absolutely rotten or fraudulent, or both; and this for the simple reason that no South African potentate dare–except under the direst pressure of circumstances, *i.e.*, Force–grant away the lands of his forefathers and of the nation or tribe at present beneath his rule. Be he chief or king his patriarchal or sovereign rights stop short there. . . . Even the elaborate lawyerese in which the deed of mining concession is drawn can, by no sort of twisting and turning, be brought to mean anything approaching a *land* concession. But the peaceable diggers come as an army, with a perfect arsenal of machine guns; forts are built, and, in a trice, the King's subjects are ordered off the King's own territory–by those who had but yesterday approached him in the guise of very subservient beggars. Verily Lo Bengúla's mind must, oft and grimly of late, have reverted to the historic "word" of his Zulu brother potentate–"*Bulalani abatagati!*" (Kill the evil-doers) which was the signal for the slaughter of Retief and his comrades. ("Side-Lights" 96-97)

In the ensuing murder and mayhem of the '96 rising that *John Ames, Native Commissioner* (1900) depicted, it was Mitford's intention both to lash out at what the government back in England did to its citizens and to attack the myth of white supremacy imported into Africa.

Cecil Rhodes and the British South African Company, also known as the Chartered Company, a commercial mining-investment consortium, contemplated total conquest of the Ndebele. After the so-called Pioneer Column in 1890–consisting of military troops, police, and black mercenaries–successfully occupied with minimal violence the area neighboring the Ndebeles, tensions on the frontier increased. King Lobengúla's peace emissaries were shot, according to Mitford, on the pretext of a misunderstanding ("Side-Lights" 99). Then in1893 Rhodes moved to gain control of the Ndebele kingdom; and although the British forcefully occupied the capital of Bulawayo, few of the Ndebele who fled north were disarmed. Lobengúla, driven into exile in 1893, died of illness early in 1894 leaving several sons but no chosen successor. The British tried to abolish the Ndebele monarchy by shipping away to England to be educated all the sons they could locate. Matabeleland came under the control of Rhodes's British South African company which appointed and paid "residents" to oversee the local chiefs–in effect, a company country. But in 1896 and 1897 the local population rose in rebellion against the settlers and the policies and police of Rhodes's Company. They wanted a restoration of the monarchy and relief from cattle levies, forced labor conscription, and police bullying–even revenge for the destructive locust swarms and rinderpest slaughter of cattle, also believed the fault of the British. The shooting of Africans' cattle to avoid the spread of deadly rinderpest caused famine, prompted the uprising (because sterile barrier precautions were misunderstood), and, possibly, promoted quicker annexation of the land by the colonists.

Among the half dozen of Mitford's novels that included Lorraine is *John Ames*, described on its title-page as "a romance of the Matabele rising." Lorraine impersonates the Voice of the "Umlimo," god of the Matabele (or Ndebele). As such, this antagonist instigates the 1896 attacks upon his countrymen for his own purposes of revenging his wife's death, a crime that goes far beyond his original gunrunning in support of the Zulus. This motif of the white man worshiped by natives, like Joseph Conrad's Kurtz, was devised by Mitford in the same year as the serial publication of "Heart of Darkness" (1899) though Mitford's novel appeared in 1900. The cult of the Umlimo originated with an oracular deity, Mwari, of the Shonas, who was approached through the intercession of ancestral tribal spirits. This god's shrine, initially at Great Zimbabwe, was relocated to diverse locations even before the Ndebele invasion of the 1830s, most importantly to a cave in the Matopo hills near Bulawayo. The Ndebele rechristened this tribal deity of fertility–both of crops and women–and extended his influence. Himself invisible, Umlimo spoke through his chosen Voice from inside his sacred cave. In many ways this duplicated a native custom of the chief's mouthpiece. In Haggard's "A Visit to the Chief Secocœni"(1877) the British are introduced, the chief then "squatted down among the head men. Secocœni took no active part in the proceedings that followed; he sat in his enclosure and occasionally shouted out some instruction to Makurupiji, who was literally his "mouth," speaking for him and making use of the pronoun "I" (*Cetywayo* 273).

In addition to supplications for rain, the priests and messengers of the Voice of Umlimo played a political role as well. Since the Umlimo traditionally had advised on weighty tribal questions, it was therefore a small step for the god to proclaim in 1896: "These white men are your enemies. They killed your fathers, sent the locusts, caused this disease among the cattle [i.e., rinderpest] and bewitched the clouds so that we have no rain. Now you will go and kill these white people and drive them out of our father's land and I will take away the cattle disease and the locusts and send you rain" (Fleming 35). The British underrated the role of Umlimo's cult in centralizing information and militarily coordinating the Shona and Ndebele chieftains (Daneel 30, 34). Their complacency was bred from ignorance of African politics, of the growing nationalism beneath a complacent racist authoritarian society (Chennells179-80). Ames called the Umlimo a "sinister abstraction" or "the Great Abstraction" because he did not believe any deity or person was behind the unrest– a significant misconception.

Mitford admired the Ndebele's cultural system, yet he also celebrated the group of simple European settlers, faced with the enormity of their fate, who could marshal themselves to defeat the *impis* of the Ndebele. The dissonant element for Mitford was the English home government's vacillating policies and hypocritical openness to manipulation by the sinister self-interest of powerful colonial cartels, the vultures that promote strife between English, Dutch, and Africans. Natural gentry, both settler and indigene, are betrayed by these get rich quick climbers, unscrupulous types who promoted expansion solely by force and fraud, "meddlesome self-seeking interlopers" (Selous 247).Whereas Olive Schreiner belatedly considered Cecil Rhodes among the most egregious of offenders, Miford, together with such scouts as F. C. Selous and J. W. Colenbrander, offered either tacit or active support for his expansionistic activities (Selous 7). Selous prefered the Chartered Company, not the Crown, because of its "sympathy" with the settlers; and thus in Mitford's fiction the finely sympathetic Ames is employed by them. Unlike lower class whites, Mitford considered the colonial upper class as not racist. Selous admits the Ndebele are governed for British interests rather than in their own interests (xiv) but he insists that they have been freed from "a most oppressive and tyrannical form of government" that has been replaced by "an orderly rule, under which every man's life and property is protected and witch-doctors are not recognised." Unfortunately, says Selous, the savage "would rather put up with all the ills from which we consider we have freed him, than be subject to the restraints of a settled form of Government" (xiv-xvi; also *Ames* 19, 113).

In his eighth chapter, ending with his "reflections on the Matabele rising," Selous restates both the pro- and anti-settler arguments with an almost prescient perspicacity for the terms of this controversy as it unfolded over the next century (65-67). His special target in *Sunshine and Storm* had been the polemical editor of the journal *Truth*, Henry Labouchère, who denounced the men of the Chartered Company as desperadoes and buccaneers. A denunciation not without reason when Selous elsewhere, perhaps because of excessively pragmatic morality, unwittingly falls into near-Swiftean absurdity describing the constructive contributions of the Boers:

> After all, as the Boers hold as large a stake in land, if not in wealth, as the British in South Africa, and as they were the first comers, and can lay claim to having killed off as many natives, and generally prepared as much country for occupation by white men, as the British, I think they are entitled to some consideration in the matter of the flag which is eventually to fly over the confederated States of South Africa. (248)

But when Olive Schreiner published *Trooper Peter Halket of Mashonaland* (1897) with a shocking frontispiece of three Matebeles apparently lynched on a tree (April 1897), her image in conjunction with her narrative suggested their innocent victimization. But to give the devil his due, an account by Selous substantially changes the import and assigns the Matebeles unequivocal guilt in the insurrection: they were "caught red-handed, looting and burning property... with assegais in their hands" (Selous 136-37). There had been a trial, Colenbrander and others testifying. Selous inquires, in the words of Molière, "What the hell were they doing in that place?"– and only rebellion could provide an answer.

Mitford's implicit stance in *Ames* contrasts the old and new Ndebele: Chief Madula (his noble customs, the habit of command) contrasted with the swagger of lower class converts to civilization, such as Inglefield's men recruited from the Holi (*Ames* 15). With the king dead and the Company in charge, the Zulu upper class is seduced by the Umlimo because it had lost its authority (20). The aristocratic Zulus loathed the Umlino hierarchy, but were willing to use it to expel the whites. In Mitford's novel, the proximate villain is the evil sorcerer Shiminya, a priest of the Umlimo from the Amaholi "slave" class. Ames and Ndebele aristocrats recognized the decadence of the younger generation who had intermarried with the Holi slave caste and were influenced by the Kalanga priests; and Mitford believed this despised class did the murdering of citizens, whereas the upper class did the fighting with the colonial troops. But the official report of the Company recognized the Rising had been led by the aristocrats– "Zansi," those from the "south."

But whereas most (or all) writers of colonial fiction presented a rebellious leader such as Lorraine as indigenous, Mitford's renegade is a British subject who finds African culture more actuating than European. Because the god Umlimo manifests himself through the Voice of the priest, Lorraine is obeyed as the revelation of the will of the divinity. This lays the blame for the rising on a revengeful white man–apart from such other reasons as colonial taxes, rinderpest that killed the tribes' cattle, and resentment by the *indunas* of Rhodes's usurpation of Lobengúla's power. Mitford does not, however, conform to that simplistic imperialism which would fail to examine this list of other political motivations. Still, if Lorraine exploited the religion of the Ndebele for private revenge, then when they rise at his instigation it is emphatically not the peaceful settlers who caused them to rebel. The whites can only defend themselves with counter-force. Further, if the bestial Kalanga priests led by this ostensibly crazy white man are responsible, then the Ndebele uppers, who were driven by rational political motives to ensure their national survival, can be exonerated of the worst excesses. Orchestrated by a white man for private purposes of revenge, the revolt was not what the Ndebele truly wanted but obvious imperial errors of judgment opened them to Lorraine's militant agenda. Mitford probably means us to suspect Lorraine is perfectly sane, only reacting to imperial *bêtise,* in particular his own criminalization back in England and the colonists' inability fundamentally to sympathize with the Ndebele.

At the last minute Mitford retitled his novel *John Ames,* crossing out on the contract negotiated by his literary agent A.P. Watt & Son the possibly puzzling original title, *The Umlimo.* The change certainly refocused the narrative's emphasis away from the white instigator of insurrection and toward the settlers and their crisis. Mitford's story began in Cape Town with Ames on convalescent leave from his Matabeleland position administering the colonial system. Ames, like Olive Schreiner's Trooper Peter, is an employee of Rhodes's Chartered Company; his duties are described as "multifarious, if ill-defined. They involved the collection of hut tax; the keeping of a vigilant eye upon the people at large; the carrying out of the disarmament programme; the settlement of all local disputes that were potient of settlement; and of about half a hundred other questions that might arise from day to day" (9-10). At Cape Town,

Ames is attracted to Nidia Commerell who intends to visit family, coincidentally in Ames's magistracy. The building local unrest grows in tandem, step by step, with the romantic attachment between these two. Nidia, along with Ames, is caught in the Rising. Mitford's heroines express a feminist will and rise above stereotyped beauties as portrayed by Violet in *Renshaw Fanning's Quest*. Nidia's face "had a way of lighting up–a sudden lifting of the eyelashes, the breaking into a half smile, revealing a row of teeth beautifully even and white. She had blue eyes, and her hair, which was neither brown nor golden, but something between, curled in soft natural waves along the brow" (42)–and so on for many more words. On the issue of Victorian standards, one thinks of the reply of Ames to his sub-inspector in charge of the Matabele Police:

> "I say, old chap, why don't you chip in for some of old Madúla's daughters–marry 'em, don't you know? He has some spanking fine ones, anyway."...
> "Because I hope to make a better thing of life, Inglefield. But that sort of thing is rather apt to stick to a man, and crop up just when least convenient. I'm no prig or puritan, so putting it on that ground alone, it's better not touched." (87)

As a liberal and "no prig," John Ames nevertheless recognizes the social practicalities that orchestrate behavior. But Mrs. Bateman's all-but-lesbian jealousy of John's growing closeness to Nidia surely would have been more candidly expressed in Haggard.

Mitford draws on descriptions of the massacred Cunningham family by F. C. Selous or Tyrie Lang to put together his own rendering. Selous describes the scene at the Cunningham farm near the Insiza river: "These poor people seem to have been attacked early in the afternoon, ... the remains of the mid-day meal were still on the table, whilst old Mr. Cunningham seemed to have been murdered whilst reclining on a couch reading a newpaper." Selous then quotes from the sworn deposition of the assistant native commissioner for the district:

> On arrival there I saw eight dead bodies lying on the ground about twenty yards from the homestead ... murdered by means

> of knob-kerries and battle-axes. . . . I identified among the dead bodies those of Mr. Cunningham senior, Mrs. Cunningham, two Miss Cunninghams, Master Cunningham, and three children whom I identified as the grandchildren of Mr. Cunningham senior. The deceased persons appeared to have been killed inside the house and afterwards dragged out and thrown outside in the position in which we found them. . . . Young Cunningham, aged about fourteen years, was still alive when we arrived, but unconscious, and died immediately after our arrival. (35-36)

Mitford changes the family name to Hollingworth and redistributes the bodies, but little else. The family is portrayed as archetypally pastoral in the tradition of Theocritus, Virgil, the Bible, right down to nineteenth-century pastoral elegies. But this story of loss leaps from these tropes of literary tradition into the stark documentary horror of violent death. On her visit to Hollingworths, Nidia returns from a pleasant walk to encounter:

> On the couch beneath the window aforesaid lay the form of Hollingworth–the form, for little else about the wretched man was distinguishable but his clothing. His skull had been battered in, and his features smashed to a pulp. . . . In one corner lay the corpse of his wife–and, in a row, four children, all with their skulls smashed, and nailed to the ground with assegais. (125)

Take a beautiful girl, put her in a world of "hideous butchery," and if she doesn't faint (or even if she does) she will improve characterologically. Suddenly, not only her circumstances but for the reader she herself becomes much more absorbing.

Ames escapes with the help of his servant-factotum, that figure often found in imperial romances, like Dirk in *Renshaw Fanning*. The problem of Pekule's loyalty to his *baas* raises the question whether he is a sentimental dupe. What sort of resistance does he make to colonial injustice? Does Pukele pander against the deepest interests of his tribal roots? Do submissive Africans serve racist and patriarchal ends? And should the Africans continue to suffer under greatly prolonged injustice without defending themselves? The likelihood here is that he was in the employ of the Umlimo from the beginning, watching and protecting Ames and

Nidia. Pukele becomes a martyr, shot for being bravely loyal to what Mitford, Ames and the Umlimo, not necessarily the Company or colonists, represented: "'Accidents will happen.' Such is the epitaph on the faithful, loyal savage, who having watched over the helpless refugee for days and nights that he might restore her to friends and safety, had found his reward" (237). This indignation echoes Mitford's description of the British shooting Dingane's emissaries, both in the "Side-Lights" essay and in *Induna's Wife* when the Boers shot Tambusa, the peace-messenger ("Side-Lights," 99; *Induna's Wife* 255). Ultimately, despite Nidia's offered reward and Umlino's hidden agenda, Pukele's assistance to Ames and Nidia was a choice made on the basis neither of self-interest nor compulsion but a freely given cooperation in the light of Ames's sympathy with tribal society. Perhaps Mitford is saying the stock figures of loyalty–those that the settlers would appreciate and endorse–are not automatically passive enablers, unwilling to speak for the victims of colonial inequalities.

Mitford shared a nostalgia with the Zulus for independent African authority and understood how much the Rebellion needed the imagery of historic Zulu kingship. But with Dinuzulu refusing to choose sides, only the god of the Ndebele, the Umlimo, could take the king's place. Mitford not only puts Ames and Nidia into Lorraine's hands, but causes Ames under emotional and physical stress to reveal signs of sympathy and loyalty to his captor. This may be less the product of a psychological survival strategy than a recognition of some resemblance to Lorraine within himself. Ames, fearing himself thwarted in love, feels sympathy as if he, like Lorraine, were also the "wild man" portrayed in Genesis 16:12: "his hand will be against every man, and every man's hand against him." Lorraine's sin is his hand "against every man" and his punishment is not only the ostricism of "every man's hand against him" but the wrath of God. In European folk tales the wild man of Genesis 16:12 is doomed to exile in wildernesses beyond the bounds of divine grace–of the earth, earthy, stigmatized, red-handed, accursed. The image of the wild man has always raised fear of the sinister unknown infecting life and inspired a desire to return to the primordial paradise before mankind fell from innocence into history. The escaped couple in the "uninhabited fastnesses of the Matopo" mountains (190) compares favorably with the graphic local color in such non-fictional works as those of Livingstone or Selous. Mitford's sharp sense of the complex social etiquette of courtship, so bizarre to contemporary experience–the hesitant use of given names, an obsessive sense of social respectability, emotional reticence, hyper-awareness of modesty in dress and gesture–all have an antiquarian appeal. Mitford's literary strengths in genre painting–the Cape resorts, the frontier homestead and trading post, a sorcerer's cave–and in his narration of military engagements are on preeminent view in *John Ames*. But if the wild man embodies this alien, uncanny existence of nature untamed, his relational counterpart is the noble savage or child of nature who bodys forth new beginnings at the world's mythical heart, a sacred zone where the divine erupts into human history. There the pilgrim finds his vision in the sacred womb of mother earth. A part of this ideal center is Umlimo's cave in the Matopos. Ames as initiate enters this sacred womb of the earth, a doctoring that is a stipulation to his rebirth.

Ames resigns his post because he unavoidably has pledged his word not to expose Lorraine as the rebel's leader, who would be seen merely as a lunatic white man impersonating a god and out to revenge himself on the colonial system as now embodied in the Chartered Company and its injustices. Early in the narrative Nidia addresses Ames:

> "I don't wonder you pioneers are proud of the part you took in extending the Empire. Isn't that the correct newspaper phrase? At any rate, it sounds something big."
>
> John Ames smiled queerly. He was not especially proud of the extension of the Empire; he had seen a few things incidental to that process which had killed within him any such incipient inflation.
>
> "Oh yes; there's a good deal of sound about most of the doings of 'the Empire,' but there–I must not get cynical on that hand, because the said extension is finding me in bread and cheese just now, and I must endeavour to be 'proud of' that."
> (57-58)

His curiously passive way of protesting the "extension of Empire" is by smiling "queerly" and choosing withdrawal. What "few things" Ames saw we never discover; but his queer smile is false, eccentric, fake. At the end, Ames is enriched by a windfall from this lunatic Ndebele *führer* and is married into the wealthy family of Nida. In short, he has become an unemployed squire back in England.

In the last chapter he savors "the outlook from the library window of the beautiful and sumptuous home," enjoying with Nidia the "golden August, with the whirr of the reaping-machine, as the yellow wheat falls to the harvest, blending with the cooing of wood-pigeons among the leafy shades of the park" (308). This image of the reaping-machine and the falling wheat has an imagistic resonance in the take-over by Rhodes of the Ndebele. Of the cruel treatment of neighboring tribes by the Ndebele, Sir Sidney Shippard confessed he would like to see the Ndebele "cut down by our rifles and machine guns like a cornfield by a reaping machine" (Pakenham 385). Olive Schreiner not long afterwards described Trooper Peter Halket's memories of the Chartered Company's brutality as he stares into his camp fire:

> Then–he saw the skull of an old Mashona blown off at the top, the hands still moving. He heard the loud cry of the native woman and children as they turned the maxims on to the kraal; and then he heard the dynamite explode that blew up a cave. Then again he was working a maxim gun, but it seemed to him it was more like the reaping machine he used to work in England, and that what was going down before it was not yellow corn, but black men's heads; and he thought when he looked back they lay behind him in rows, like the corn in sheaves. (Schreiner, *Trooper Peter* 39-40)

The stuttering of Schreiner's maxims haunts our readerly sense of an ending in Ames's so ostensibly unironic scene of "happily-ever-after." But Mitford's, Schreiner's, and similar imperial narratives assume in historical hindsight ironic dimension: the world they envisioned, a great Anglo-Saxon empire in Africa, is a very different one from that which actually emerged and which continues to define itself today in the land of Cecil Rhodes's nineteenth-century British *imperium*.

§

John Buchan's *Prester John* (1910) is set at the time of the uprising in 1896-97 approximately in the territory historically in dispute between the Ndebele and the Transvaal colonists. The novel's ideology reflects the discourse of the British empire in the decade of South African unification–the fear of black conspiracy, rebellion, and disorder threatening the tenuously imposed order of white Africa. Its plot features an American Episcopalian, John Laputa, who becomes a charismatic "Ethiopian" preacher supporting "Africa for the Africans" (131). As early as Marco Polo, who described Ethiopia as a strong Christian nation, Europeans had recounted the legend of a mythical priest-king Prester (or Father) John who had gone to Ethiopia to convert the Africans, accumulated a fortune there, and crowned himself Emperor. By the nineteenth century the missionary effort had extended beyond the colonial frontier, and ordained converts led indigenous services more African than English. In *The White Hand and the Black* (1907) Mitford introduced the "Ethiopian" black Christian preacher Magwagwa. Tension with and challenge to dominant colonial views are portrayed in Magwagwa, who is both despised as a "rogue" and praised for saving whites. His separatist "patriotic" movement which spurned white authority had discerned in Ethiopia an uncolonized yet historically Christian nation: "Ethiopia shall soon stretch out her hands unto God" (Psalms 68:31). Although many separatist churches in Rhodesia may have been largely apolitical, missionaries and administrators felt Ethiopian churches were agents of political subversion in the growing power of African nationalism. Now it was the turn of the British, after the Boers, to see themselves as Israelites given the task of mastering and transforming the God-given land of the heathens. Their divine mandate conflicted with the "Ethiopian Movement" of "Africa for the Africans" and a reclamation of old national pride. Laputa as Christian preacher presents himself as the reincarnated spirit of the fifteenth-century Abyssinian king, Prester John, validated by his ownership of the Queen of Sheba's collar of rubies and gold. Laputa also links his political authority to claims of legitimate magic in the miraculous power of Christianity, *viz. Acts* 19:13-20, not demonic connivance. Ancient but modern, Christian but pagan; civilized but savage; American in education but African in power; spiritual and political; idealized father-figure but dangerous to empire–all these seemingly antithetical roles combine to define a complicated state of mind in this renegade.

The background for Buchan's narrative is drawn initially from his Scottish Calvinism and afterwards from his service as private secretary to Lord Milner, High Commissioner for South Africa. David Crawfurd's father is a Scottish Presbyterian minister–an autobiographical echo of Buchan's father's vocation, to which is owing that wonderful and frequently cited aphorism from the novel, "Perfect love casteth out fear, the Bible says; but, to speak it reverently, so does perfect hate" (Buchan, *Prester John* 161; 1 John 4:18). Davy's father has died and he is sent by his uncle to be a storekeeper in the Northern Transvaal at the time of the uprising. Analogous to Mitford's Lorraine, Laputa is the single force behind this rebellion; also, like Lorraine, he presents himself as "the Great Great"–or the voice of God: "they believed him, that he was the Umkulunkulu, the incarnated spirit of Prester John" (134). Buchan masterfully builds the sense of suspense as the number of Africans in the bush, but not in the towns, increases. Their uncanny drumming destabilizes David's pacific world of an imperially prefigured destiny: "I have never heard an eerier sound. Neither natural nor human it seemed, but the voice of that world between which is hid from man's sight and hearing" (110). Between man and nature lie hidden daemonic "ancestral voices prophesying war!" ("Kubla Khan" 297).

David, by foiling Laputa's plot, is similar to Buchan's later character Richard Hannay in *The Thirty Nine Steps*, and is ultimately instrumental in the failure of the united black uprising. The defeat and death of this last African king becomes the final stage in the historical process of displacing the traditional government of tribal chiefs, depriving the African of his heritage and historical identity, and acquiring the dark continent for the colonizer. David's reward is the treasures accumulated for the rebellion, with which he endows a school to retrain the blacks in white citizenship as preparation for their commercial, industrial future. Probably this final disposition of affairs should not be taken as ironically antithetical to the outcome that Buchan endorses. And when David describes his newly found wealth as bought with men's blood, yet "like fairy gold out of the void" (370), one should connect "void" with the colonists' perceptual ethnocentricity. David's African servant-girl, Zeeta, becomes a metonymy for colonized Africa–but not in the form of that "barbarous and superb woman" who "stretched tragically her bare arms after us over the somber and glittering river" (Conrad, "Heart of Darkness," *Youth* 166). Withal, Davie's partner Aitken establishes "a great native training college. It was no factory for making missionaries and black teachers, but an institution for giving the Kaffirs the kind of training which fits them to be good citizens of the state" (373). In this image of a unitary Africa at peace, the white/black division of the contested landscape is healed–the imperial ideal of a wealth knit from the interwoven relationships of the Africans and British envisioned in his *A Lodge in the Wilderness*.

§

After the final battle of the Zulu War in 1879 at which the army of Cetywayo (or Cetshwayo) was crushed, Zululand was divided, with only the weakest central authority, into kinship groups or "septs" under different chiefs paired with British "residents." The "Bambatha Rebellion" in Zululand and Natal began in 1906. Following the war of 1879 and that initial Zulu resistance to British conquest, the ensuing injustices of colonialism–land dispossession, impoverishment, labor conscription, and a poll tax–prompted the 1906 Bambatha Rebellion. Historically a minor Natal chief, Bambatha, had appealed to the ailing, alcoholic Zulu king, Dinuzulu kaCetshwayo, for assistance. Although the fence-sitting king probably gave him little more encouragement than sympathetic words, Bambatha ambushed mounted police and a local magistrate of Greytown and then fled from Natal to Zululand. Mitford's *The White Hand and the Black* (1907) has an agenda subtly critical of imperial relations with the amaZulu. In that novel's culturally eclectic morality, the Zulu antagonist's power to blackmail is credible because a murder did occur, but this dark secret is ultimately nullified at the feast on Christmas. When white and black together drink a Euro-African champagne-*tywala* mix, friendship replaces hostility and absolution trumps accusation. But as lived values, neither friendship nor hostility, innocence nor guilt are entirely good or evil. To escape from judgmental preconceptions and to embrace life requires that one absolve the other of the guilt one attributes to him, affirming that oneself and the other are ontologically linked beyond the parochial values of good and evil. Whites and blacks bury their differences and escape the self-deceptive moral, political and religious preconceptions of dogmatic and absolutist views by accepting the abyss that swallows life and by affirming existence in spite of its guilt, despair, and temporal loss.

On the governmental level this also implies a relationship different from the *Weltpolitik* of "might makes right." It replaces imperial force as the definition of who the colonist is and wants to be with a softer power rooted in in the settlers' awareness of what the indigenous inhabitants think and expect of him. Heroism and treachery, innocence and guilt, lose their absolute standings and constitute a relativistic morality in which Mitford insists upon replacing the voice of the imperial script and the voice of violence from the rebellious locals to create a softer mouthpiece for political action. He wishes to supplant the settler mentality with a sensitivity to the African's perspective, theorizing an anti-ethnocentric paradigm beyond socially constructed values of innocence and guilt or power and submission. In the twentieth century, these visionary speculations became a center-piece of social change. In the place both of passively suffering subjugation or of armed aggression and militancy, the recognition that political power is grounded in cooperation and consent of the governed should become the basis of social change. Whether those who defend the *status quo* accept or reject such behavioral change, it has been an effective strategy of reform, past and present–from Lysistrata's scheme of collective abstinence until the Greeks forsook war to Mahatma Gandhi's principled and pragmatic resistance to the British Raj–and beyond.

Mitford's following novel about this rebellion is set in the remote fastnesses of northern Zululand during increasing tribal unrest. Its title, *Forging the Blades* (1908), is a metaphor of traditional arts lost to capitalism. Old Malemba is an assegai-maker:

> Such blades he turned out, such splendid blades, keen as razors, the fluting in perfect symmetry. . . . By and by Birmingham-forged blades were imported, surreptitiously, by the traders; but the assegai turned out by old Malemba and his son never fell in reputation. . . . For years Malemba's trade had been in abeyance, if not practically extinct. . . . Sapazani, the ultra-conservative, had no use for assegais fabricated across the seas. He know the balance and the temper of the home-made article to a nicety, especially that made by Malemba. (153-155)

Among his people, Sapazani discouraged European clothing and customs, preferring instead the traditional way of life. But old Malemba lectures the young warriors:

> I made blades for . . . Dingana, who scourged the Amabuna as a whip-lash scourges an ox, until he had to take flight when our nation was divided. But then the guns of the Amabuna shot but feebly and there was opportunity to run in and make an end. But now, when the white man's bullets fall thick as the stones in the fiercest hail-storm, what chance have ye with these?" pointing to a row of blades which awaited the binding. . . . "Well, I have naught to do with it, I who am old. I can but make you the weapons, it is for yourselves to wield them. And most of you have never learned the art. You were born too late." (156-57)

When one recalls the attempts of Mitford himself to collect historic and beautifully made assegais described in the prologues of his two first Ndebele-Zulu novels, these "blades" represent an authorial nostalgia for an old world of native weapons and the disappearing traditional life-ways owing to European industrial technology. In one demonstration in Haggard's *King Solomon's Mines*, of who belongs where in the power hierarchy, Quatermain fires on the flat side of an assegai blade at forty paces–"the bullet struck the flat of the spear, and broke the blade in fragments" (146). This definitive demonstration of the superiority of the white man's modern weapons over those traditional ones of the Africans seems almost too vivid not to have originated in an actual occurrence.

In the Natal-Zululand Rising depicted in *Forging the Blades*, Lorraine has taken the name Opondo ("horns"; in *The Gun-Runner* he had been Zimpala, "antelope") and befriends the story's protagonist, Alaric Denham, a British naturalist who escapes the blackmailer Golding by shooting him in self-defense and disposing of both him and his horse in the crocodile infested Income river. To his readers, Mitford justifies Alaric's action on natural moral grounds of self-protection, but in the eyes of the law he most likely would have been found guilty. Unbeknownst to Alaric, his killing has been observed by spies serving chief Sapazani who will use this knowledge in an even more sinister blackmail. As a hidden impresario outside social and moral limits, Lorraine has adopted tribal ways and can understand black consciousness; he assists Denham in reaching Ezulwini on condition that this assistance remains strictly anonymous. Also later Lorraine saves Alaric's life on several occasions, partly to honor the memory of his lost love of Lynette though Alaric's love of Verna, partly to send by him a mysterious package back to England. The British mentality was hostile to old-style Zulu life (76), but insofar as Mitford supported the maintenance of tribal customs, criticized forced Europeanizing of the Africans, and critiqued underlying injustices of colonial policy toward both the Africans and social dissidents, he sympathized with Lorraine while deploring his thirst for vengeance and violence. Because Lorraine, not Mitford, oversteps colonial limits, the author can placate the colonists by lauding their troopers and police while subverting self-righteous colonial rationalizations. Mitford ironically applies the phrase "the ruling race" (78, 182).

The scene next shifts to Ben Halse's daughter, Verna, kneading bread and visiting with the noble-looking Sapazani: "chatting, easily, merrily, even banteringly–that to any one unaware of the stern and rigid line of demarcation in such matters, between white and coloured, which has ever saturated public opinion throughout South Africa, it might have seemed that she was carrying on a sort of mild flirtation with this splendid savage" (33). Ben Halse, who runs guns and liquor to the locals, very much approves of Sapazani, only he will not supply guns to the Zulu if they are to be used against the settlers. The uprising is attributed to naively pacifist British "home" attitudes that encouraged the Africans to believe incorrectly that their massacre of the settlers if sufficiently sweeping would result in the total withdrawal of imperial forces. This is what James Bryce in his talk to the Anglo-African Club may have meant by the need to explain the colonial situation to the British in England.

When describing the old Africa of traditional weapons and strong chiefs free of imperial control, it is not difficult to assess Mitford's sympathies. Sapazani bitterly complains to Verna:

> "But what is a chief in these days? *I* am no chief. Every white man is chief now, if he is sent by Government–every white *boy*, rather. There are no chiefs left in the land of Zulu. Even those of our people who act as dogs to the courts of the white magistrates think they are chiefs over *us. Hau!*" And Verna had answered consolingly–"No one, in all the land of Zulu–white or not–could mistake Sapazani for anything but a chief" (41-42).

When later Sapazani refused to salute the local magistrate, Downes, Mitford provided his readers an echo of Bambatha's defiance of the magistrate at Greytown. The rising will be a 1906-style reclamation of old national pride–Africans the white man's dog no longer.

Denham, who back in England had been an avid purchaser from Ben Halse of museum specimens of African fauna, unexpectedly turns up at this juncture. Not long before this, Verna had shot a record-size bull koodoo, its horns a valuable trophy that Denham will buy. Given that Lorraine's native name, Opando, means "horns," and its primary reference is to the Zulu attack pattern of Shaka, perhaps the trophy horns of the dead koodoo imply that the military power both of Lorraine and that of the great Zulu kings is past. During his visit to Ben's trading station, Denham falls in love with Verna. She is like Africa's spirit–the rolling country covered with game or the Lumisana forest haunted with mysterious life.

Several times Verna fears she may be thought to be an Amazon (or perhaps a Diana, shooting the koodoo by moonlight?)–a female great white hunter. But that wilder era was already gone; permits now are needed to hunt. Her defiance of game laws–and that of Ben and Alaric–is a return to Africa's earlier era. Her native name is Izibu, water lily (32). Whether or not Mitford was thinking of the North American *Iris Verna* as the origin of her name, it clearly aligns her with nature: its Latin root *vernus*, meaning "springtime," or *verno*, "young in heart." A name especially popular in the late nineteenth-century, a thousand years earlier the Chinese poet Chou Tun-I called the water-lily "Lady Virtue," an emblem of purity and truth, rising stainless from its long-stemmed root in the fertile bed below, nesting freely on the clear waters–"something to be regarded reverently from a distance and not to be profaned by familiar approach"(Giles 219).

The most problematic figure in *Forging the Blades* is Sapazani. Alaric would resent Sapazani's erotic glances at Verna (241) if he believed the chief's looks were genuinely meant. Alaric might have been less complacent had he heard the talk among warriors of taking white "wives" at the Rising (159). Sapazani, who recognizes a native wildness in Izibu, who speaks fluent Zulu, determines to add her to his *isigodhlo*. His effort to force Verna to become his wife had been the subject of an earlier short story by Mitford, "The Dilemma of Verna Halse" (1895). There the chief has a conscience that prompts him to "renounce" his coercive scheme; but in the novel, he is grudgingly thwarted only by the orders of Opondo, who sides with Verna and Alaric. It might be speculated that Sapazani's effort to blackmail Izibu by offering eye-witness testimony to Alaric's crime is a slipping of the chief's characterization into a stock melodramatic cliché, the two-dimensional treacherous native, regularly deployed to illustrate civilized British superiority. But both Sapazani's political rebellion and his demand upon the girl are predicated on a mistaken assumption of reclaiming lost powers, analogously futile efforts to escape status deprivation as the white man's dog. Mitford seems to be implying that historical change is irreversible and that Sapazani cannot wield a power or recoup a status that he no longer has. As his assegais forged for rebellion represented an anachronistic harking back to noble Zulu traditions of war, so also his blackmail of Verna carries the pathos of a recognizable, understandable response to emasculation. His performance of *gwaza*, defying death (219, 137), was almost a challenge to Verna to shoot him. He has seen her stainless beauty, but like the primordial earth in its changes, prolific and creative, she is also nature's wild and deadly child.

Another suitor pursuing Vena jealously had encouraged the police to collect evidence of Alaric's Income crime and the inspector and constable in consequence had found the victim's rotted gorgon-like head in the river's mud. Fortunately the uprising diverts everyone's attention from the murder. Ironically, both Sapazani and the treacherous Golding are killed by their intended blackmail victims, suggesting that they are destroyed by their lack of conformity to the colonial codes, aliens whose values, customs, and beliefs exclude them from dominant Christian society. Perhaps the admirable Jewish figure in *Legacy of the Granite Hills* (1909) connotes that not race but class solidarity is important–he is a gentleman and if he profits from the war, like Ben Halse it will not be by betraying his countrymen.

In *The White Shield* Lalusini is Mitford's mouthpiece saying that the British "voice" with its message of a greater kingdom under the Queen must be listened to and obeyed. The British child spared by the Ndebele is acknowledged by all to be regal; and "when her voice again shall be heard, neglect it not, lest a nation be a nation no more" (216). First as an empire with Kings Mzilikazi and Lobengúla, now their dominion is succeeded by a yet greater empire with a Queen to bring both settlers and indigenes into orderliness as allies–an ideal unexpectedly shattered by the July Rising. The fact of this rebellion that occurred between the writing of the short story in 1895 and the publication of the romance in 1908 allowed Mitford to add political conflict as a dramatic counterpart to his romance. Sapazani clearly does not heed the voice of Britannia. In both the story and romance, however, Verna's "dilemma" is a forced choice between two possibilities that go in radically differing directions–wife of Sapazani or Alaric's death. The outlandish possibility in 1908 of Sapazani as her husband could only be entertained from a less socially constructed vantage point of fantasy or from a perspective decades in the future. But her personal and socially approved "right" choice as Alaric's wife results in her irrevocable loss of Africa's strengths–an unresolvable conflict in Mitford's vision.

One motif in this story–as indeed is found long prior to Mitford's novels in Harriet Ward and also in the expository writings of such contemporaries such as Olive Schreiner as well as in the twentieth-century novels of Sarah Gertrude Millan–is the issue of racial mixing, the "half-caste." Here in *Forging the Blades* Denham commends the coloured Charlie Newnes "'I should think he and his like would count for something in this country, in the long run.'"And Ben Halse responds: "'Oh, I don't know. They are rather between the devil and the deep sea . . . There are quite a lot of them about–decent, respectable chaps for the most part. Neither one thing nor the other'" (202). Olive Schreiner theorized that the child of such mixing inherited the worst character traits from each side, not the best of both; others, such as the African chief Umzilikazi, seemed to be more concerned with preserving the cultural and physical traits of the amaZulu from mixing with the Shona. In Mitford's single effort to write a classic late nineteenth-century "Western," *Golden Face: A Tale of the Wild West* (1892), maintenance of the upper-class blood line is the single most important thing that takes place; those who muddle the lineage are eliminated. When in *King Solomon's Mines* Ignosi invites the trio to remain and marry tribal wives (repeating Twala's earlier offer), they choose instead to take the recovered diamonds to London. The dying African maiden, Foulata, had asked Quatermain to tell Captain Good that "'I love him, and that I am glad to die because I know that he cannot cumber his life with such as me, for the sun cannot mate with the darkness, nor the white with the black" (281). Quatermain priggishly considers her death "a fortunate occurrence" that avoids the complications of racial miscegenation; but upon the trio's return to London the sterility of wealth and the impossibility of heroic action suggests they have lost their primal connection to the land and its fertility. As will emerge in the next chapter, this is precisely the problem-ending of Mitford's *Sign of the*

Spider (1896)–the protagonist loves a princess; her social caste is impeccable but her lineage is black.

This issue is a subdivision of the yet more problematic issue of the integration of cultures, European and African. One of the most painful later assessments of Euro-African interaction is "An African Tragedy" (1928) by R.R.R. Dhlomo who addressed the corruption of Johannesburg. Although Dhlomo set his moralizing story of urban slum life among African youths, his analysis of drink and prostitution as underlying sexual activites creates a conflict in his thinking. Ostensibly attacking from the Christian perspective the custom of wife-purchase, *lobola*, he simultaneously finds that the youth of Africa has lost as its behavioral model the tribal, mythopoeic past. It may be that *lobola* in a detribalized Western context is problematic, but the change in social contexts itself contributes greatly to the problem. When a socially homogenizing Christianity disrupts continuity with specific tribal origins, the young men and women languish in a partial acculturation, caught precisely as Ben Halse described Charlie, "between the devil and the deep sea." European religion may have replaced superstitious practices with precepts and abstract laws, but Western practices also brought the vices of drink and prostitution into the slums of the gold-mining industry. The land to which there is a spiritual connection and from which the inhabitant has been exiled has ceased to exist.

Although Africa "glows with life" (172) in contrast to the drab monotony of England, Verna wishes to be a tame Victorian wife, taken back almost as one of Alaric Denham's trophies. Alaric's whistle to tame a snake and kill it as trophy is what he does with Verna–or, for that matter, what Mitford does with his collection of assegais. These dead animal specimens are not unlike old Malemba's artistic but obsolete assegais. Almost comically, *Forging the Blades* ends with Alaric and Verna touring his dead animal museum, contemplating not the exhilarating dangers of living beasts, but their stuffed doubles. The appearance of liveliness is not life itself. The bull koodoo and the mamba are the trophies of untamed Africa Verna laid at Denham's feet. She herself could become Denham's ultimate prize, if not literally to be stuffed in his museum. By her shot through the chest of Sapazani, the chief who dies with her name on his lips, the last of the great warriors to resist the march of European penetration, she chooses the drawing-room culture of opulence rather than the primordial energies of Africa.

CHAPTER 8
CANNIBALS AND SLAVES

Joseph Conrad's "Outpost of Progress" was written in same the year that Bertram Mitford's *Sign of the Spider* was published:1896. Both are accounts of slave-raiding, and both have a contemporary setting in the Congo basin, "one of the dark places of the earth" (*Youth 50, Spider 128,* an allusion to Psalm 74:20). The first British novel to link slaving with cannibalism was Daniel Defoe's *Life and Adventures of Robinson Crusoe* (1719). After Crusoe's slave ship was wrecked in a storm and his life established on the island, he rescues Friday from cannibal captors and teaches him English and the Christian faith. Even earlier, Prospero in Shakespeare's *The Tempest* had introduced the savage Caliban to language and Western values. At issue, however, is not only the effectiveness of such cross-cultural communication but equally of words and rituals used to bolster authority among the citizens of empire itself. In colonial discussions, says Conrad, "We talk with indignation or enthusiasm; we talk about oppression, cruelty, crime, devotion, self-sacrifice, virtue, and we know nothing real beyond the words" ("Outpost" 153). Mitford's novel actually opens with the language of non-communication:

> She was talking *at* him.
> This was a thing she frequently did, and she had two ways of doing it. One was to talk at him through a third party when they two were not alone together; the other to convey moralisings and innuendo for his edification when they were–as in the present case. . . . His spouse, exasperated by his silence, continued to talk at–his back. (1-2)

Everyone understands that owing to its rigid master-servant dualism, "imperial-speak"anesthetizes its users to possibilities for real cross-cultural communication–opportunities are everywhere but dialogue is nowhere. Without converse, the husband here is recast as his wife's lackey, like a colonized native emasculated by his pseudo-feminine subjection.

In *Sign* Miford's ironic authorial voice is a distinguishable presence within his protagonist's outlook, presented as almost nihilistically skeptical of traditional values. Conrad, a more overt voice than Mitford, editorializes, mimics in parody, and frames his condemnation of slavery in what one might call an "allegorical realism," moralistically blunt but symbolically as intricate as that of Mitford. As novelists, they both describe the irony of false illusions without offering any overt creed or ideological antidote to explain or redeem. The reader senses the failure of characters to understand their destinies, their aspirations blasted by randomness of circumstance, turned into quixotic aberrations. Thus the work of both writers embraces dysfunctional socio-economic institutions and the loss of values, prompting a sort of existential Catholicism of guilt–for Conrad perhaps owing to his early upbringing, though as an adult he renounced his religious heritage, and for Mitford from his youthful conversion to Catholicism from Anglicanism.

Mitford's narration, as a romance, is a classic in the tradition of legendary fantasy monstrosities, from Grendel onwards. But both "Outpost" and *Sign* explore the irony of the social code's illusions of respectability and the self-deceptions of the imperial enterprise in ivory trading, gold mining, and slaving. Such crimes against persons as Conrad's and Mitford's tales describe in the Congo areas during the 1890s period are amply documented. In the *Congo Report* of Roger Casement (1903) both slavery and cannibalism in the Congo basin were observed:

> The towns around the lower Lulongo River raided the interior tribes, whose prolific humanity provided not only servitors, but human meat for those stronger than themselves. Cannibalism had gone hand in hand with slave raiding, and it was no uncommon spectacle to see gangs of human beings being conveyed for exposure and sale in the local markets. I had in the past, when travelling on the Lulongo River, more than once viewed such a scene. On one occasion a woman was killed in the village I was passing through, and her head and other portions of her were

brought and offered for sale to some of the crew of the steamer I was on. (Casement 138)

Mitford's first novel, *The Fire Trumpet* (1889), also contained an extended episode on slaving. As a topic, slaving in empire romances runs from well before R. M. Ballantyne's *The Gorilla Hunters* (1865) all the way to the end of the nineteenth century in Conrad's "Outpost of Progress" (1897) and "Heart of Darkness"(1899).

§

Joseph Conrad's "An Outpost of Progress" (1897) is set at an isolated ivory trading post on a navigable tributary of the Congo River, which together with his slightly later novella, "Heart of Darkness" (1899), represents a redaction of his personal experiences as a steamer captain on the Congo. Of "Outpost" Conrad wrote:

> It is a story of the Congo. There is no love interest in it and no woman–only incidentally. The exact locality is not mentioned. All the bitterness of those days, all my puzzled wonder as to the meaning of all I saw–all my indignation at the masquerading philanthropy–have been with me again, while I wrote. The story is simple–there is hardly any description. The most common incidents are related–the life in a lonely station on the Kassai. I have divested myself of everything but pity–and some scorn– while putting down the insignificant events that bring on the catastrophe. Upon my word I think it is a good story–and not so gloomy–not fanciful–alas! I think it interesting–some may find it a bore! (Davies 1: 294)

Some critics say that "Outpost" is a more "obvious" story than "Heart of Darkness" with a less sophisticated handling of narrative point of view; others say it is a "brilliant overture" to the better-known tale; however, "Outpost" is certainly more than an ingenious prologue. Its overt attack on progress and empire is fleshed out by an original and highly subtle allegorical strategy. Conrad alludes to the stronger focus on characterization in "Outpost" when describing "Heart of Darkness": "The criminality of inefficiency and pure selfishness when tackling the civilizing work in Africa is a justifiable idea. The subject is of our time distinctly–though not topically treated. It is a story as much as my *Outpost of Progress* was but, so to speak 'takes in' more–is a little wider–is less concentrated upon individuals" (2: 139-40). Conrad's narrative voice noticeably editorializes in "Outpost" on the faults of his central characters: "They were two perfectly insignificant and incapable individuals" (*Unrest* 128); "the two men got on well together in the fellowship of their stupidity and laziness" (133). Or his voice will offer exegetical opinions: "we know nothing real beyond the words" (153). However, these apparently overly-explanatory assessments of the literal events, frequently considered unartistically didactic, camouflage an underlying level of correlated allegorical meanings, sustained but tacit, shelving off in the narrative's final scene into subliminal depths of significance.

Finished in 1896, it was serialized in two parts the following year in the briefly-running *Cosmopolis* and was collected in *Tale of Unrest* (1898). "'An Outpost of Progress,' at first called 'A Victim of Progress,' [was] written in July in about three weeks" (Davies 1: 292 n.2). Later, Conrad's friend, Edward Garnett (14 August 1896), identified a false "artistic simplicity" in the opening pages that, presumably, Conrad meant to correct (1:300). Conrad's then-publisher, T. Fisher Unwin, had arranged with the editor of the *Cosmopolis*, which Unwin also published, for the story's placement. Its satire of the shameful management of trade within the Congo Free State fitted the magazine's wide-ranging and "international" agenda. But the division of the tale into the June and July 1897 issues did not please Conrad, who solicited Garnett's advice:

> As soon as I get my 2^d proof of story for the *Cosmopolis* I shall send it to you. I want to know what you think of it. I also wished to ask where it could best be cut without spoiling the effect too much. It is too long for one number they say. I told the unspeakable idiots that the thing halved would be as ineffective as a dead scorpion. There will be a part without the sting–and the part with the string–and being separated they will be both harmless and disgusting. But if they must cut, then You will help me to minimize the disaster. (1: 319-20; also 288, 299, 330, 335, 338, 363 n.6)

Ironically, in the July 1897 issue of *Cosmopolis* in which Conrad's novella concluded, an essay entitled "The Globe and the Island" appeared, remarking upon on the festival of Queen Victoria's Diamond Jubilee:

> Britain is imperialistic now. The "Little Englander" has wisely decided to efface himself. The political party which should talk of reducing the navy or snubbing the Colonies would have a short shrift. We are Imperialists first, and liberals or Tories afterwards. I said this, for my own part, years ago, when the sentiment was not quite so popular. Now it has happily become commonplace. The Jubilee is its culminating expression, and foreign observers should not fail to take note of this underlying significance of our national fête to-day. (Norman 81; Lugard 1: 585)

Such rhetoric of imperialism as the "culminating expression" of Victoria's age of empire reflects the impact of its long arm on far-flung societies and uninvolved individuals: thus the chief agent's reason for being in the Congo is "to earn a dowry for his girl" (132). Henry Norman in his next pages turns to "President McKinley's treaty for the annexation of Hawaiian Island to the United States," discussing the future of American imperialism at considerably greater length. Conrad's issue-mate observes with a kind of complacent fatalism: "It is the inevitable nature of expansion of this kind, once begun, to go on;. . . it is certain that the annexation of Hawaii will be followed by other annexations, or other attempts at annexation" (Norman7: 81-82).

"An Outpost of Progress" is a parody of "the sacredness of civilising work" (137), of bringing a Christian way of life to savage inhabitants, because such "progress" is actually a loss of salvation. All the characters in Conrad's novella are capable of evil but they disguise the guilt of their dark-heartedness in ornate rhetoric, outright lies, or silence. The third man on the staff, "Henry Price" or Makola, is the most diabolic; however, as with the other the names in this story, "Makola" seems determinedly neutral–merely an African place name both in the East Kasai district of the Congo and in Sierra Leone.

One might almost suppose that the article in an old copy of a home newspaper the two station operatives begin to read, entitled "Our Colonial Expansion" was a sardonic commentary on the contribution of Conrad's issue-companion. The two new station agents, Kayerts and Carlier, who had also been reading tattered copies of the swashbuckling exploits of such romantic heroes as Alexander Dumas or Balsac, found glory in the fantasy of the empire's expansion, especially their role in it:

> "In a hundred years, there will be perhaps a town here. Quays, and warehouses, and barracks, and–and–billiard-rooms. Civilisation, my boy, and virtue–and all. And then, chaps will read that two good fellows, Kayerts and Carlier, were the first civilised men to live in this very spot." Kayerts nodded, "Yes, it is a consolation to think of that." They seemed to forget their dead predecessor. (137)

This tendency to minimize the differences between fictional and real lives suggests a failure of aesthetic understanding, a confusion of illusion with reality.

Conrad's personal opinion of empire was starkly realistic: disintegrating civilized norms and moral regression, unethical policies and dehumanizing commerce, ethnocentricity and incompetence. And one shouldn't forget the physical and psychological concomitants: fever, hunger, slavery, homicide, suicide. In this political posture, Conrad of course was not alone. The poet Wilfred Scawen Blunt wrote in his diary on 9 January 1896:

> The British Empire is the great engine of evil for the weak races now existing in the world–not that we are worse than the French or Italians or Americans–indeed, we are less actively destructive–but we do it over a far wider area and more successfully. I should be delighted to see England stripped of her whole foreign possessions. We were better off and more respected in Queen Elizabeth's time, the "spacious days," when we had not a stick of territory outside the British Islands, than now, and infinitely more respectable. The gangrene of colonial rowdyism is infecting us, and the habit of repressing liberty in weak nations is endangering our own. I should be glad to see the end. (1: 212-213)

The fate of the snuffed out "energetic artist" (126), predecessor of the two white traders, leaves each wondering if they too will be buried at the station. Surely this dead artist is an anticipation of Fresleven in "Heart of Darkness" who, when Marlow finally had a chance "at last to meet my predecessor, the grass growing through his ribs was tall enough to hide his bones" (*Youth* 62). When Kayerts passed near the artist's grave he commented "Poor devil!" to Carlier. If "devil" is taken literally, perhaps the artist-agent was not unrelated to the god of Makola, who "cherished in his innermost heart the worship of evil spirits" (124). But the "tall cross" above his mounded grave, poorly raised by the Director, had leaned "much out of the perpendicular" (125)–*per + pendere*, to hang. Carlier "planted it upright" and then *hung* with both hands on the cross-bar to weight-test it for stability. Conrad's words, "replanted the cross firmly" (137), recalls all the crosses ritually planted in the cause of imperialism on foreign shores. Its tilt suggests Christianity's irrelevance for the dark places of Africa. If Adam's tree and Christ's cross stood in one place (John Donne, "Hymn to God, My God") then this cross suggests an unredeemed wilderness. The supposed bringers of civilization's "light and faith" revert, at the distant outpost of the imperial Gospel of Trade, to humanity's barbarous origins.

In the Congo, then, Christ is incarnate in a dead artist. The mediævals compared the Supreme Being to an artist to illustrate His creative power; Christ as artist expresses God's creativity in the universe. The creative impulse of the earthly artist as the *imago Dei*, the image of God, reflected this divine activity. But in the Renaissance, Ludovico Ariosto in *Orlando Furioso* (1532) called Michelangelo "*il divino*," the divine one, thus inverting the traditional comparison by now likening God's *Fiat* to the artist's creative activity. It did not take a great leap to imagine Christ no longer the dynamic voice of God by whom all things are made (John 1:1-5; Psalm 33; Colossians 1:16; Hebrews 1:2-3). In such an absence of divine presence, creation collapses back, symbolically, into a world without form and void:

> The river, the forest, all the great land throbbing with life, were like a great emptiness. Even the brilliant sunshine disclosed nothing intelligible. Things appeared and disappeared before their eyes in an unconnected and aimless kind of way. The river seemed to come from nowhere and flow nowhither. It flowed through a void. (133)

All that is left of the ancient Christian faith seems to reside in the old chief Gobila's primitive fetichism–or in the storehouse "called the fetish, perhaps because of the spirit of civilisation it contained" (134-135). To the failed artist who preceded Kayerts and Carlier, Gobila had ascribed a Christ-like role of death and resurrection. This is probably one of the most arrestingly sardonic and irreverent passages of colonial literature:

> The two whites had a liking for that old and incomprehensible creature, and called him Father Gobila. Gobila's manner was paternal, and he seemed really to love all white men. They all appeared to him very young, indistinguishably alike (except for stature), and he knew that they were all brothers, and also immortal. The death of the artist, who was the first white man whom he knew intimately, did not disturb this belief, because he was firmly convinced that the white stranger had pretended to die and got himself buried for some mysterious purpose of his own, into which it was useless to inquire. Perhaps it was his way of going home to his own country?.... In short, they behaved just like that other white creature that had hidden itself in a hole in the ground.... Perhaps they were the same being with the other– or one of them was. He couldn't decide–clear up that mystery; but he remained always very friendly. (138-139)

The God of Christianity re-emerges as the subordinate devil-deities of animistic polytheism in an unconscious parody of the doctrine of the Trinity. The three white agents–the buried artist, Carlier who swung on the cross and Kayerts who at the story's end will hang dead upon it–are a parody in old Gobila's mind of God the Father, Christ the Son, and God the Holy Spirit, the consubstantial and co-eternal Persons in the Trinitarian Godhead. Never having encountered any missionary explanations of these metaphysical "divisions" in the Creator–not that it would have been less of a "mystery" for him to have inquired into this creedal cornerstone of the First Council of Nicaea–old Gobila flounders around between three gods in One or one God in three persons. He wonders if the Artist, a sort of primorial God the Father, has gone home or now as Christ the Son lives in the ground ("*descendit in inferna*,"as in the Apostles' Creed) or has risen by the power of the Holy Sprit and come again?

Makola's sale of the "station men" to the slavers is merely service to his personal devil, if indeed Kayerts' labeling him a "fiend" (151) doesn't suggest Makola himself is the diabolic spirit of trade. His wife, who speaks "with great volubility" (141) to the armed strangers, is from Loanda, a Portuguese colony. The subtitle of Livingstone's *Missionary Travels* (1858), that Kayerts and Carlier probably should have read, told his readers that it would be about his "residence in the interior of Africa, and a journey from the Cape of Good Hope to Loanda on the west coast, thence across the continent." For several centuries before Livingstone and Conrad, Loanda had been the principal port for slave trading between Portuguese West Africa and Brazil. But Kayerts and Carlier naively have no idea that the armed men, whom they are told by Makola "are traders from Loanda" (147), might be slavers. Before the ten station men and an indeterminate number of Gobila's men are sold by Makola in exchange for a magnificent haul of prime-quality ivory, Kayerts, at the urging of Makola, unwittingly had supplied them liberally with palm wine. One is tempted to read their drunken entertainment as an ironic last supper, inasmuch as Makola's alias is Henry Price, thus suggesting an equivalence between the ivory and the thirty-pieces of silver that Judas received as the "price" of Christ's betrayal. Christ is here collectively embodied in the station men, the home-sick blacks drunk on palm wine yet made in the "image of God" and in whom God is made manifest: "They were not happy, regretting the festive incantations, the sorceries, the human sacrifices of their own land; where they also had parents, brothers, sisters, admired chiefs, respected magicians, loved friends, and other ties supposed generally to be human." (146). Conrad's ironic description of their awkward plight is not racist as some have suggested, commenting particularly on the final words in his passage; rather, it is the voice of imperialism exposing an incongruity, understood by the reader as the author intended, between their situation and the tenor of the words used. Europe of the 1890s had a collective imperial voice of the spirit of civilization that Conrad mimics–with the addition of a subtly mordant barbed irony. By the simple device of employing the identical verb– Kayerts "regretted" (132) his European life just as the station men were "regretting" their lost community–Conrad links the white agent and black Africans through their poignant sense of lost human ties.

Kayerts and Carlier, though they profess to be shocked by Makola's betrayal, rather quickly make themselves his accomplices by accepting the profit-motive as paramount, thus rationalizing the crime and resolving not to "blab" (158) about it. The dapper Makola who has betrayed the station men covers the barbarity of his act with civilized customs:

> Across the yard they saw Makola come out of his hut, a tin basin of soapy water in his hand. Makola, a civilised nigger, was very neat in his person. He threw the soapsuds skilfully over a wretched little yellow cur he had, then turning his face to the agent's house, he shouted from the distance, "All the men gone last night!" (149)

Conrad creates an almost mock-epic juxtaposition of the bizarre and the archetypal to lash out at Makola's opportunistic act and to assert a countervailing set of values. This hand and dog-washing turns back upon Pontius Pilate's ceremonial drama in the gospel of Matthew, a parody of purification by a washing of hands to evade responsibility. It echoes the white traders' lip-service in characterizing as "deplorable" the equation between the men and the ivory: "It's deplorable, but, the men being Company's men, the ivory is Company's ivory" (154).

And not long after, owing to no relief by the overdue river steamer, as the two European traders are reduced to a diet of boiled rice and coffee, an argument breaks out over whether Carlier can use the sugar Kayerts has been holding back for sickness or a similar exigency. If the rice and coffee are the bread and the wine of communion, then the sugar over which the two fight becomes the narrow theological dispute of Protestant and Catholic–is the sacrament only a symbol or does it contain the real Presence of Christ? Since "Christ" as the *Imago Dei* has already been sold off, the sugar in the coffee (Hawaiian sugar of imperialism?) is an absurd quarrel that mocks all religious strife and that lacks the very morality it professes to defend. Carlier calls Kayerts a "slave-dealer" who, his delusions of superiority thus laid bare, loudly resents the charge; Carlier throws a stool and their chase around and around the station evokes both a paranoid nightmare and a children's game, a contrastive insanity or immaturity, that is suggested not for the first time in this narrative. Devil worship, slaving, and imperial trade come together much as Kayerts and Carlier "came into violent collision" (163) as Kayerts's revolver goes off.

The shot is so sudden, at first Kayerts thinks he himself has been mortally wounded; but in fact he has killed Carlier "who lay there with his right eye blown out" (165). Makola preposterously declares he died of fever–a convenient lie that turns a blind eye to homicide, accidental though it may have been. Perhaps this is Matthew 5:29: "And if thy right eye offend thee, pluck it out, and cast it from thee: for it is profitable for thee that one of thy members should perish, and not that thy whole body should be cast into hell." Or, alternatively, as in Egyptian mythology, is Kayerts as chief and Carlier as his assistant the sun and moon? Here Carlier would be Horus, who is blind in his right eye because the moon was weaker than the sun; as in myth, attacks on friends are thus explained because Horus and Carlier are impaired and mistake them for their enemies. That Kayerts's and Carlier's predecessor died of "fever" is only the allegation of Makola–perhaps it was more like the "fever" of Carlier's bullet in the eye. "What is truth? said jesting Pilate; and would not stay for an answer" (Bacon "Of Truth"). What had Truth to do with the politics of the Roman Empire about which Pilate was questioning Christ–or with the politics and trade of nineteenth-century Europe?

Just after Kayerts has jettisoned his moral beliefs as nothing more than a "rubbish heap" (168), the whistle of the riverboat is heard in the mist; the station bell joins its ringing to create a din comparable to the sounding trumpets at the Last Judgment, though here perhaps with its high C a little off center. The mist is ironically "white and deadly, immaculate and poisonous" (168), this oxymoron repeated in the "cross-shaped stain" (169) of the artist's shaft; but at the Last Judgment, as Conrad's fellow Catholic observed, such ambiguities and incongruities are sorted out:

> . . . twó flocks, twó folds–black, white; | right, wrong; reckon but, reck but, mind
> But thése two; ware of a world where bút these | twó tell, each off the óther. . . . (Hopkins 105)

To the skewed and tilted morality of "progress" will come a "justice" (168) greater than society's that will discriminate into two basic domains for eternity the innocent and the guilty. In the morning fog, the artist's rood is a "stain" at the entrance to the station. And as the Director toils up the steep bank he finds Kayerts

> hanging by a leather strap from the cross. He had evidently climbed the grave, which was high and narrow, and after tying the end of the strap to the arm, had swung himself off. His toes were only a couple of inches above the ground; his arms hung stiffly down; he seemed to be standing rigidly at attention, but with one purple cheek playfully posed on the shoulder. And, irreverently, he was putting out a swollen tongue at his Managing Director. (170)

The stiff arms and rigid body are now as effectively "perpendicular" as the imperially implanted cross itself. But Kayerts appears less a suffering savior than a grotesque marionette–playful, irreverent– expressing in death a profound want of respect for the imperial enterprise, only mockery and petulance.

Conrad reacted strongly to cutting his story into two installments because this ending was the "sting in the tail" (Davies, 1:299, 320, 335). He whimsically characterized this "tail" or "tale" upon publication of the second installment as "not half-bad" (364). Clearly envenomations from jungle and desert areas have a capacity to create a forceful, even lethal, effect. Does this story aspire to kill illusions, even those of a watchful providence? Writing to R. B.

Cunninghame Graham, Conrad associated this climactic image with an impersonal "machine" universe in which the "ardour for reform, improvement for virtue, for knowledge, and even for beauty is only a vain sticking up for appearances as though one were anxious about the cut of one's clothes in a community of blind men":

> "Put the tongue out" why not? One ought to really. And the machine will run on all the same. The question is, whether the fatigue of the muscular exertion is worth the transient pleasure of indulged scorn. On the other hand one may ask whether scorn, love, or hate are justified in the face of such shadowy illusions. The machine is thinner than air and as evanescent as a flash of lightning. The attitude of cold unconcern is the only reasonable one. Of course reason is hateful–but why? Because it demonstrates (to those who have the courage) that we, living, are out of life–utterly out of it. (2:16-17)

Although a skeptic in so much, Conrad, on his deathbed, returned to his devout beginnings in romantic Polish Catholicism; suggestive, perhaps, of an almost self-contradictory intuition of Christian values even at the heart of his dubiety.

§

Possibly the most popularly successful of Mitford's novels, *The Sign of the Spider* (1896), has strong affinities with Haggard's occult mysteries. It combines ethnic conflict with such late nineteenth-century concerns as the discovery and rush to exploit Africa's mineral resources; slavery and cannibalism; social Darwinism; a new anthropological interest in myths; the vogue of psychic phenomena then under scientific scrutiny; and–most exotically–the "cryptozoological" horror of the vampire Spider. This last was an important milestone in the elaboration of high Victorian dark fantasy of which Beowulf's Grendal was perhaps the distant precursor. In the novel's climactic struggle, the protagonist is confronted with a hairy bear-sized arachnid fed with living men, a giant *vagina dentata* that he stabs and bludgeons into submission–his phallic club a human leg bone with a massive band of gold at the extremity that in a putative deathblow he hurls into the spider's eye. What gives imaginative force and artistic structure to *The Sign of the Spider* is its brilliant fusion of the classic quest for wealth and love with the exotically dangerous yet inviting "dark continent," its darkness metaphoric of the association of the feminine with the moistened earth and its secret recesses: "This wonderful land–the dim, mysterious recesses of its interior–what possibilities did it not hold?" (98). In this respect, although Mitford's novel in large part certainly reflected colonial life as it actually was in nineteenth-century South Africa, its presentation of ethnic rituals and beliefs in tribal societies is an intentional parable of the internal economic and class tensions at the metropolitan centers of empire. The Ba-gcatya cannibals, "The People of the Spider" (Zulu: *Ba*, they, of + *gcatya*, "Venomous spider, which is often seen running nimbly about he road" [Colenso141]), are a dystopian parallel to colonial and European society, the new cannibalism of industrial capitalism. Mitford's vampiristic spider, like all fictional monsters that inhabit liminal spaces, embodies the worst possibilities of society, of ourselves.

To measure the reality of human sacrifice against its thematic use in high romance, it must be construed against the historical backdrop of actual tribal practices. Among the most vivid of eye-witness historical accounts of evil priests is that in Fred Fynney's *Zululand and the Zulus* (1880). As chief interpreter on Sir Theophilus Shepstone's staff–and inspector of Natal native schools and former border agent–Fred Fynney's description of a Zulu "smelling-out" makes it evident that Mitford's portrays without exaggeration the historical fact of the *izanusi* in *The King's Assegai*:

> There are among the natives a class known as the *Izanusi* or *Abangoma*, who profess to have direct intercourse with the spirit-world, and to practice divination. Their influence is invoked in the "smelling-out" or finding out of the *abatakati*. . . . I can, perhaps, best explain by relating an incident that happened within my own knowledge in the year 1856. During that year, I went to Zululand, accompanied by a staff of carriers, for the purpose of hunting and trading. We formed a large party, and it was

therefore necessary, in looking out for a resting place at night, to secure the most commodious kraals along our line of travel.

Having arrived at chief Nobeta's kraal,

> I mentioned incidentally that it was by mere chance that we had got that far, as we had purposed staying at a kraal farther back, only we had found it deserted. The old reptile thereupon callously observed, "Oh, yes; I wiped them all out two days ago. They were all *abatakatis*; they killed my mother, or assisted in doing so; but there are more *abatakatis* to be smelt out yet." . . .
>
> Next morning, on my proceeding to bid the chief good-bye, I was surprised to find that he would not hear of my going just then. He wanted my presence at his kraal that morning, he said, as they had a great piece of business on, and I must see how he punished evil-doers. I pleaded the urgent necessity of our getting forward on our journey, but all to no purpose, so we made a virtue of necessity and remained with the chief, as requested.
>
> I noticed, about 10 o'clock that morning, that batches of natives began to arrive outside the kraal, from all directions. They came with sullen, downcast looks, and observed an ominous silence; each enveloped in a blanket, and carrying only a short stick. After some little time a bevy of girls came out of the kraal, and began a sort of chant, to the music of which they kept time by clapping their hands; young men, armed with knob kerries, next came upon the scene; and last of all, five of the fearful *abangoma* advanced toward where the sable throng was seated. The appearance of these fearful creatures, enveloped as they were in everything which tended to make them hideous, in the shape of snake skins and portions of reptiles and other animals, would baffle description. Reluctant observer of such a scene as I was, they inspired me with a feeling of awe and disgust, for I then realized what their presence foreboded.

There is little doubt but that the bloodshed about to begin was a major way of controlling headmen who were a threat to the chief's control; moreover, such killing added to the number of beasts in the chief's cattle posts:

> Each carried in his left hand a bundle of small assegais and shield, whilst in the right hand was the tail of a gnu,–their gaunt forms according well with their panther-like actions. The young

> warriors drew round the terror-stricken lines of defenceless natives. The chant was struck up, and the smelling out began. Victim after victim was revealed by the aid of the spirits as an *umtakati*, upon which, the *umgoma*, bounding over each, switched him with the Gnu's tail; this was the signal for his being seized upon the spot and dragged away, as food for the ever-ready vultures and wolves. No sooner were the different victims disposed of, than a band of warriors were dispatched to the several kraals to continue the work of destruction, and seize the cattle. I do not know the number of those killed, but I believe there were seventeen, all kraal owners, together with their families, which constituted a total, in one day, that makes one's very heart revolt at the thought of it.
>
> Whilst compelled to sit by Nobeta in the kraal, I observed a lot of vultures settled on a tree above our heads, and I was so disgusted with the old fellow's mercilessness, that I indiscreetly remarked that he had not yet satisfied his friends the vultures, asking if he could not find another *umtakati*. He flew into a fearful rage, charged me with ingratitude, and bade me begone. I obeyed at once. (2: 8-11)

However, as noted in connection with Haggard's biographical novel of Shaka, such intragroup bloodshed also contains a mythic dimension–an element, one should add here, not limited to Africa; the Aztec earth goddess, Tlaltecuhtli, is depicted with a stream of blood running into her mouth as she crouches to give birth; thus she consumes life to renew it.

In Africa one encounters many uncanny events not scientifically explainable: visions, premonitions, and–notably–ambiguous meanings. Thus if the hue of black symbolized fears of night-time spirits and underworld ghosts, it contrastingly could represent fertility and resurrection–the dark soil of Africa in its mysteriously renewed life. Death in Zulu terms as described by Mitford or Haggard is a "going down into the darkness," into "the Dark Unknown." Although such phrases may seem nihilistic to the Western observer, it is possible that Mitford reserved judgment on the limits of African spirituality and that Haggard credited the Zulu darkness with being the "yet unknown." His Africa is one of physical forces tinctured with magic; but such mythic patterns and powers are hidden, almost beyond the scope of human manipulation, never obtrusive. Spiders in antique legends of Athena and Arachne are less relevant than those in tales from the west African forest regions who in their anti-heroic qualities seem almost analogous to Stanninghame himself. The spider is the monster that reflects fear of the "other," such as the Empire's colonized peoples, but is also like Olive Schreiner's cannibalistic John Bull who embodies what the imperialist fears as the worst parts of himself, as in her caricature in *Thoughts on South Africa*: "seated astride of the earth, his huge belly distended with the people he has devoured and his teeth growing out yet more than ever with all the meat he has bitten and looking around on a depeopled earth and laughing" (354). The face of the Ba-gcatya's vampire spider is a reflection of the face of society itself, a "cruel human face"–the uncanny embodiment of the price one pays for belonging to any closed social group.

The protagonist in *The Sign of the Spider* is Laurence Stanninghame of "sixteen quarterings"(310).[28] Disgruntled with loss of wealth, prestige, and living in genteel poverty in overcrowded London housing, he leaves wife and children for Johannesburg to make his fortune or die. Mitford presents the contradictions and unrest of Victorianism owing to growing urbanization and the global expansion of the British empire, particularly a capitalist world of multiplying markets where person to person social relations are reducible to material self-interest and people, not only as African slaves, are defined by a cash value. Stanninghame in pursuit of the "oof-bird" of wealth and its economic freedom (note that as a gentleman he never for a moment entertains the possibility of manual labor) is not unlike many historical and fictional colonial figures with brave but flawed ambitions. The time is 1890 (dated by internal references to railway construction, population figures, and the recent Republican revolution in Brazil), approximately four years after the

---

28. "A *seize quartiers* man ... could prove his sixteen heraldic quarterings, which is the open sesame to every chapter, community, and court in Europe. It ... implies that the individual belongs to the old nobility, entitled to bear arms for five generations on both sides of the house" ("Rome and the Romans" X-8).

first discovery of gold at Johannesburg. Aboard the *Persian* on his voyage to Africa, Stanninghame's routine of daily domestic strife is replaced by relaxing private moments in a tropical climate of sun and stars; even the ship's Oriental name suggests a legacy of mystery and passion, "Ah Love! could thou and I with Fate conspire . . .". Laurence, in spite of himself, falls in love with Lilith Ormskirk, a beautiful young woman of superior intellect. Seemingly irrevocably ruined by stock speculation after he arrives, Stanninghame is about to shoot himself when a vision of Lilith appears to him. At this crisis he resolves to join a slave-trading party into the far interior, raising for the reader the complex moral issue of how to sympathize with an anti-hero of this ilk.

The dark continent is the site for acts that elsewhere are cloaked in a heavily sublimated adherence to the façade of civilized respectability. Stanninghame's journey becomes an expedition into the unknown, battling the horrors of a psychic and physical darkness, either to triumph over them or to be consumed by them. For an untraceable but profitable interval he tears off the social and religious masks of conformity to indulge the less respectable but ever-present animal-like rapacity of human desire, confronting in this way the apocalyptic manifestation of his own bestiality. Together with his companions, Hazon and Holmes, he carries to the extreme the exploitative aspect of imperialism–if gold speculators are vile but socially respectable, then Stanninghame will be viler than all and, for the nonce, bourgeois respectability be damned. Johannesburg is the corrupt Jerusalem of Isaiah, as Hazon's name suggests. The opening words of Isaiah 1:1, the prophet's "vision" or "revelation" (Hebrew: *hazon*) is of Judah and Jerusalem as religiously empty, self-indulgent, and under judgment of God. Whatever the facts of Isaiah's vision, for Stanninghame the corresponding hypocritical morality of the empire is its materialistic rhetoric of duty and honor neither natural nor beneficial:

> Duty? Hang duty! He had made a most ruinous muddle of his whole life through reverencing that fetish word. Honour? There was no breach of honour where there was no deception, no pretence. Consideration for others? Who on earth ever dreamt of

considering him–when to do so would cost them anything, that is? Unselfishness? Everybody was selfish–every*thing* even. What had he ever gained by striving to improve upon the universal law? Nothing. Nothing good. Everything bad–bad and deteriorating–morally and physically. (78)

The background to *Sign of the Spider* owes more than a little to the new values of evolutionary ethics, and to its debates concerning species selection and social Darwinist assumptions. Mitford embeds a quotation from Alfred Lord Tennyson's *Maud*, about "a world of plunder and prey" (1: 173). Unlike Wordsworth, Tennyson the scientific modernist saw no divine spirit of love in nature; for him evolutionary survival meant a ravening nature:

> For nature is one with rapine, a harm no preacher can heal;
> The Mayfly is torn by the swallow, the sparrow speared by the shrike,
> And the whole little wood where I sit is a world of plunder and prey. (1: 123-25)

Although the speaker in *Maud* is palpably an imperfect moralist, "a morbid poetic soul" confined to a madhouse, his bitterness prepares the way, even while it casts doubt upon his sanity, for a social philosophy of the struggle for existence and the survival of the fittest.

Indeed, perhaps Mitford's world of "preyer or preyed upon" is consistent with the ideas of Friedrich Nietzsche. Nietzsche posited a will to power beyond good and evil, denying absolute criteria in morals and presenting a master-slave world-view:

> Life itself is *essentially* appropriation, injury, overpowering of what is alien and weaker; suppression, hardness, imposition of one's own forms, incorporation and at least, at its mildest, exploitation . . . "Exploitation" does not belong to a corrupt or imperfect and primitive society: it belongs to the *essence* of what lives, as a basic organic function; it is a consequence of the will to power, which is after all the will of life. If this should be an innovation as a theory–as a reality it is the *primordial fact* of all history: people ought to be honest with themselves at least that far. (Nietzsche, Section 259)

In Nietzsche's slave morality, the stronger individual's assertive creativity is defied by the weaker's notions of conformity to duty, authority, and rules of emotional expression; and those who brush aside such societal limits are impugned and vilified. In this sense the slaving expedition of Stanninghame is a *reductio* of Nietzschean philosophy–a literalistic application of its principles. However, although Nietzsche had little use for any altruistic morality, Stanninghame keeps his word, believes one good turn deserves another, intercedes for Lutali's life, and out of loyalty and friendship substitutes himself for Holmes. These are chivalric virtues, and Mitford's caste-like social views–very much akin to those of H. Rider Haggard–are ultimately not in competition with the scientific morality of Darwin or such English utilitarian philosophers as Bentham, Mill, and Spencer. Between cannibals and Anglican bishops there exists a common moral substrate; and attempts at ethical consensus between majorities and minorities may have mutually compatible features. In this, Mitford follows the utilitarian belief that altruism was a biological phenomenon opposed to the unmitigated self-assertion of the physical universe.

In *Sign of the Spider* the meaning and morality of an idea or a proposition seems to lie in its observable practical consequences. However there is a whole basketful of "ifs," "buts" and "maybes" between the permissible and the immoral in terrestrial affairs. Animals may be rational, but consider them within a nature "red in tooth and claw" (Tennyson again): for the prey, being eaten is a disaster; for the predator, without food for self or brood, eating the prey is commonsense. On the human level compare the enemy who would seize for himself and his clan one's possessions (and destroy one's life if practical)–an obligatory duty for him, wrongful to oneself. Mitford exempts from his readers' opprobrium hunters of treasure if they betray no trust; also the economically desperate are tolerantly evaluated, not only if they follow a gentleman's code, a chivalrous, honorable moral vision, such as the titular hero of *Renshaw Fanning's Quest*, but apparently even if, like Stanninghame, they are driven to shockingly primitive immorality by the economic barricades of "home," what Mitford in *Averno* (1913) calls the drab, unhealthy life of "stuccodom" (94). In *Sign of the Spider* Mitford even provides Stanninghame and Hazon the grotesquely familiar moral rationalization given by Archibald Dalzel: "Whatever evils the slave trade may be attended with . . . it is mercy . . . to poor wretches, who . . . would otherwise suffer from the butcher's knife" (xxiv-xxv). Not only does the readers' repulsion to cannibalism allow Stanninghame's slaving to seem less criminal by contrast–better to be a slave than a cannibal's dinner–but perhaps Stanninghame is simply a reverse evangelist, sending the Africans to civilization rather than coming as a civilizing missionary to them. Late in the previous century when British slavery was the focus of a growing abolitionist movement, anti-slavery writers such as Robert Burns sentimentalized the noble African in his idyllic African landscape, as in "The Slave's Lament" (1792), to counter any rationalization that transportation to a fairer clime was desirable.

Mitford's description of white slaving and black cannibalism might be impeached as being derived from sources that validate or reinforce racist and colonial notions of European superiority. In those days few, if any, missionaries, traders, hunters, scientific explorers, soldiers, or settler-colonizers believed that what was heinous in their society might not be so in another. Stanninghame, like Robinson Crusoe, confronts an unfamiliar culture and is disgusted with its practices, though unlike Crusoe he holds the cannibals entirely blameworthy. Yet often some blame also extends to one's own culture. In Evelyn Waugh's morbidly comic satire *Black Mischief* (1932) the dependents at the Azania Legation, including Basil Seal's fiancée Prudence, have been evacuated by aircraft; but when her plane is reported missing, Basil goes cross-country in search of her, only to be stunned by the blackest irony that the Africans have fed him his fiancée from their stew pot (290-92). Such "Christian anarchism" as Waugh's is focused primarily on the cultural decadence and incompetence of British colonial rule, not tribal ritual practices: "Waugh's African novels reserve their savage indignation for those arrogant Westerners who seek to replace the old barbarism (cannibalism, paganism) with the new (birth control, animal rights,

Bauhaus architecture)" (*American Spectator* 19 November 2002). Similarly for Mitford.

Among the high romances of Africa, Mitford's is possibly the most historically graphic account of slaving although H. Rider Haggard's account in *People of the Mist* (1894) runs a close second. Mitford incidentally manages to convey a great deal of ethnographic data in his descriptions of slavery and cannibalism, harking back to his sources for *The King's Assegai*, 1894. In writing *The King's Assegai* two years before *Sign*, Mitford in its third chaper had drawn on the first-person description of physical and oral evidence for past and recent cannibalism in South Africa by his second cousin, J. H. Bowker, to whom he dedicated that novel. Henry Callaway, in the 1860s, observed that "It is probable that the native accounts of cannibals are, for the most part, the traditional record of incursions of foreign slave-hunters" (Callaway, 155-64). But in response to more-recent positions that severely minimize the extent of African cannibalism by blaming the disappearance of inhabitants on European slave-hunting, one could point out that the old Zulu name for South Africa is *Ningizimu*, meaning literally "the place of many cannibals." W. C. Scully's splendid short story, "Ghamba," in *Kafir Stories* (1895) describes this post-Shaka practice in Natal and Basutoland: "Many people have heard or read of the cannibals of Natal who turned large tracts of the country into a shambles in the early part of this century, . . . but many do not know that some of the cannibals fled to Basutoland where, among the almost inaccessible mountains, they carried on their horrible practices for many years" (159-61). Mitford's colonial biases, however, were corrected or qualified by oral traditions of the Africans themselves, highly figurative accounts presented in African poetry and song, evidence strongly rooted in historical places and events. The referential content of such thematic and imagistic patterns may have been explained to him by the performers or intended auditors.

Other of Mitford's multiple sources are not directly traceable, but coincidentally in the same year that *The Sign of the Spider* was published, the Swiss priest Émile Jacottet, published his transcriptions of the Basuto tales of Kholumolumo, an ogre-cannibal

(Jacottet 107-151; Guma 194-201). F. D. Ellenberger later quoted a Christianized cannibal: "I am Kholumolumo, the horrible beast of our ancient fable, who swallowed all mankind, and the beasts of the field" (226). The Zulus have a similar devouring figure, Usilosimapundu, emblem of the earth and its "eating up" of man, as well as other tales and traditions encoding cannibalistic scenes (Callaway 159). As frightening personifications, Usilosimapundu and Kholumolumo are similar to the devouring Spider of the Ba-gcatya (perhaps more than affinities, less than influences). The figurative leap from a literal cannibalism to capitalistic consumption is an easy step for Mitford who only needed to adapt the satiric trope of Jonathan Swift's "Modest Proposal" relating to the English landlords of Ireland: "who, as they have already devoured most of the parents, seem to have the best title to the children" (88). From the anthropophagoi, the "man-eating savages" of the geographer Claudius Ptolemy in the second-century AD, to the voracious mining consortiums and stock markets of Jo'burg in the nineteenth century, the once-literal horror of cannibalism becomes a rhetorical trope for industrial victimization, especially a metaphor of the earth that swallows its miners. Throughout the novel, the human body as a material commodity reflects a range of socially constructed cultural meanings even beyond cannibal food or slaves to be bought: it supplies weapons of bone against the Spider; and Stanninghame himself is for wife or children merely a financial provider.

So much is made on-board ship of Lilith's name as that of Adam's first wife, the reader would be obtuse indeed not to suspect a deeper connection to her mythic namesake. (Her family name of Ormskirk is Old Norse, derived from *Ormr*, a Viking name which means serpent or dragon, and *kirkja*, church; certainly this figure of a serpent's church supports her given name in the novel's plot). It is almost certain that Mitford would have known D. G. Rossetti's sonnet "Lilith" either upon its first appearance as paired with his painting "Lady Lilith" (1867-68) or, more likely, later from "The House of Life" (1870) when Rossetti retitled this sonnet "Body's Beauty" to contrast with its contrary, "Soul's Beauty." In these paired sonnets, he attempts the ideal unification of flesh and spirit. His painting-*cum*-poem recasts the pre-Biblical Lilith, an aggressive and outright evil demon, as a "*Modern Lilith* combing out her abundant golden hair and gazing on herself in the glass with that self-absorption by whose strange fascination such natures draw others within their own circle" (W. M. Rossetti 2: 850). Olive Schreiner perceptively reads such narcissism as the hypnotism of a social web shaping women from childhood: "we go and stand before the glass. We see the complexion we were not to spoil, and the white frock, and we look into our own great eyes. Then the curse begins to act on us." Complection and dress advertise her as a marriageable commodity. Though seemingly the constructor of her web, she is actually its victim, trapped in a narrow reproductive role—the "curse" is both the Fall *and* her menses. The child sees herself exactly as society expects, invisibly distorted according to a patriarchal script of self-hypnosis (Monsman, *Haggard* 46-47):

> Of Adam's first wife, Lilith, it is told
> > (The witch he loved before the gift of Eve,)
> That, ere the snake's, her sweet tongue could deceive,
> And her enchanted hair was the first gold.
> And still she sits, young while the earth is old,
> > And, subtly of herself contemplative,
> > Draws men to watch the bright web she can weave,
> Till heart and body and life are in its hold.

Lilith, temptress of mankind, and Eve, temptress of Adam, are akin: both are beautiful, seductive, and deadly. Earlier in *Faust* Goethe (1808-32) had turned this medieval legend of Lilith as Adam's first wife into the new romantic "femme fatale" of ensnaring sexuality:

> Faust: Who's that there?
> Mephistopheles: Take a good look. *Lilith*.
> Faust: Lilith? Who is that?
> Mephistopheles: 'Tis the first wife of the first man. Adam's first wife, Lilith. Beware, beware of her bright hair.... Many a young man she beguileth, smiles winningly on youthful faces but woe to him whom she embraces!

On the back of his picture of "Lady Lilith," Rossetti inscribed Shelley's translation from Goethe's *Walpurgis-Nacht* in *Faust*:

> Hold then thy heart against her shining hair,
> If, by thy fate, she spread it once for thee,
> For, when she nets a young man in that snare
> So twines she him he never may be free.

After Mephistopheles gives this warning, he nevertheless encourages Faust to dance with "the Pretty Witch" (1: 4206–4211, 4216 – 4223).

Only great saints or necromancers can bind or exorcize spirits and devils, and Lilith Ormskirk's "unholy spells" are those of a modern enchantress. From Goethe, Rossetti took his idea of Lilith's "strangling" golden hair that ensnares and chokes the emotional life of the young Adam. Like a spider she "Draws men to watch the bright web she can weave." Indeed, one orb-web spider is called *Araneus circe*–and like Circe with her pigs, Lilith Ormskirk is surrounded by her admirers, her "poodles." Lilith's "enchanted hair" belongs as a doppelgänger to the two worlds of death and beauty. Her sinister side as the spider's web expresses nature's cruelty, killing those who see, approach, or woo her. But also the "modern Lilith," in the spirit of John Keats' "Lamia" or his "La Belle Dame," is less the murderously jealous or selfish temptress than one whose beauty unintentionally, though ineluctably, destroys. Icon of the temptress though she may be, she too has become the victim of her own power, her own helpless humanity caught in the common grip of social conformity.

Mitford did not read Sigmund Freud on "The Uncanny" or *Dreams in Folklore,* but psychoanalysis has attested that the spider, like the serpent, is an over-determined or highly condensed symbol expressing the core fantasies and conflicts from various developmental levels. Spiders emblematize feelings of repulsion and anxiety, of being "caught in the web" of desires, emotions and personal feelings of dependence and need. When an intensely ambivalent person battles against a break with reality, the spider often emerges as a symbol of the feared and deeply repressed aspects both of the self's potentially psychotic core and of the parasitic woman who subtly debilitates and drains her prey. The spider-woman is the *femme fatale* that lures men to their doom—psychological or financial—by enchantment without love in return. A psychoanalytic interpretation suggests that to define the feminine as innately predatory merely conceals a misogynistic aberration: she appears in dreams of men disgusted or guilty about sexuality for whom the lure of the web-entrapping woman represents a threat of sexual engulfment. On the other hand, a mythic interpretation stresses that the dangerous woman is like the primordial earth in its changes, prolific and procreative yet also wild and deadly. This figurative interpretation entails two sides to love: the demonic and the angelic, both representative of phases in the energies of nature, the earth-mother's cycle of life, death, rebirth. The spider, presented here in the novel as a grotesque, monstrous chimera, a Chthonian eater of men's raw flesh that looms like a massy *vagina dentata*, is a trope of the "sarcophagus" (*sarco*, flesh + *phages*, eating) or grave, that old and œcumenical cannibal with mouth wide open who consumes all living things.

In addition to psychoanalytic and mythic overtones, there is also the related social symbolism of the spider. Disgust with predatory sexuality paralleled societal fears of devolution, of the species in social decline. Such *fin de siècle* anxieties, loosely based on the theories of Max Nordau and Cesare Lombroso, saw in the streets of London a frightening blurring of boundaries between the hidden pathological self and its respectable public image. In the Gothic novel, the woman's body is frequently the locus of masculine anxiety about a new sexuality invading her domestic sphere and her emasculating challenge in the workplace. Mina Harker in *Dracula* (1897) is the "new woman," able to use the technology of the typewriter but in imminent danger of becoming sexually rapacious like Lucy, her friend-turned-vampire. Mitford's spider thus symbolizes the castration of the male by the female's enlarging sphere of activities. Stanninghame began his African expedition as a wanderer in untamed nature, free of domestic space; he then defeats this spider of the "new domesticity" and possesses Lindela with a passion that bodies forth a new beginning at the world's mythical heart, ostensibly having shaken off matrimonial and domestic entanglements.

The detestable superstition of the People of the Spider is analogous to nineteenth-century British respectability–both cultures have strangling webs the spider does not allow to be broken easily and that must be escaped to live and love. In this the Ba-gcatya cannibals are an ironic parallel to Victorian society. Both demand obedience and both feed people to a devouring maw, the vampire spider or mass consumerism. Spiders in the novel represent the constructedness of social values that proscribe individual identities–speech, opinions, modes of dress as embodied in personal choices–by customs, institutions, and penal codes regulated by fetishists or amoral cadres structured by collusion and connivance. The man-eat-man morality of the slavers is morally not unlike the South African settlers' exploitation of the indigenous inhabitants. Colonial society concocts a mask of respectability, but demands an involuntary behavioral servitude akin to the literal enslavement of Stanninghame's victims. In his fierce desire for wealth, Stanninghame transforms himself into a lawless huntsman who has sold his soul to the diabolic spider. He becomes in his hunt for humans the apocalyptic manifestation of his own darkest possibilities, El Afà, the poisonous serpent, even as Hazon, Sanninghame's partner, bore the sobriquet of El Khanac, the strangler.

The Ba-gcatya maiden, Lindela, rescuing Laurence from the spider's lair, becomes a perfected reincarnation of Lilith Ormskirk. Although initially merely an expedient way of avoiding his death-by-spider, she not only assumes the role of his savior but conducts him safely through the nether regions of passion towards a perfection more than mortal, a heroic love glimpsed beyond the flaming ramparts, a neo-Platonic "Beauty" enthroned. He had lacked this imaginatively ideal love until "at the twelfth hour" Lilith and he each came to realize the catastrophe of a socially dictated propriety; but now he attains it. During Stanninghame's and Lindela's love-idyll, they enjoy the fruits of freedom, a perfection of physical and spiritual love that cannot last in a world of getting and spending. Disentangled from the conventions of civilized femininity, Lindela had represented that ideal in the final couplet of Goethe's *Faust*, "the Eternal Feminine that draws us ever onward" (Haggard, *Finished* 258)–*das Ewig Weibliche* that in the person of Gretchen had redeemed Faust. Numerous times Mitford observes that Lindela defied convention as she knew it–her clan, its laws, its priests, even its protocol of emotional feelings: "We girls of the Ba-gcatya do not love–not like this" (239). But Stanninghame cannot convey Lindela back to civilization, not just because she is a "savage" African, nor merely because he already is married, but because neither her love nor his could fit the bourgeois and proletarian paradigms of contemporary society. Just as his entrapment in an unsatisfactory marriage and a degrading poverty seemingly had impeded his love for such as Lilith Ormskirk, so now Lindela's love is checked not long before Stanninghame crosses the frontier back into civilization. Stanninghame's descent into hell and ascent with this African "Beatrice" into the possibilities (or impossibilities) of the future is thwarted by his second spider encounter. In the first clash Stanninghame had wounded the hideous creature, but not as fatally as supposed; now he cannot save Lindela and vents his fury by pounding her deadly nemesis to death. Its fatal bite expresses indirectly the poison against which even their elite individualism, their disdain, boldness, and profound indifference to the self-delusions and materialism of society, will be no antidote. On a narrative level, the nineteenth-century author had no other plot options for such as Lindela but death.

Unsullied by the inhibitions of modern capitalistic culture, Lindela was an emblem of love without entrapment in relationships organized in terms of conformity to cultural, religious, or racial codes. Such love Lilith Ormskirk could not provide. Stanninghame had reproved her for waiting too long to declare her affection for him at the twelfth hour, although in this dissembling of feelings he too is guilty. We may suppose Lilith and Laurence to be childishly and ruinously proper; however, in Victorian society (and, one might add, in anthropophagite or any other culture) who can express what, and when, and where was and is a closely controlled matter of precept and proscription. In the end Lilith accedes to an illusory "duty" of self-sacrifice by betraying her first love and marrying her boorish cousin

George. This "life-time of the awful pain of loss" (122) already surrounded her as she entrusted to Stanninghame her monogram, its decorative floral "O" like a spider's outline or "sign," indicating her protective love by spiritual affinity. A "sign" is an external mark carrying a meaning, derived etymologically from its incised, i.e., cut, figure; and spider amulets traditionally had been charms inscribed with a magic incantation worn to protect against evil. But unlike the sign of the cross which invokes divine protection or blessing, Lilith Ormskirk's monogram shares "commonalities" of socially constructed values with the Ba-gcatya spider; hers is an apotropaic talisman, and not notably different in significance from the primitive fetish god. After Stanninghamme seemingly has won his freedom from the webs of thraldom–both from the economic entrapments of civilized society and the literal prison of the spider's cave–he returns to civilization only to encounter a forlornly enslaved Lilith, victim of her own beauty. His love for Lilith thus is swallowed by what he left England to evade–the snare of a humdrum and deadening existence, a sacrifice of passion to family obligation. Not so inconsistently, in the light of Lilith's capitulation and society's censure of unfaithful wives, the lovelorn Stanninghame accepts her unhappy marriage as final– "for your own sake" (304)–despite her misplaced motive of self-denial.

Beyond the imperial frontier, behind which the codes of Victorian respectability are enshrined, lie both the worst of human violence, cannibalism, and the best of human love, expressed in Lindela's perfectly unconditional commitment. From the outset Stanningham's goal was not spiritual meaning and purpose in life but wealth, *material* sustenance. Then the profound, the miraculous, and the disastrous happened, buoying him with a renewed longing and energy. Lilith had opened to him the possibility of something more than his dream of affluence; and Lindela truly gave that "more" to him–until the spider of social constructionism reappeared, a power not merely indifferent, but unjust, morally blind, even cruelly mocking. Mitford, as novelist, could never have contemplated his protagonist bringing Lindela back to Johannesburg to live happily ever after. As author, Mitford knew there were no admissable scenes available that could include Lindela at Stanningham's side. The spider has determined the story's outcome. Enmeshed by the spider of his original ideal, wealth, nothing more remains in life for Stanningham. His death is one of spirit and purpose.

Stanninghame–"selfish cynic" (25) as Mitford describes him and supporter of the gender double standard–is nevertheless a believable, sympathetic character–perhaps too much so (one recalls, possibly, John Milton's not-always-successful editorializing against a rebellious Satan in *Paradise Lost*). Yet the reader still struggles to disconnect the corrupt maxim that "the end justifies the means" from Stanninghame's return home. As has been noted, the readers' repulsion to cannibalism (not to mention also the Zulu Ba-gcatya) allows Stanninghame's slaving by contrast to seem less criminal; and, moreover, certainly some of his new-found affluence is owing to the diamonds he unoffendingly picked up in the spider's lair, the result of his original altruistic rescue of Holmes. He is admirable to such a degree that the abstract legalities of slaving are seen as less important than the parade of troubles he finally overcomes. Still, why does Mitford invite the reader to endorse Stanninghame's goal of wealth if his actions perpetuate and reward racist and imperial practices? Mitford's authorial sentiments at first sight seem impenetrable, inasmuch as at the end his wealthy protagonist is one for whom slaving has amply paid off. Mitford remarks, in what perhaps is "a" moral of Stanninghame's tale: "he fell to thinking on what strange experience had been his–of the consistent and unswerving irony of life as he had known it. Every conventionality violated, every rule of morality, each set aside, had brought him nothing but good–had brought nothing but good to him and his" (310-11). Yet–and here is "the" specific moral posture of the author–for Stanninghame, rusticated from the circle of sociality, Lindela is dead; Lilith, her "charm" locked away never to be worn again, has vanished into an unhappy marriage; and his tenure on the newly-rented estate is provisional–not because he could not buy it but because he is clueless about his future, has no home in the ultimate sense. Rich after four years, he is now also decisively alienated from the primordial energies of love.

However, "nothing but good" is ironic. Once returned from beyond the frontier, society offers neither hellish violence nor heavenly love–only a limbo. Throughout, Stanninghame confused the significance of life with a wealthy life. Hazon at the outset had told Stanninghame he would come back a rich man or never come back at all. Both eventualities occur: wealth and limbo, for with wealth nothing more remains to attain in life. Nor does the journey into the heart of his own darkness prompt a penitential retelling and recognition of good and evil, like S. T. Coleridge's ancient mariner to the wedding guest or (just three years in the offing) like Conrad's Marlow on the yacht. Rather, his wealth, even without his recognizing it, has absorbed him back into the spider's web of conventional mores. Stanninghame is very much like Mitford's character Maurice Sellon at the end of *Renshaw Fanning's Quest*. In that novel Sellon appropriates the great diamond "eye" of the Bushmen with its wealth but loses the future happiness that will be Fanning's.

Stanninghame's story ends with his child Fay's new-found idyll of leisure and play misting over his memories of violence and passion. Now vastly more wealthy and with the last perils of his criminality blotted out by Holmes's marriage, he ends where his wife always wanted him to be, in a world where basic attachments between people assume the form of a relationship between things, in which material self-interest, not such intensities as his African loves, defines the ties that bind. Stanninghame has sacrificed his manhood to this domesticity, as truly emasculated as when he lived in stuccodom. H. Rider Haggard's landed and gentrified hero, Allan Quatermain, had observed: "no man who has for forty years lived the life I have, can with impunity go coop himself in this prim English country, with its trim hedgerows and cultivated fields, its stiff formal manners, and its well-dressed crowds. He begins to long–ah, how he longs!–for the keen breath of the desert air; he dreams of the sight of Zulu impis breaking on their foes like surf upon the rocks, and his heart rises up in rebellion against the strict limits of the civilized life" (*Quatermain* 4). Stanninghame's world is now the drawing-room culture and its emerging mass consumerism of accumulated possessions. Of course, from the first he had been complicitous with this system, inasmuch as the new money at Johannesberg and those who put economic gain above other values remained his exclusive focus; he even tried to shun love's "spell." Curiously, the novel's final pages omit all mention of the nagging wife to which Stanninghame has been fated to return, almost as if she has evaporated from his life, which indeed figuratively she has–or, rather, she together with him and their children have been eaten up by the spider's maw of opulence. If the primordial energies flow anew, it will only be in the next generation, perhaps with his daughter Fay, who may become the next Lilith or Lindela–or not.

AUTHOR'S AFTERWORD

At the outset of this study, I said of authors, colonists, and tribal members that "each voice must be construed against the backdrop of all the other voices, not to mention the roaring of beasts and the thunder that is the voice of God." I would like to conclude these chapters with a South African folktale of the voice of God, a story that challenges a fixed connectedness between literal content and interpretive meaning and that foregrounds a way of critically revaluing the fiction of empire. This story, as contributed by Thomas Bain, first appeared in the March 1880 issue of the *Folk-lore Journal* (21-23) and was subsequently collected in 1910 in James Honey's *South-African Folk-tales* (5-6). The following is its *Journal* form, with its original notes:

> The Distribution of Animals, &c., &c., After the Creation, as Related by a Kafir.[1]
> (Contributed by Mr. Thomas Bain.[2])
>
> A very intelligent old Kafir once told me, in a conversation about the Creation, that the Kafirs fully believed in a Supreme Being or *Teco* (click on the *c*),[3] and that their version of the distribution of animals, &c., &c., after the Creation, was thus–
> *Teco* had every description of stock and property.
> There were three nations created, *viz.*, the whites, the *Amakosa* or Kafirs, and the *Amalouw* or Hottentots. A day was appointed for them to appear before the *Teco* to receive whatever he might apportion to each tribe. While they were assembling, a honey bird,[4] or honey guide, came fluttering by, and all the Hottentots ran after it, whistling and making the peculiar noise they generally do while following this wonderful little bird. The *Teco* remonstrated with them about their behaviour, but to no purpose. He thereupon denounced them as a vagrant race that would have to exist on wild roots and honey beer,[5] and possess no stock whatever.
> When the fine herds of cattle were brought, the Kafirs became very much excited,–the one exclaiming, "That black and white cow is mine!" and another, "That red cow and black bull

are mine!" and so on, till at last the *Teco*, whose patience had been severely taxed by their shouts and unruly behaviour, denounced them as a restless people, who would only possess cattle.

The whites patiently waited until they received cattle, horses, sheep, and all sorts of property. Hence, the old Kafir observed, "You whites have got every thing. We Kafirs have only cattle, while the Amalouw or Hottentots have nothing."[6]

(Signed)   T. Bain.

[1] Whether this story is originally a Kafir one, is not yet clear. A Bayeye version, given to the Rev. C. H. Hahn by Mr. Edwards, will be found on page 34 of the present number.

[2] With regard to the above, Mr. Bain, in a letter dated *Rondebosch, 15th Febry.* 1880, writes as follows:

> "Enclosed is a Kafir version of the distribution of animals after the creation, which I have a distinct recollection of, although it is many years ago since it was related. It struck me at the time as being rather a good version, and perhaps on that account I have such a good recollection of it."

[3] Probably *u'Tixo*.

[4] [Bain:] The Hottentots look upon it almost as a sacred duty to follow the honey guide. I have known them to neglect important duties, while I have been out Road-surveying, on the sudden appearance of a honey bird, regardless of consequences.

[5] [?Bain:] This is a most intoxicating beverage.

[6] Apparently the Kafir who narrated the above to Mr. Bain can only have had impoverished specimens of the Hottentot race before his eyes.

This seemingly modest contribution by Thomas Bain (1830-1893), a road builder of national standing in southern Africa, is not greatly fleshed out by the editors' printing of its Bayeye version.

The Bayeye were a tribe inhabiting the country near Lake Ngami. In "Tradition of the Bayete" this "distribution of animals" incident is a minor part of a larger narrative. It reads:

> They account for the white men being so much richer and wiser, by saying the whites were not so greedy as the black. At the creation, the black men were impatient, and cried out, "Give us our things, and let us go." The whites were patient, and waited,

and so received all the best gifts, wisdom, riches, &c., &c. (35-36)

That "the whites were not so greedy as the black" is amusing, to say the least.

The most evident interpretation of this story may be styled nineteenth-century "imperial ideology" because Teco is cast as the voice of a British imperialist God. This is especially evident in the use of *Teco/u'Tixo*, of which Bishop J. W. Colenso observed that at the local missionary station

> people were unanimous in their disapproval of the word for God, now commonly in use among the Missionaries–*uTixo*,–which, they said, 'had no meaning whatever for the Kafirs. They used it because they found it in their Bibles; but it was not a word of their language at all.'. . . The origin of this word is very uncertain; but it is said to be the name of a species of mantis, which is called 'the Hottentot's god.'. . . Dr. Vanderkemp, who first laboured among the Hottentots some sixty years ago, adopted this word in his teaching as the name of God; . . . and it must be long before they [the parishioners] can become able, as it were, to bridge over the gulf, and make out for themselves, that this strange name, which is preached to them, is only the white man's name for the same Great Being, of whom they have heard their fathers and mothers speak in their childhood. (*Ten Weeks* 52-60)

Colenso insists that in the place of this non-native missionary word the indigenous form, *umKulunkulu*, be used. Ironically, Colenso elsewhere observed that "the name for Deity among Zulus . . . is derived [from] the word *umlunga*, commonly used in this colony for 'white-man'" (*Zulu* 2). If the *umKulunkulu* and *umlunga* are linked after the fashion of *Teco* and the culture from which the missionaries came, the voluble "voices" of the Africans competing with each other or whistling to the honey-bird suggest a child-like simplicity incapable of appreciating modern capitalistic values. Assuming this story is a sort of ersatz folk tale generated within the earlier colonial era, then its imperial interpretation simply implies that Africa was for the settlers an ideal world in which, according to Isaac Dinesen, "the white pioneers lived in guileless harmony with the children of the land" (*Shadows* 14).

But outside of that cultural and historical situation this folktale's archetypes can carry a radically different interpretation. Since colonized peoples often concealed their thoughts and motives from the whites to survive in colonial cultures, it is likely the nineteenth-century form of the tale followed its function as indoctrination. But however much its rendition as we have it may be colored by Western religious and imperial values, another reading not only is possible but actually has been established. At my request, Msizi Biyase, a bilingual clergyman of KwaZulu-Natal, asked six of his advanced catechumens what other meaning this story might have either for them or for their community. He reported (19 April 2006) that these lads found it an ironic tale of the trickster-figure who bides his time, perhaps even waiting with the patience of a guileful predator. They observed that the essential hunting tactic is *ukuthula*– "to be quiet" or what the great white hunter, H. A. Bryden, in the story discussed in chapter six, called "motionless silence" (44) and "infinite patience" (46)–which will allow the prey to betray itself. The "Hottentots" and "Kafirs" forfeit "stock and property" by impatiently breaking the silence with whistling and exclamations, like a noisy herd that offers its predators an easy mark.

Now in *this* interpretation the natives no longer are seen as England's children but instead as victims of England's colonial greed. Here the "script" that allowed the imperialist to establish control over the Africans by framing intrusion with guile is recognized and rejected by these contemporary young African scholars. The white man is the predator, the Xhosa and Khoi are the prey, and Teco, as the voice of imperialism, is an analogue to the wolf's "law of the jungle." Interestingly, given this post-colonial construction, the tale might also be seen as having roots in some pre-colonial cosmogonic myth that was modified after the advent of the missionaries and colonists. In such an *Ur*-form the "whites" could be originally (among other possibilities) any dominant group that practiced patience to gauge precisely the ambit of its quarry; and *Teco* would be their imperious chief commanding his regiments to ambush and eat up the undisciplined warriors and their cattle.

Through its simplicity, this myth of the distribution of animals highlights social and political interpretive differences between colonial and indigenous perspectives. The etymology of "politics" is *polis*, Greek for "city" or "state"; and, as Aristotle said, "man is by nature a political animal" (*Politics* I: 2). Precisely because of those political roots, the meanings that rhetorical forms carry are inherently equivocal. Facts and their interpretations are differentiated but interconnected presences underlying each other. All histories contain qualitative judgments as to evidence, every assertion is socially based, each datum is a discursive construct open to interpretation, and every account consists of more than the facts. Any set of images or events, in folklore as in history, is open to multiple viewpoints reflecting the beliefs of its users. The political insistence on language as a univocal instrument only valid when it is a product of *self*-representation sets up a binary focus on one group's perspective against all the others; it discourages dialogue and empties it of content. The empire writers understood on some level that attitudes are culturally situated and that a recognition of the subaltern's perspective was essential for meaningful engagement. Drawing on the co-relations and connections within their common historical moment, they strove for a culturally contextualized understanding and empathy in which differing perspectives would fit into a wider historical picture.

At a time when no indigenous fiction writers in southern Africa were on the horizon, English had long been one of the *lingua francas* for the communication of intellectual, technical, or business information. Because they were writers *in* Africa, the empire novelists wrote *of* Africa; but their language was the language of empire, a magnificent voice yet one nonetheless inflected by the acts and self-justifications of economic globalization. Even before a more progressive "federation of the world" could be articulated in the place of older get-rich-quick imperial ambitions, guileful words of greed had poisoned trust in European motives. The empire authors required from English a capacity for conveying the speech and import of indigenous speakers in the face of their lack of trust or of a common cultural framework between them. And because the colonized subjects of empire often hid their motivations and actions from the colonizers, English authors had diminished opportunities to transmit expressive and affective African experiences into their English texts. Nevertheless, these colonial writers labored to validate their efforts by assessment and reassessment, by questioning such ideological dogmas as may rule the moment, and by pegging their insights to multiple historical tethers. On their terms they succeeded; on contemporary terms of identity politics they failed. Yet if the twenty-first century reader is able to put all definite histories and dogmatic interpretations back into play, so as to find beneath the surface of one interpretation the antithetical surface of another, then that individual will be both a good philosopher and the best of readers.

BIBLIOGRAPHY

A

"About Men and Women." *Eastern Daily Press* (Norwich) 17 November 1896: 8.
Abrahams, Peter. *Wild Conquest*. New York: Harper, 1950.
African Review 15 (21 May 1898): 311-313.
Alden, W. L. "London Literary Letter." *New York Times* 11 June 1898: BR388.
"Anglo-African Writers' Club." *Times* (London) 17 May 1898: 11.
"Anglo-African Writers' Club Dinner." *African Review* 25 June 1898: 476-18.
"Anglo-African Writers' Club." *Times* (London) 22 December 1898: 8.
"Anglo-African Writers' Club." *Times* (London) 17 October 1899: 6.
"Anglo-African Writers' Club–A Dinner." *Times* (London) 27 March 1900: 6.
"Anglo-African Writers." *Daily News* 13 November 1900: 5.
"Anglo-African Writers' Club." *Times* (London) 13 November 1900: 10.
"Anglo-African Writers' Club." *Times* (London) 18 December 1900: 10.
"Anglo-African Writers' Club." *Times* (London) 15 October 1902: 12.
"Anglo-African Writers' Club." *Times* (London) 12 February 1903: 8.
Archives and Records Service of South Africa, National (Pretoria). 203 CSC 2/2/2/798; 204 MOOC 6/9/805; 205 MOOC 6/9/8995.
Archives, UK National (Hertfordshire). DE/Z118/C11/7 12 May 1898.
Archives, UK National (Kew). Gentle Divorce File. Ref.: WO 13/1606.
Archives, UK National (West Sussex). Mitford Archives: MS. 3.
Aristotle. *Politics of Aristotle*. Trans. B. Jowett. 2 vols. Clarendon: Oxford University Press, 1885.
Armstrong, Nancy. *Fiction in the Age of Photography: The Legacy of British Realism*. Cambridge: Harvard University Press, 2000.
Augustine, Saint. *The Confessions of Saint Augustine*. New York: Dover, 2002.

B

Ballantyne, R. M. *The Gorilla Hunters: A Tale of the Wilds of Africa*. London: T. Nelson, 1861.
Barrow, John. *Account of Travels into the Interior of Southern Africa*. 2 vols. London: Cadell & Davies, 1801.
"Bettington, Fanny." *Women of South Africa*. Ed. Thos. Lewis. Cape Town: LeQuesne and Hooton-Smith, 1913.
Bhebe, Ngwabi. *Christianity and Traditional Religion in Western Zimbabwe, 1859-1923*. London: Longmans, Green, 1979.
"Births." *Times* (London) 19 June 1891: 1.
Biyase, Msizi. "Re: Myth," E-mail to author. 19 April 2006.
Blackburn, Douglas. *Richard Hartley, Prospector*. Edinburgh: Blackwood and Sons, 1905.
Blavatsky, Helena. *Isis Unveiled: the Mysteries of Ancient and Modern Science and Theology*. Ed. Boris deZirkoff. 2 vols. New York: Bouton, 1877.
Blunt, W. S. *My Diaries: 1888-1914*. New York: Alfred Knopf, 1921.
Bowker, James Henry, Dr. Bleek, John Beddoe. "The Cave Cannibals of South Africa." *Anthropological Review* 7 (April 1869): 121-128.
Bryant, A. T. *Olden Times in Zululand and Natal*. London: Longmans, Green, 1929.

----------. *A Zulu-English Dictionary with Notes.* Pinetown, Natal: Mariannhill Mission Press, 1905.
Bryce, James. *Impressions of South Africa.* London: Macmillan, 1899.
Bryden, H. A. "A Bushwoman's Romance." *Tales of South Africa.* Westminster: Archibald Constable, 1896. 41-62.
----------. "Schreiner v. Rhodes." *Saturday Review.* 80 (5 October 1895): 435-36.
Buchan, John. *A Lodge in the Wilderness.* Edinburgh: William Blackwood, 1906.
----------. *Memory Hold-the-Door.* Toronto: Musson Book Company, 1940.
----------. *Prester John.* London: Thomas Nelson, 1910.
----------. *The Thirty-Nine Steps.* Edinburgh: William Blackwood, 1915.
Bulpin, T.V. *The White Whirlwind.* Johannesburg: Thomas Nelson, 1961.
Burton, Richard F. *Two Trips to Gorilla Land and the Cataracts of the Congo.* 2 vols. London: Low, Marston, and Searle, 1876.

C

Callaway, Henry. *Izinganekwane, Nensumansumane, Nezindaba Zabantu / Nursery Tales, Traditions, and Histories of the Zulus.* Springvale, Natal; Pietermaritzburg; London: Blair; Davis; Trübner, 1866.
Casement, Roger. *The Black Diaries.* Ed. P. Singleton-Gates and Maurice Girodias. New York: Grove, 1959.
Chennells A.J. "The Treatment of the Rhodesian War in Recent Rhodesian Novels." *Zambezia.* 5 (1977): 177-98.
Chrisman, Laura. *Rereading the Imperial Romance.* Oxford; Clarendon Press, 2000.
Cohen, Morton. *Rider Haggard: His Life and Works.* London: Macmillan, 1960.
"Colenbrander, Johan." *People Directory.* <http://pipl.com/directory/>.
Colenso, J. W. *Zulu-English Dictionary.* Pietermaritzburg: Davis, 1861.
----------. *Ten Weeks in Natal: A Journal of a First Tour of Visitation Among the Colonists and Zulu Kafirs of Natal.* Cambridge: Macmillan, 1855.
Coleridge, S. T. "Epitaph on an Infant." *Coleridge: Poetical Works.* Ed. E. H. Coleridge. London: Oxford University Press, 1967. 68.
Conrad, Joseph. *The Collected Letters of Joseph Conrad.* Ed. L. Davies and F. Karl. 9 vols. Cambridge: Cambridge University Press, 1983-90.
----------. "Heart of Darkness." *Youth and Two Other Stories.* New York: McClure, Phillips, 1903. 47-184.
----------. "Henry James–An Appreciation–1905." *Notes on Life and Letters.* London: Dent, 1921. 13-23.
----------. *Tales of Unrest.* London: Unwin, 1898.
Corbett, Edward. *The French Presence in Black Africa.* Washington, D.C.: Black Orpheus Press, 1972.
Cruchley, G. F. "Royal Naval School." *Cruchley's London: A Handbook for Strangers.* London: G.F. Cruchley, 1865.

D

Daneel, M.L. *The God of the Matopo Hills.* The Hague: Mouton,1969.
Darwin, Charles Robert. *Variation of Animals and Plants under Domestication.* 2 vols. London: John Murray, 1868.
"Death of Mr Bertram Mitford." *Eastern Daily Press* (Norwich) 15 October 1914: 4.
"Dinner to Captain Lambton." *Times* (London) 11 June 1900: 11.

Doyle, Sir Arthur C. "The Mystery of the Sassassa Valley." *Stories by English Authors: Africa.* New York: Scribner's Sons, 1897. 11-29.

"Dr. Conan Doyle on Mr Kruger." *North Otago Times* (New Zealand) 27 November 1899: 4.

E

"Eglinton, W." *Encyclopedia of Occultism and Parapsychology.* Ed. Leslie Shepard. Detroit: Gale, 1978.

Eliot, T. S. "Baudelaire." *Selected Essays, 1917-1932.* New York: Harcourt, Brace, 1950. 422-425.

----------. "The Metaphysical Poets." *Times* (London). Section: Literary Supplement. 20 October 1921: 669-670.

----------. "'Ulysses,' Order, and Myth," in *Selected Prose of T. S. Eliot.* New York: Houghton Mifflin, 1975. 175-178.

Ellis, Peter. *H. Rider Haggard: A Voice from the Infinite.* London: Routledge, 1978.

F

Firmat, Gustavo. "The Facts of Life on the Hyphen." *Remembering Cuba.* Ed. Andrea O'Reilly Herrera. Austin: University of Texas Press, 2001: 173-176.

Fleming, Peter. *The Siege of Peking.* London: Rupert Hart-Davis, 1959.

Flint, John. *Cecil Rhodes.* Boston: Little, Brown, 1974.

Folk-lore Journal. "Distribution of Animals." 2: 2 (March 1880): 21-22.

Foucault, Michel. *Discipline and Punish: The Birth of the Prison* (1975). Trans. Alan Sheridan. New York: Vintage Books, 1995.

Freud, Sigmund. *Studies in Parapsychology.* Ed. Philip Rieff. New York: Collier, 1963.

Fynney, Fred B. *Zululand and the Zulus.* 2 vols in 1. Maritzburg: Horne Brothers, 1880.

G

"Gentle, Alexander. " Office for National Statistics, General Register Office (London) 22 October 1874: No. 145.

"Gentle *v.* Gentle and Blennerhassett." *Times* (London) 4 April 1884: 3.

Giles, Herbert. *A History of Chinese Literature.* London: Heinemann, 1901.

Glendinning, Victoria. *Edith Sitwell: A Unicorn Among Lions.* London: Weidenfeld and Nicolson, 1981.

Goethe, Johann Wolfgang von. *Faust.* Trans. Carl Mueller. Hanover, N.H.: Smith and Kraus, 2004.

Gojwana, Mbodlomani. 4 October 2002 <www.inkundla.net / indonsakusa / Leadership>.

Grace, Michael. "The Hundred Years Waugh." <spectator.org/archives/2003/11/19/the-hundred-years-waugh>

"Grant of Administration for the estate of Edward Ledwich Osbaldeston-Mitford." Probate Registry (Family Division of the High Court of Justice, England). 12 November 1912.

"Grant of administration for the estate of Bertram Mitford." Probate Registry (Family Division of the High Court of Justice, England). 24 March 1915.

Green, Martin. *Dreams of Adventure, Deeds of Empire.* New York: Basic Books, 1979.

H

Haggard, H. Rider. "About Fiction." *Contemporary Review* 47 (February 1887). 172-180.

----------. *Cetywayo and his White Neighbours.* London: Trubner, 1882.

----------. *The Days of My Life: An Autobiography*. 2 vols. London: Longmans, Green, 1928.
----------. *Finished*. London: Ward, Lock, 1917.
----------. "*In Memoriam." Life and its Author* by Ella Haggard. London: Longmans, Green, 1890. 3-12.
----------. *King Solomon's Mines*. London: Cassell, 1885.
----------. *King Solomon's Mines*. Ed. Monsman. Peterborough: Broadview, 2002.
----------. *Mr. Meeson's Will*. London: Longmans, Green, 1888.
----------. *The Private Diaries of Sir H. Rider Haggard*. Ed. Stephen Coan. London: Cassell, 1980.
----------. "Who is 'She'?" *Pall Mall Gazette*, London, 22 January 1887: 13-14.
----------. "A Zulu War-Dance," *Gentleman's Magazine*, 243 (July 1877): 94-107.
Hamilton, Carolyn. *Terrific Majesty*. Cambridge: Harvard University Press, 1998.
Hart, John. MS letter #6602 "Haggard." 22 July 2007 <www.rrauction.com/content/pdf/295pdf/artlit.pdf>
Heliodorus. *Aethiopica Historica*. Trans. Thomas Underdown. New York: AMS Press, 1967.
Henty, G.A. *With Roberts to Pretoria*. London: Blackie, 1902.
Homer. *The Odyssey*. Trans. Robert Fitzgerald. New York: Doubleday, 1961.
Honey, James. *South-African Folk-tales*. New York: Baker and Taylor, 1910.
Hopkins, G. M. *Poems*. Ed. W.H. Gardner. New York: Oxford University Press, 1948.

J

James, William. *The Varieties of Religious Experience*. New York: Longmans, Green, 1902.
Jowell, Phylis, Adrienne Folb. *Into Kokerboom Country: Namaqualand's Jewish Pioneers*. Vlaeberg: Fernwood, 2001.
Jung, C. G. *The Archetypes and the Collective Unconscious*. Trans. R.F.C. Hull. 2nd ed. Princeton, NJ: Princeton University Press, 1980.

K

Kenyatta, Jomo. *Facing Mount Kenya: The Tribal Life of the Gikuyu*. London: Secker and Warburg,1938.
Kearney, J. A. "Bertram Mitford and the Bambatha Rebellion." *Natalia* 25 (1995): 43-53.
"Khama and the Chartered Company." *Saturday Review* 80 (26 October 1895): 496-37.
"Kipling's South African Talk." *New York Times*. Section: Saturday Review of Books and Art. 11 June 1898: BR385.

L

Laertius, Diogenes. *Lives of Eminent Philosophers*. Trans. R.D. Hicks. 2 vols. Cambridge: Harvard University Press, 1925.
Layard, Austen Henry. *Adventures in Persia, Susiana, and Babylonia*. New York: Longmans, Green, 1887.
----------. *A Popular Account of Discoveries at Nineveh*. New York, J. C. Derby, 1854.
"Mr. Layland." "The Cave Cannibals of South Africa." *The Journal of the Ethnological Society of London* 1:1 (March 1869): 76-80.
Leach, Henry. "In London's Lesser Club-land." *Living London*. Ed. George R. Sims. Vol. 3. London: Cassell, 1906. 159-165.
Leslie, David. *Among the Zulus and AmaTongas*. Edinburgh: Edmonston and Douglas, 1875.
Letters Addressed to A. P. Watt. Ed. A. P. Watt. London: Watt, 1929.
Lewis, C. S. "Haggard Rides Again." *Time and Tide*. 3 September 1960: 1044-1045.

Lieven, M. "Contested Empire: Bertram Mitford and the Imperial Adventure Story." *Paradigm* 25 (May 1998): 1-13.

"Literature in England's Colonies–James Bryce's Views." *New York Times*. Section: Saturday Review of Books and Art. 14 January 1899: BR23.

Livingstone, David and Charles. *Narrative of an Expedition to the Zambesi and its Tributaries*. New York: Harper, 1866.

Low, Gail. *White Skins / Black Masks*. London: Routledge, 1996.

Lucan. *Pharsalia*. Trans. Jane Wilson. Ithaca, NY: Cornell University Press, 1993.

Lugard, F. J. D. *The Rise of Our East African Empire*. 2 vols. Edinburgh: W. Blackwood and Sons, 1893.

M

MacDonald, George. "The Gifts of the Child Christ." *Stephen Archer and Other Tales*. London: Dalton, 1908. 26-78.

Mahlangu, Peter. *uMthwakazi*. Salisbury: Longmans Rhodesia, 1978.

McClintock, Anne. *Imperial Leather: Race, Gender, and Sexuality in the Colonial Contest*. London: Routledge, 1995.

Mill, J. S. *The Subjection of Women*. Ed. Susan Okin. Indianapolis: Hackett Publishing Company, 1988.

Milton, John. *Poetical Works of John Milton*. Ed. Helen Darbishire. 2 vols. Oxford: Clarendon, 1952.

"Mitford, B." *Allibone's Critical Dictionary of English Literature: A Supplement*. Ed. J. F. Kirk. Philadelphia: Lippencott, 1891.

"Mitford, B." *The Anglo-African Who's Who and Biographical Sketchbook*. Ed. Walter Wills and R. J. Barrett. London: Routledge, 1907.

"Mitford, B." *Anglo-African Who's Who*. Ed. Leo Weinthal. London: Walter Judd, 1910.

"Mitford, B." *Biographical and Bibliographical Record of South African Literature in English*. Ed. E. A. Seary. Grahamstown, SA: National Library of Australia., 1938.

"Mitford, B." *Cassell's Encyclopaedia of World Literature*. Ed. J. Buchanan-Brown. New York: William Morrow, 1973.

"Mitford, B." *The Catholic Who's Who and Yearbook*. Ed. Sir F.C. Burnand. London: Burns and Oates, 1910.

"Mitford, B." *A Dictionary of Literature in the English Language*. Ed. Robin Myers. Oxford: Pergamon Press, 1970.

"Mitford, B." *Dictionary of South African Biography*. Ed. W. J. KeKock. Pretoria: National Council, 1987.

"Mitford B." Her Majesty's Courts Service, British Probate Registry (Family Division of the High Court of Justice), Grant of Administration: 24 March 1915.

"Mitford, B." *The Men Behind Boys' Fiction*. Eds. W. Lofts and D. J. Adley. London: Howard Baker Pubs., 1970.

"Mitford, B." *The People of the Period*. Ed. Alfred T. C. Pratt. London: Neville Beeman, 1897.

"Mitford, B." *South African Bibliography*. Ed. Sidney Mendelssohn. London: Mansell, 1979.

"Mitford, B." *The Stanford Companion to Victorian Fiction*. Ed. John Sutherland. Stanford CA: Stanford University Press, 1989.

"Mitford, B." *Times* (London) 29 March 1915: 11

"Mitford, B." *Who Was Who 1897-2004*. British Library Electronic Database: Xreferplus, 2006.

Mitford, Bertram. *The Curse of Clement Waynflete*. London: Ward, Lock, 1894.
----------. *Forging the Blades*. London: Eveleigh Nash, 1908.
----------. *A Frontier Mystery* (London: White,1905).
----------. *The Induna's Wife*. London: F. V. White, 1898.
----------. *The King's Assegai*. London: Chatto and Windus, 1894.
----------. *Renshaw Fanning's Quest*. London: Chatto and Windus, 1894.
----------. "Side-Lights on the Amandebili (Matabili) Question." *The Imperial and Asiatic Quarterly* 1894-1895: 96-102.
----------. *Sign of the Spider: An Episode*. London: Methuen, 1896.
----------. *Through the Zulu Country: Its Battlefields and Its People*. London: Kegan Paul, 1883.
----------. *The Triumph of Hillary Blanchland*. London: Chatto and Windus, 1901.
----------. "A Veldt Vendetta," *The Windsor Magazine*, 2 (July to December 1895): 451-97.
----------. *War and Arcadia*. London: F. V. White, 1901.
----------. *The Weird of Deadly Hollow*. London: F. V. White, 1899.
----------. *The White Shield*. New York: Frederick Stokes, 1895.
Mitford, Edward. *The Arab's Pledge–A Tale of Marocco in 1830*. London: Hatchard, 1867.
----------. *A Land-March from England to Ceylon Forty Years Ago, Through Dalmatia, Montenegro, Turkey, Asia Minor, Syria, Palestine, Assyria, Persia, Afghanistan, Scinde, and India, of which 7000 miles on Horseback*. 2 vols. London: W. H. Allen, 1884.
"Mitford, Roland." Office for National Statistics, General Register Office (London) 17 June 1891: No. 146.
"Mitford, Yseult." Office for National Statistics, General Register Office (London) 3 June 1887: No. 204.
Moffat, Robert. *Missionary Labours and Scenes in South Africa*. London: John Snow, 1842.
Monsman, Gerald. *H. Rider Haggard on the Imperial Frontier*. University of North Carolina, Greensboro: ELT Press, 2006.
----------. *Olive Schreiner's Fiction: Landscape and Power*. New Brunswick: Rutgers University Press, 1991.
Muddock, Joyce E. *The Savage Club Papers*. London: Hutchinson, 1897.

N

Ngugi, Wa Thiong'o. "Minutes of Glory," *Secret Lives, and Other Stories*. New York: L. Hill, 1975. 82-96.
Norgate, Matthew and Alan Wykes. *Not so Savage*. London: Jupiter Books, 1976.
Norman, Henry. "The Globe and the Island." *Cosmopolis: An International Review*. July 1897: 81-86.

O

"Opinions of the Press." *Golden Face: A Tale of the Wild West*. London: Trischler, 1892. i-iii.
Oppenheim, Janet. *The Other World and Psychic Research in England, 1850-1914*. Cambridge: Cambridge University Press, 1985.

"Osbaldeston-Mitford, Edward Ledwich." Her Majesty's Courts Service, British Probate Registry (Family Divison of the High Court of Justice), Grant of Administration. 12 November 1912.

P

Pakenham, Thomas. *The Scramble for Africa.* New York: Random House, 1991.

Parsons, Neil. *King Khama, Emperor Joe, and the Great White Queen.* Chicago: University of Chicago Press, 1998.

Pater, Walter. *Greek Studies.* London: Macmillan, 1925.

----------. Introduction. *The "Purgatory" of Dante Alighieri.* Trans. Charles Shadwell. London: Macmillan 1892.

----------. *The Renaissance.* London: Macmillan, 1910.

Plaatje, Solomon. *Mhudi.* Alice, SA: Lovedale Press, 1930.

Pliny (the Elder). *Natural History.* Trans. H. Rackham. 4 vols. Cambridge, MA: Harvard University Press, 1944.

Porter, Bernard. *Critics of Empire: British Radical Attitudes to Colonialism in Africa.* London: Mcmillan, 1968.

Pratt, M. L. *Imperial Eyes: Travel Writing and Transculturation.* London: Routledge, 1992.

R

Review of *Between Sun and Sand* (Scully). *The Athenæum* 23 April 1898: 491.

Review of *The Red Derelict* (Mitford). *The Sketch* 9 November 1904: 8.

Reznikoff, John. MS letter #883 "Doyle." 22 July 2007 <John Reznikoff@www.university archives.com>.

"Rudyard Kipling at the Anglo-African Writers' Club: His Views on South Africa." *African Review* 21 May 1898: 311-13.

Ruskin, John. "Lectures on Art" (1873). *The Complete Works of John Ruskin,* Eds. E. T. Cook and Alexander Wedderburn. Vol. 20. London: George Allen, 1905. 41-43.

-----------. *The Crown of Wild Olive* (1866). London: Allen, 1906.

S

San Francisco Call (San Francisco, Calif.) 1 July 1895: 6.

Schreiner, Olive. *From Man to Man.* Ed. S. C. Cronwright-Schreiner. London: Fisher Unwin, 1926.

----------. *Stories, Dreams, and Allegories.* London: Unwin, 1923.

----------. *The Story of an African Farm.* 2nd ed. London: Chapman and Hall, 1883.

----------. *Thoughts on South Africa.* New York: Stokes, 1923.

----------. *Trooper Peter Halket of Mashonaland.* London: Unwin, 1897.

----------. *Woman and Labour.* London: Unwin, 1911.

Scully, W. C. *Between Sun and Sand: A Tale of an African Desert.* Capetown: Juta, 1898.

----------. "Ghamba." *Kafir Stories.* London: Unwin, 1895. 131-161.

----------. *Lodges in the Wilderness.* London: Jenkins, 1915.

----------. *A Vendetta of the Desert.* London: Methuen, 1898.

Selous, F. C. *Sunshine and Storm in Rhodesia.* London: Rowland Ward, 1896.

Sidney, Philip. *New Arcadia.* Ed. Victor Skretkowicz. Oxford: Clarendon, 1987.

"Smoking Room." *African Review* 16 November 1895: 867.

Smuts, J. C. Introduction. *Voices of Africa.* By W. C. Scully. Durban: Knox Publishing, 1943. [vii-ix].

"Speech in Reply to Mr. Winston Churchill." *Daily News* (London) 13 November 1900: 5.

Spenser, Edmund. *Faerie Queene. Spenser: Poetical Works.* Ed. Smith, J. C. and E. De Selincourt. London: Oxford University Press, 1969.

Stiebel, Lindy. Review of *H. Rider Haggard on the Imperial Frontier* (Monsman). *Victorian Studies 45*:2 (2007).
Stoker, Bram. *Dracula.* New York: Grosset & Dunlap, 1897.
Swift, Jonathan. *A Modest Proposal*. Dublin: S. Harding, 1729.

T

Temple, Robert. "*Heath Hover Mystery*–MITFORD (Bertram)." 23 March 2007. <http:// www. biblio.com / books / 21915163.html>.
Tennent, James Emerson. *Ceylon: An Account of the Island*. London: Longmans, Green, 1860.
Tennyson, Alfred. *The Poetical Works of Tennyson*. Ed. G. Robert Stange. Boston: Houghton Mifflin, 1974.
Thoreau, H.D. *Journal*. 2 vols. Boston: Houghton Mifflin, 1949.
Trimen, Roland. *South-African Butterflies: A Monograph of the Extra-Tropical Species*. 3 vols. London: Traubner, 1887-89.

U

Uzanne, Octave and Albert Robida. *"La fin des livres." Contes pour les Bibliophiles*. Paris: Quantin, 1895.

W

Watt, A. P. *Letters Addressed to A. P. Watt*. London: Watt, 1929.
Waugh, Evelyn. *Black Mischief*. London: Chapman and Hall, 1932.
Wittenberg, Hermann. "Occult, Empire and Landscape." *Journal of Colonialism and Colonial History.* 7:2 (2006): 8-10.
Wright, Peter. "Sons of the Air." *Cross & Cockade International.* 34 (January 2003): 9.
Wylie, Dan. *Savage Delight*. Pietermaritzburg: University of Natal Press, 2000.

INDEX

A
"About Fiction" 11, 281.
Abrahams, Peter, 113, 129-130, 134.
Achebe, Chiuna, 7, 25, 100-101, 113.
African Review, The, 11, 19-21, 40, 279.
Amin, Idi, 80.
Anglo-African Writers' Club, 3-5, 7, 9-11, 13, 15, 18-19, 23-24, 29, 34, 37-39, 44, 69, 81, 279.
Anglo-Boer War, 18, 22, 24, 198, 279.
Aristotle, 42, 277, 279.
Armstrong, Nancy, 75, 279.
Augustine, Saint, 157, 279.

B
Bailey, Benjamin, 45, 47-48.
Bailey, Janet, 45.
Bain, Thomas, 273-274.
Ballantyne, R. M., 50, 79, 243, 279.
Bambatha Rebellion, 65-66, 216, 230, 234, 282.
Beard, Madeleine, 49.
Bettington, R. A. and F., 56-58, 60, 279.
Between Sun and Sand, 10, 175, 178-179.
Bible, 30-31, 95, 98, 121, 128, 156, 186, 189, 196, 224, 229, 275.
Blackburn, Douglas, 145, 279.
Blavatsky, Helena, 86-87, 110, 204, 279.
Blennerhassett, M. T., 61-62, 281.
Blunt, Wilfred, 246.
Boers, 5-6, 23, 25-26, 65-66, 76, 81, 113-116, 119-121, 129, 131-133, 136-140, 175, 178-179, 184, 187, 189, 211, 220-221, 225, 228.
Bowker, Bertram, 56-57.
Bowker, J. H., 102-103, 107, 145, 262, 279.
Bowker, Miles, 50-51, 57.
British South African Company, 11, 93, 122, 213, 218.
Bryant, A. T., 33, 80, 106, 123, 279.
Bryce, James, 20-22, 25-27, 37, 39-40, 75, 234, 280.
Bryden, H. A., 3, 10-13, 15, 17, 21, 175, 179, 191-193, 276, 280.
Buchan, John, vi, 3, 17-18, 22, 29-30, 36, 75, 132, 137, 228-230, 280, 283.
Bulpin, T. V., 68, 280.
Bulwer, Henry, Sir, 19, 75-76.
Burnham, Frederick, Major, 23.
Burton, Richard, 40, 69, 102, 280.
"Bushwoman's Romance, A," 175, 180, 191, 280.

C
Callaway, Henry, Bishop, 88, 95, 103, 262-263, 280.
Cannibalism, 97, 102-103, 241-242, 253-254, 261-263, 269-270.
Casement, Roger, 242-243, 280.
Cetywayo, King, 6, 99, 219, 230, 281.

"Child's Day, The," 146, 150, 161.

Chrisman, Laura, 75, 109, 113, 280.
Churchill, Winston, 23, 285.
Colenbrander, Johan, 33, 67-68, 102, 123, 220-221, 280.
Colenso, J. W., Bishop, 51, 98, 254, 275, 280.
Coleridge, S. T., 103, 152, 271, 280.
Colonial Civil Service, 43, 52, 81, 199.
Conrad, Joseph, 8, 35, 91, 100, 138, 195, 218, 230, 241-247, 249-250, 252-253, 271, 280.
Crown of Wild Olive, The, 16, 285.
Curse of Clement Waynflete, The, 6, 212, 284.

D
Dante, 15, 165, 167, 170, 172, 285.
Darwin, C. R., 44, 47, 157, 253, 259-260, 280.
Days of My Life, The, 10, 282.
Décle, Lionel, 11-13.
Devil, 3, 20, 46, 167, 169, 181, 201, 203-205, 221, 237-238, 247-249, 251, 265.
Dickens, Charles, 9, 199, 214.
Dingane/Dingaan/Dingana, King, 65, 131-133, 137-140, 225, 232.
"Distribution of Animals, The," 273-274, 277, 281.
Doyle, Conan, 4, 18-19, 70, 194, 281, 285.
Dracula, 14, 24, 266, 286.
Dr. Jekyll and Mr. Hyde, 29, 171, 195.

E
East London Advertiser, 50, 53, 55-56, 60, 65, 162.
Eden, Garden of, 66, 116, 121, 134, 145, 147, 149, 155-156, 167, 183, 193, 195, 204, 206.
Eglinton, William, 10, 281.
Eliot, T. S., 3, 30, 165-166, 183, 281.
Ethiopian Movement, 228.

F
Facing Mount Kenya: The Tribal Life of the Gikuyu, 7, 282.
Forging the Blades, 36, 197, 212, 232-233, 235, 237-238, 284.
Frazier, J. G., 35.
Freud, Sigmund, 152-53, 200-201, 265, 281.
Frontier Armed and Mounted Police, 51, 65, 102.
Fynney, Fred, 33, 82, 90, 138, 254, 281.
Fynn, H. F., 81.

G
Gentle, Alexander, 61, 63.
George V, King, 47.
Gerard Ridgley, 34.
Girard, René, 90.
Goethe, 264-265, 268, 281.
Golden Face, 40, 64, 237, 284.
Gordon-Gorman, W. J., 49, 70.

Green, Martin, 39, 76, 281.
Gun-Runner, The, 33, 36, 44, 68, 81, 83, 166, 196, 200, 212-214, 233.

H
Haggard, H. Rider, 3-4, 6, 10-11, 18-28, 30-34, 39, 41-45, 58-59, 63-64, 66, 75-88, 90, 92, 94, 99, 106, 109-110, 112-114, 124, 128, 134, 137-138, 141, 162, 166, 172, 184, 194, 200, 203-206, 212, 219, 223, 232, 253, 256, 260, 262, 264, 268, 271, 280.
Hamilton, Carolyn, 75, 282.
Haussmann, Baron Georges-Eugène, 9.
"Heart of Darkness," 100, 195, 219, 230, 243, 247, 280.
Henty, G. A., 4, 6, 69, 78, 282.
Homer, 7, 9, 282.
Honey, James, 273-274, 282.
Hood, Thomas, 162-163.
Hopkins, G. M., 171-172, 252, 282.
Horace, 35, 205, 289.
H. Rider Haggard on the Imperial Frontier, 6, 284, 286.

I
Impressions of South Africa, 21-22, 26, 39, 280.
Induna's Wife, The, 28, 36-37, 79, 96, 111, 122, 132, 134, 137-138, 140-141, 197, 225, 284.
Isis (goddess), 110, 202, 204, 279.

J
James, William, 86-87, 90, 282.
John Ames, Native Commissioner, 64, 67, 197, 212, 217-218, 222-223, 226.
Jung, C. G., 110-111, 282.

K
Kafir Stories, 10, 24, 262, 285.
"Kellson's Nemesis," 24.
Kenyatta, Jomo, 7-8, 282.
"Khama and the Chartered Company," 13, 282.
Khama, King, 11-13, 285.
King's Assegai, The, 25, 34, 51, 65, 75, 79, 92-94, 96-98, 101-103, 123-124, 126, 132, 134, 140, 254, 262, 284.
King Solomon's Mines, 28, 41, 43, 76-77, 88, 90, 106, 109, 113, 194, 206, 232, 237, 282.
Kotzé, Chief Justice, 19-20.
Kruger, Paul, 19-20, 167, 281.

L
Lang, Andrew, 33, 77-78, 85, 89.
Lalusini (fictional character), 36, 112-113, 132-135, 140-141, 197, 236.
Layard, A. H., 46, 282.
Lectures on Art, 14, 285.
Leopold II, King, 9.
Leslie, David, 84-85, 28, 282.
Lewis, C. S., 75, 282.
Lieven, Michael, 39, 283.

Lilith (character and demon), 215, 258, 263-265, 267-270, 272.
Livingstone, David, 13, 40, 69, 113, 118, 120, 123, 128, 151, 226, 249, 283.
Lobengula (dog), 12.

Lobengúla, King, 65, 68, 90, 128, 137-138, 213, 218, 222, 236.
Lodge in the Wilderness, A, 29-30, 230, 280.
Lorraine (fictional character), 36, 68, 196, 212-218, 221-222, 225-226, 229, 233-234.

M
MacDonald, George, 151, 283.
Mahlangu, Peter, 104, 283.
Matheson, Greville, 18.
Maud, 14, 61, 168, 259.
McClintock, Anne, 75, 109, 283.
Memory Hold the Door, 280.
Mhudi, 78, 93, 112-119, 121, 130, 141, 156, 285.
Mill, J. S., 112, 260, 283.
Milner, Alfred, Lord, 17.
Milton, John, 58, 75, 114, 121, 195, 204, 270, 283.
Mitford, Bertram, vi, 3, 6, 10, 12, 39, 50, 63, 68, 71, 75, 79, 122, 158, 166, 194, 213, 241, 280-283.
Mitford, Edward, 46-48.
Mitford, Rowland, 71.
Mitford, William, 50-52.
Mitford, Yseulte, 63, 65, 72.
Mitford, Zima, 60-63, 70-72.
Moffat, Robert, 98, 104-107, 113, 117, 123, 127-128, 130-131, 140, 176-177, 191, 284.
Monsman, G., 13, 33, 63-64, 71, 200, 264, 282, 284, 286.
Morley, John, 160.
Mzilikazi/Umzilikazi, King, 22, 36, 39, 75, 79, 90, 93, 97-98, 100, 104-108, 116-119, 123-124, 126-134, 137-138, 140, 236-237.

N
Nada the Lily, 41, 75-77, 89, 94, 124.
Napoleon Bonaparte, 84, 154.
Napoleon III, Emperor, 9.
Ngugi, W. T., 101, 284.
Nietzsche, Friedrich, 259-260.
Ninth Frontier War, 65, 161, 199.

O
Odysseus/Ulysses, 6-7, 44.
Olive Schreiner's Fiction, 284.
Oppenheim, J., 85, 284.
Osborn, Melmoth, 76, 82.
Our Arms in Zululand, 58.
"Outpost of Progress, An," 35, 241, 243-245.

P
Parsons, N., 11, 285.
Pater, Walter, 90, 135-137, 165, 285.

Pearce, Joseph, 49.
Persephone (goddess), 89, 111, 257.
Plaatje, Sol, vi, 8, 25-26, 78, 93-94, 112-120, 122, 130, 134, 141, 156, 285.
Poe, E. A., 121, 162-163.

"Political Situation, The," 12.
Polyphemus (Homeric character), 6-7.
Pratt, M. L., 4, 285.
Prester John, 36, 228-229, 280.
Pringle, Thomas, 21.

Q
Quatermain, Allan (fictional character), 28, 41, 77-78, 80, 87, 109, 205-206, 212, 232, 237, 271.

R
Renshaw Fanning's Quest, 36-37, 103, 176, 194-195, 198-206, 214, 223-224, 260, 271, 284.
Retief, Piet, 137-139, 217.
Reynolds, Joshua, 41.
Rhodes, Cecil, 4, 11-13, 15-17, 25, 29, 65, 68, 93, 122, 137, 176, 199, 213, 216-218, 220, 222, 227-228, 280.
Roberts, Frederick, Field Marshal, 23.
Ruskin, John, 13-17, 29, 40, 75, 154, 203, 285.

S
Schreiner, Olive, vi, 4, 8, 10-13, 17, 21, 27, 34, 79, 112, 119, 121, 137, 146, 148-149, 151-153, 155-156, 159-161, 181, 184, 198, 220-222, 227, 237, 285.
"Schreiner v. Rhodes," 12, 280.
Scully, W.C., vi, 3, 9-10, 21-22, 24, 82, 92, 175-176, 178-189, 191, 194, 262, 285.
Selous, F. C., 10-11, 177, 220-221, 223, 226, 285.
Shaka, King, 75, 77-78, 80-81, 83-84, 87-90, 93, 97, 113, 119, 123, 132-133, 234, 256, 262.
Shakespeare, William, 4, 119, 163, 166-167, 201, 241.
She: A History of Adventure, 76, 110, 281.
Shepstone, T., Sir, 81-82, 254.
"Side-Lights on the Amandebili (Matabili) Question," 137-139, 217-218, 225, 284.
Sign of the Spider, The, 10, 15, 34, 41, 64, 68, 196, 212, 214-215, 241, 253-254, 257, 259-262, 284.
Slaves, 105, 127, 241, 257, 263.
Smuts, J. C., 5, 285.
Spenser, Edmund, 201, 285.
Stevenson, R. L., 24, 195.
Stiebel, Libby, 11, 286.
Stoker, Bram, 14-15, 24, 286.
Stokes, Charles Henry, 12.
Story of an African Farm, The, 10, 36, 79, 121, 146, 285.
Swift, Jonathan, 220, 263, 286.

T
Tales of South Africa, 10, 175, 191, 280.

Tauana/Taune, King, 116-117, 129, 192.
Tennyson, Alfred Lord, 7, 14, 44, 58, 106, 132, 259-260, 286.
Thompson, Leonard, 33.
Thoreau, H. D., 157, 182, 286.
Thoughts on South Africa, 136, 285.

Trimen, Roland, 51-52, 286.
Through the Zulu Country, 43, 52, 67, 201, 284.
Touré, A. S., 27.
Trooper Peter Halket of Mashonaland, 119, 221-222, 227, 285.
Tylor, E. B., 29-30, 35.

U
"Ulysses," 7, 30, 44, 281.
Umlimo, The (divinity), 64, 218-219, 221-222, 224-226.
Umslopogaas (fictional character), 77, 87-91, 134.
Umkulunkulu (divinity), 87, 229, 275.
Untúswa (fictional character), 25, 36, 65, 92-94, 96-97, 99-108, 122, 124, 126, 132-136, 138-141, 211.

V
Vendetta of the Desert, A, 9, 175, 188-190, 285.
Victoria, Queen, 4, 8-9, 11, 29, 32, 34, 42, 44, 46, 76, 79, 81, 109-110, 112, 118, 134, 147-148, 153-155, 158, 161, 164-165, 167, 192, 211, 223, 238, 245, 253, 257, 267-269, 283, 286.

W
War and Arcadia, 64, 284.
War of the Worlds, 14.
Watt, A. P., 44, 64-66, 162, 197, 199, 222, 286.
Waugh, Evelyn, 45, 172-173, 261, 286.
Weird of Deadly Hollow, The, 23, 49, 64, 69, 161-163, 165, 214, 216, 284.
Wells, H. G., 14-15, 24.
White Hand and the Black, The, 33, 43, 65, 228, 230.
White Shield, The, 49, 79, 96, 107, 111, 122, 124, 127, 129-130, 132-133, 137, 140, 211, 236, 284.
Wilde, Oscar, 24.
Wilmot, A., 12, 145.
With Buller in Natal, 6.
With Roberts to Pretoria, 6, 282.
Wittenberg, Hermann, 29, 286.
Wolseley, Garnet, Sir, 76.
Word of the Sorceress, The, 63, 79.
Wordsworth, William, 163, 259.
Wylie, Daniel, 75, 80, 286.

Z
Zambezi River, 132.